MANAGEMENT AND ORGANISATIONAL BEHAVIOUR

A Student Workbook

MANAGEMENT AND ORGANISATIONAL BEHAVIOUR

A Student Workbook

THIRD EDITION

Karen Meudell & Tony Callen

Revised by Heather Lussey

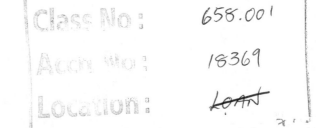

FINANCIAL TIMES
PITMAN PUBLISHING

Pearson Education Limited
Edinburgh Gate
Harlow
Essex CM20 2JE
England

and Associated Companies around the world

Visit us on the World Wide Web at:
www.pearsoned-ema.com

First published in Great Britain in 1995
Third edition published 1999

ISBN 0 273 64142 5

British Library Cataloguing in Publication Data
A CIP catalogue record for this book can be obtained from the British Library

10 9 8 7 6 5 4 3 2 1

Typeset by Pantek Arts, Maidstone, Kent
Printed and bound in Great Britain by Redwood Books Ltd, Trowbridge

The Publishers' policy is to use paper manufactured from sustainable forests.

Contents

Preface to the third edition

The third edition of this workbook has been reorganised to follow the fifth edition of Laurie Mullins's *Management and Organisational Behaviour* chapter for chapter, making it easier to use in conjunction with that book.

While retaining many of the features from the second edition of the workbook – case studies, activities, assignments and debates – these have been updated to take into account current issues. In addition, three of the sections from the previous edition – 'Look, it really works!', 'Pause for thought' and 'Still not convinced?' – have been combined to create a new feature, entitled 'Applications'. Taking the form of short cases, newspaper and journal articles, this section is intended to provide students with the raw material for discussion and debate.

1 Introduction

This workbook has been written to complement *Management and Organisational Behaviour* by Laurie Mullins. Following the fifth edition of that book chapter for chapter, the third edition of this workbook builds upon many of the assignments and activities in Mullins's main text, provides numerous new and additional cases, and a wealth of *Financial Times* newspaper articles which can be used as short case illustrations or as a basis for discussion.

AIMS AND OBJECTIVES

This book is for lecturers and students. It will help lecturers build a learning programme that is both fun and interesting, while for the student it will bring the subject of organisational behaviour (OB) to life by illustrating its importance and relevance to the real world of organisations. The problem for many first-time students of OB, whether undergraduate or postgraduate, is getting to grips with what must seem like a baffling quagmire of theories and research studies which obscure each topic and its relevance to working life. This book addresses this particular difficulty and will save the OB lecturer the time it takes to invent interesting and stimulating activities.

The aims of this book, therefore, are fivefold:

1. To provide lecturers with a planned and flexible scheme of work to complement a formal lecture programme for one or two semesters.
2. To give students some topical debates and real-life examples of how the various theories can actually work in practice.
3. To allow students the opportunity to research the various subject areas and to relate them to 'real world' situations.
4. To encourage the development of student skills in the areas of research, critical analysis, and oral and written presentation.
5. To allow opportunities for group-working wherever possible.

DISTINCTIVE FEATURES

- The workbook is extremely flexible in approach. It can be used by both lecturers and students, in part or in entirety, to complement both lecture and seminar programmes.
- It can be used on both undergraduate and postgraduate/post-experience courses.

- In these days of ever-increasing class sizes, its contents and layout present the lecturer with ready-thought-out exercises, assignments and examples.
- It is 'real world' related, with case studies from academics, industrialists and trainers, as well as from the *Financial Times*.
- It encourages students to research topics for themselves, facilitating the development of critical analysis by asking them to analyse their findings against the various theoretical models and frameworks.
- It deliberately provides a mix of activities, assignments and debates, some of which are more demanding of the student than others.

PLAN OF THE BOOK

The book has been designed to complement a one- or two-semester lecture programme and follows the traditional 'micro to macro' approach. It can be used in several ways:

- As an addition to formal lecture input by using parts of each chapter as considered appropriate.
- As a complete seminar programme: each chapter provides a variety of seminar-type topics and these can be either lecturer- or student-driven.
- As a combination of the above whereby, for example, an application could be taken as the lecture topic and the remainder of the chapter used in a subsequent seminar.
- As an additional text to aid student learning and understanding and as a revision aid.

CHAPTER OUTLINE

Each chapter takes the same format, as follows.

Case studies

These are all 'real world' related and wherever possible the actual companies have been named. However, there are occasions when, for the purposes of maintaining confidentiality, the name of the organisation has been changed.

Activities and assignments

These can be completed individually or in groups and are based on a 'learning by doing' approach. We have not generally specified a word length and lecturers can decide their own requirements.

Debates

These can either be used for discussion or as a formal debate with the audience voting at the end. For each topic we have included a couple of starting points both for and against the proposition together with some further reading that we strongly recommend students use.

Applications

These take a variety of forms – short cases, newspaper and journal articles – and are intended to provide the raw material for discussion and debate.

INSTRUCTOR'S MANUAL

Lecturing colleagues will find the Instructor's Manual for this workbook at the end of each corresponding chapter in the Instructor's Manual for Mullins's main text. This enables a full learning programme to be constructed which incorporates a variety of exercises for each stage of the course.

The Instructor's Manual offers guideline answers for many of the cases, assignments and activities in the book and provides comments, teaching suggestions and references to Mullins. It provides suggestions on how assignments and exercises might be incorporated into the teaching programme.

2 The Nature of Organisational Behaviour

CASE STUDY

The organisational setting in Spain

In the forty years after the Second World War, Spain underwent important changes in business, political and social environments. These changes were instrumental in helping both public and private organisations make the transition from the authoritarian/bureaucratic style of organisational control to being dynamic and outward-looking. However, this organisational change was not able to keep up with the pace of change in the external environment, and Spain still lagged behind her European partners in many areas, having a negative effect on the competitiveness of Spanish businesses.

Traditionally the culture that has predominated has been characterised by the size and importance of the state sector under the aegis of the Instituto Nacional de Industria (INI), and a rigid, monolithic state bureaucracy which offered civil servants at all grades a job for life; a large number of small and medium-sized firms, many with strong family links that led to a static hierarchical organisational structure; a pool of cheap and compliant labour which removed the impetus to invest in and develop new technologies; and an inward-looking productive structure which was highly protected and therefore denied the challenge of competition. The stability provided by the authoritarian regime of General Franco before 1975, and the cosy relationship between business, banks and government, allowed business organisations and government agencies to forgo long-term planning. Spanish firms thus failed to identify long-term strategic objectives and short-termism, insularity and quick profits for business became the norm.

One significant event which helped force organisations in Spain to change in the second half of this century was the abandonment of the policy of autarky in the late 1950s which led to a partial lifting of government controls on the location and expansions of business and fewer restrictions on foreign investment in Spain. The post-war economic prosperity in Western Europe provided Spain with an influx of tourists and an outlet for workers looking for better pay and conditions abroad. Income from tourism, emigrant remittances and foreign investment led to an economic boom in the country which led to a proliferation of new private business organisations and a more pragmatic approach to the control of the political economy. However the influence of these factors only laid the groundwork for future changes. Foreign investment led to 'a modern, dynamic component of large firms grafted on to the pre-existing world of predominantly small companies' (Shubert, 1990), while new ideas on forms of social interaction brought in by tourists and returning emigrants were repressed or rejected by the narrow, authoritarian, blinkered view of the administration and many managers. On the surface at least, there was little movement from the mechanistic organisation and its rigid structures to the organic organisation, more appropriate in a changing environment, identified by Burns and Stalker (see Mullins, pp. 563–5).

Even after the collapse of the authoritarian regime in Spain in the mid 1970s, the political and economic turmoil was not conducive to the introduction of innovative management structures. While the emphasis was on political change, the machinery of state administration changed very little and another layer of bureaucracy was added with the creation of seventeen autonomous communities each with their own regional parliaments and their own administrative structure. The oil crises of 1974 and 1979 left Spanish companies reeling, unable to come to terms with the speed and scope of the changes taking place in the external environment, and unwilling to risk significant changes in internal management structures. This period of crisis led to even greater government intervention in private companies, with the state taking over companies which were in danger of collapse in order to save jobs. This corporatist and paternalistic response from a weak government was allied to a general disenchantment in the business community, which was compounded by the election victory of the Spanish socialist party in the 1982 general elections. There were fears that the government would initiate a policy of nationalisation, support union wage claims and adopt a model of central planning for the economy. In fact these fears were unfounded. When the socialists came to power 'The Spanish economy was based on an inefficient, backward productive structure. Industry was biased towards consumer goods and traditional sectors, was labour intensive, used outdated technology and had low levels of productivity and competitiveness' (Ferner and Hyman, 1994). In order to tackle these problems the government adopted a tight monetarist approach and applied market principles to cut inflation, reduce the balance of payments deficit and promote greater flexibility in business. Another of the commitments of the government was to reduce bureaucracy and initiate a policy of privatisation through a policy of industrial reconversion, that is, restructuring the state sector enterprises to make them more efficient and responsive to market forces.

Not all the government's measures were successful. Public administration fell prey to the party machine and management was again hooked on short-term objectives, governed more by sectoral interests than market principles. On the other hand the adoption of a free market philosophy revitalised the faith in private enterprise as a motor for growth and prosperity and started a shift of young professionals away from the public to the private sector.

These measures that the government took were also aimed at bringing the Spanish economy in line with the other Western European countries in the EU. By 1985 the economic indicators had begun to show a recovery but it was Spain's accession to the EU in 1986 which was the primary impulse for change. Membership of the EU was widely seen as a positive move, which would lead to a process of modernisation and to Spain gaining her rightful place in the Western world. However, there were problems. Membership subjected Spanish companies and industries to a level and intensity of competition that was unheard of, and these changes in the external environment forced organisations in Spain to review the technological, structural, personnel and management systems with which they worked. Some feared that Spain's accession to the EU and the corresponding loss of the protection of tariff barriers would lead to Spain's industries being overwhelmed, while others accepted that the internationalisation of the Spanish economy would provide the stimulus that business people needed to change attitudes, renovate the industrial base and learn to compete in foreign markets. Initially, during the difficult period of adjustment, many companies were forced to close in the face of foreign competition, but the last half of the 1980s saw Spanish growth rates surpass other EU member states, averaging almost 5 per cent between 1987 and 1990.

Although the economy slumped at the beginning of the 1990s, competition and government policy have gone some way towards modernising the organisational structures. The government carried out a policy of privatisation, creating a new holding for profitable state industries and a semi-privatised banking group for the different state banks. Private banks were not slow to adopt practices that had been introduced by foreign banks such as Barclays and NatWest, offering a wider range of services and changing the industry from one based on the bank–client relationship to that of 'an industry based on competition, price and service' (Canals, 1994). The liberalisation of the banking sector led to mergers between and greater competition from savings banks, and banks were at the forefront of new technology in Spain.

The attitudes and skills of the personnel in organisations in Spain are still anchored in the past. 'It would appear that conservatism and paternalistic employment relations remain the dominant characteristics of small-scale capital in Spain' (Ferner and Hyman 1994). The individualism which militates against group work, the acceptance of authority and the mistrust of new ideas are attitudes which need to be overcome if Spanish work organisations are to become more competitive. Another of the serious problems is the quality of education and training in Spain. Only 17 per cent of the working population in Spain between the ages of 16 and 65 have the qualifications that employers are looking for. The demand for university graduates and qualified postgraduates in business outstrips the supply by three to one, and there is a proliferation of MBA courses on offer in the main urban centres.

Given the short supply of skilled personnel, one would expect that the commitment to in-house training in Spanish firms would be high. However, training is not a priority in Spanish firms, coming sixth on the list of priorities. The proportion of overall labour costs in companies dedicated to education and training is 0.2 per cent, compared to an average of 1.5 per cent in other EU countries. Training is often given on an *ad hoc* basis as a 'reward', and not included in the overall corporate strategy of companies, indicating that Spanish companies still have a long way to go in developing the skills that are required to be competitive. New managers are coming out of Spanish Business Schools at a rate of some 11 000 a year, however, with an international outlook and speaking one or two foreign languages. They are learning to be more flexible in the organisational environment and to work outside a narrow, precise sphere of responsibility.

Fears have been expressed that foreign investment and the sale of Spanish companies to foreign firms is leaving the Spanish economy dangerously dependent on decisions taken abroad. The introduction of foreign capital has, though, meant a change in management structures in Spain, while direct foreign investment has brought with it new working practices and new organisational structures. In Spain there are still organisations with 14 to 16 different organisational levels, which slows down internal communication and promotes inflexibility, but multinationals such as General Electric have reduced these to four levels in Spain. Companies are also decentralising their operations. This, given the authoritarian and hierarchical structure of organisations to date, has often met with opposition from regional managers who are not accustomed to taking important decisions without approval from head office.

The level of technological innovation in an organisation is another of the subsystems that can be used to analyse the competitiveness of a work organisation. Traditionally in Spain low labour costs have been the cornerstone of the competitive advantage of firms. Now, with the widespread application of technology and with spending on research and development programmes, low labour costs have become less of a competitive advantage. Again Spain still spends less than 1.0 per cent of her gross domestic product on research and development, compared to an average of 2.33 per cent in the four leading countries in the European Union – France, Great Britain, Germany and Italy. EU membership has thus had a positive impact, prompting greater official recognition of the need for research and development, but too much is still spent on importing foreign technology.

These are just some of the internal and external environmental influences that are affecting Spanish organisations. The pace of change in the past thirty years has been dramatic, and public and private organisations are struggling to adapt. In many respects Spain is still ten to fifteen years behind the leading member states of Europe, but the commitment to organisational change is coming from local, regional and national government bodies, the education system, and from large and small Spanish and foreign businesses.

Activity brief

1 Prepare an environmental audit of the political, economic, social and technological factors which have most affected organisations in your country or region.

2 Discuss how the management functions in your country, region or immediate organisation differ from those outlined above.

3 Suggest how cultural forces accelerate or slow down changes in organisations in your own country or another country with which you are familiar.

Further reading

Almarcha Barbado, A. (1993), *Spain and EC Membership Evaluated*, Pinter.

Canals, J. (1994), *Competitive Strategies in European Banking*, Clarendon Press.

Ferner, A. and Hyman, R. (1994), *Industrial Relations in the New Europe*, Blackwell.

Randlesome, C. (1993), *Business Cultures in Europe*, Butterworth-Heinemann.

Shubert, A. (1990), *A Social History of Modern Spain*, Unwin Hyman.

Case study provided by Bob Gould, University of Portsmouth.

ACTIVITY 1

In small groups of not more than five people, design an activity which illustrates one of the topics considered in Chapter 2 of Mullins. For example, this could be a group exercise, a card game, a quiz or a 'Question Time' type group discussion.

Play out the activity with the rest of the group and then prepare a verbal presentation based on the following points:

- How successful was the activity? Why or why not?
- What modifications, if any, would you make to your activity?
- How does the success (or otherwise) of your activity link with issues concerning the study of OB?

ACTIVITY 2

Using the text in Mullins (pp. 10–12) and information from the reading list below, prepare a students' guide to undertaking case studies from *one* of the following two perspectives:

1 A first-year undergraduate with little or no work experience.

2 A mature part-time management student with considerable work experience.

Further reading

Cameron, S. (1994), *The MBA Handbook*, 2nd edn, Pitman, Chapter 10.

Easton, G. (1992), *Learning from Case Studies*, 2nd edn, Prentice Hall.

Mullins, L. J. (1984), 'Tackling Case Studies', *Student Administrator*, 1 (5).

DEBATE

'The study of organisational behaviour is really an art which pretends that it is a science and produces some spurious research findings to try to prove the point.'

Starting points

For

- OB deals largely with intangibles. Not only is it difficult to observe and measure, it is also difficult to establish links between cause and effect.
- Science aims to be able to control. There are moral and ethical considerations in OB which militate against this.

Against

- The problems of considering OB as a science occur only if we try to apply rigid scientific practices to the subject.

- OB is a science in that it follows similar principles (i.e. to describe, explain, predict and control) but it is a *different* type of science – a social science – and thus cannot be compared directly.

Further reading

Mohr, L. (1982), *Explaining Organizational Behavior*, Jossey-Bass.

Ryan, A. (1970), *The Philosophy of the Social Sciences*, Macmillan.

Shipman, M. (1981), *The Limitations of Social Research*, Longman.

ASSIGNMENT 1

Using the metaphors suggested by Gareth Morgan (Mullins, pp. 19–20), apply one or more to your own organisation. If you are not currently working, take any organisation that you know – this could be a sports club, the Students' Union, or somewhere where you've worked during your vacation.

Prepare either a verbal or written (maximum 1500 words) report of your findings.

ASSIGNMENT 2

In small groups, using Application 3 in this chapter (see below, p. 11), the text in Mullins (pp. 28–33), and the reading list below:

- Explain why certain business activities have become increasingly harmonised across the world.
- In what ways would you expect work organisations to vary in different societies? Will these differences always exist?

Present your findings to the other groups in whatever format you consider appropriate to the topic.

Further reading

Torrington, D. (1994), *International Human Resource Management*, Prentice Hall.

Trompenaar, F. (1993), *Riding the Waves of Culture*, Economist Publications.

Welford, R. and Prescott, K. (1994), *European Business,* 2nd edn, Pitman.

Assignment provided by Dr Ray French, University of Portsmouth.

APPLICATION 1

One of our students on our part-time MBA course came to the Stage 1 OB unit with a degree of trepidation and cynicism. A systems engineer by training, she expressed grave reservations about successfully completing a unit in 'such a fuzzy, unquantifiable subject'. The introductory lecture, 'The Nature of Organisational Behaviour', did very little to change her opinion. In fact, if anything, it reinforced it – this was definitely a subject that Lyndsey felt uncomfortable with. A quick straw poll of the class showed that she was not the only one to feel this way – over 50 per cent of the students thought the same (we'd like to think that it was because they were all engineers and scientists rather than because we were lousy lecturers . . .).

Anyway, we ploughed on and about two-thirds of the way through the course Lyndsey came up to one of us after the lecture and said, 'You know, it actually works!' 'What does, Lyndsey?' (you get a bit gobsmacked after three hours of 'Great Leadership Theories I Have Known' . . .). 'This whole thing,' she replied. 'I had to do a presentation on performance-related pay to the main board last week and to back up my point that we didn't need it, I used all the research findings on motivation and money. The board ended up agreeing with me and said afterwards that it was largely because I could prove my points with research data – I'd never have done that prior to the course.'

Hopefully this not only provides an example of how OB *can* work in practice but it might also be useful to look at the model of attitude change here (see Mullins, pp. 324–7).

APPLICATION 2

Steve White is the head chef in a large London hotel. He's been in the industry for twenty-five years, starting off as a 'button boy' (a kind of junior hall porter-cum-gopher) before moving into the kitchen and gradually working his way up. He's been a head chef in various hotels for the last ten years and in his last three jobs he's been recruited prior to the opening of the hotel so he's been required to help design the kitchen, recruit his brigade, sort out menus and generally get the show on the road. There is a limit to how many times anyone can do this and, frankly, Steve is bored. He joined his current company because they seemed to offer wider opportunities than just kitchen work and, having opened the hotel, he is now looking to change.

Before we go any further and for those not intimately connected with the hotel industry, perhaps we ought to establish a few facts:

- Tradition says that 'once a chef, always a chef' – they're experts in their own field but can't (or don't want to) move into any other.
- Rule 1 says that 'the chef is always right'.
- Rule 2 says that if the chef is wrong, Rule 1 applies.
- Chefs are not, generally, known for their democratic approach to managing people. This can range from a slight raising of the voice when contradicted to hurling whatever is in the hand at the time (if you've ever been on the receiving end of a red-hot wok, as one of the authors has, you'll know what we mean).
- Having said all that (and to avoid having one's kneecaps filleted at the table and served with a vinegar and mustard *timbale*), chefs are known for their undying devotion to their craft. They are synonymous with training, development and maintaining their networks – all chefs know each other and can point to who they have trained and to who they have encouraged to leave for a promotion which they've organised.

Back to our bored Steve . . . he's now been at the hotel for two years (and is breathing a sigh of relief because he now can't be sacked without a good reason). He's seen two food and beverage managers (his immediate boss) come and go and he is looking for something else. The hotel manager approaches him one day and asks him if he would like the job of food and beverage manager. He jumps at the chance because he knows that he can promote his existing sous chef and still keep control in the kitchen whilst furthering his own career.

A few weeks later a former colleague of his rings him up to congratulate him on his promotion and to ask how things are going. He replies: 'I hate it. I have to wear a suit all day, carry a bleep, I'm at the beck and call of everybody, the bar and restaurant staff don't understand where I'm coming from and I've had two waitresses and one barman in tears – I'm thinking of jacking it in.'

Can you see where the psychological contract might fit in here? When he joined the company Steve clearly had his *own* psychological contract, as did the company. Where did it go wrong?

APPLICATION 3

The world is getting smaller. No, not an example of catastrophe theory in physics or the message of a religious sect predicting the demise of the planet; rather this statement reflects for many the opening up or demystifying of the rest of the world.

Few significant businesses do not think of themselves as international and the concept of a global business environment is accepted by more and more commentators.

There is a paradox. Increasingly products, services and the means of providing them are becoming more homogeneous. Japanese-owned car producers such as Nissan and Toyota have not only set up manufacturing plants in Britain but have also 'imported' their own organisational practices. McDonald's have opened outlets in the former Eastern bloc, to great initial demand from the local clientele. In the summer of 1994, that archetypal French event, the Tour de France, came to the south coast of England. That first year, an estimated three million spectators witnessed the event over two days – and they said it would never catch on!

But if many aspects of life which were once culturally distant are now similar, most of us recognise that culturally derived attitudes and patterns of behaviour remain significant across the world. We continue to believe, with justification, that Italians, Australians and Swedes display distinctive cultural identities which will impinge upon the business world. Few would expect these to disappear even in a truly global environment. Torrington's advice (1994) to 'think globally and act locally' perhaps comes closest to explaining this paradox.

Provided by Dr Ray French, University of Portsmouth.

APPLICATION 4

It's 9.10 on a rainy Monday morning in February. The lecture theatre is filling to capacity with wet first-year students who will, judging by the already gently rising steam cloud, dry themselves off during the next hour.

Into the lecture theatre walks a middle-aged man who goes to the lectern and begins to speak: 'Good morning, ladies and gentlemen, my name is Michael Morris and I'd like to welcome you to this introductory lecture in Behavioural Science. Indeed, that is as good a starting point as any – is it a science at all? Pedagogically speaking the critics would argue . . . .' The voice droned on, the steam rose, heads began to droop and eyelids began to close.

At the end of a seemingly endless hour the lecture was over and groups of students filed out: the keen ones to the library, the majority to the refectory. Over coffee, Julian said to his friends: 'Well, if that's what we've got for the rest of this semester, then it confirms everything I ever thought about the subject – boring, dry, lifeless and uninspired. I suggest we get a rota going, take it in turns to attend and copy each other's notes. What do you reckon – one lot turn up and the rest have a lie-in and watch *The Big Breakfast*?'

Not convinced about OB? Well, given this scenario, you'd probably be very justified. However, give the subject a chance. OK, not all lecturers (for whatever reason) are going to make it into an earth-moving experience (the thought of students at 9.15 on a Monday morning is frequently no more attractive than your thoughts of having to face us !). Not everyone sees OB as the exciting and dynamic subject that we do, but try and look for examples of how it might relate to the 'real world'.

APPLICATION 5

Sit cross-legged on the floor, circle your thumb and forefinger together and repeat after us: 'OB is dynamic, OB is exciting, OB is real-world related . . . .' Not working? OK, follow one set of the following instructions:

1 Tune in and follow regularly any soap opera, drama or other series. Each week, take one concept of OB and apply it to whatever you're watching. Some suggestions to get you going might be:

   (a) *London's Burning* (leadership, informal groups, organisational bureaucracies, organisation culture).
   (b) *Neighbours* (attitudes, motivation, perception).
   (c) *Casualty* (non-profit organisations, groups, informal leadership, motivation, attitudes).
   (d) *The Original Star Trek* (leadership, groups, cultural differences, perception, personality).
   (e) *Blind Date* (perception, personality, attitudes).
   (f) *Coronation Street/Brookside* (all of the above and then some).
   (g) *Question Time* (attitude change, communication).

2 Take any novel or play and analyse it in OB terms. As an example, let's take *Hamlet*:

   (a) **Hamlet** thinks the rest are out to get him (perception, personality).
   (b) **Ophelia** (the female love interest) is infatuated with Hamlet (attitude and motivation, gender stereotyping) but doesn't know if he feels the same (perception).
   (c) **Gertrude** has recently remarried and so remains Queen (organisation theory, motivation).

(d) **Polonius** wants everyone to like him (attitude, perception).
(e) **Horatio** tries to pour oil on troubled waters and protect his friend (perception, attitude, motivation).
(f) **The gravediggers** have a lousy job to do but manage to make the best of it (job satisfaction, motivation, attitudes).
(g) **Rosencrantz and Guildenstern** are trying to cope in a turbulent and changing environment and to stay together without having to do the Elizabethan MBA (motivation, attitudes, perception, groups, organisational culture).
(h) **Fortinbras** – the 'born leader' (leadership, motivation, personality).
(i) **The ghost of Hamlet's father** – is he there at all? (perception, attitudes, personality, paranoia?).
(j) **'Something is rotten in the state of Denmark . . . .'** (organisational misbehaviour!).

Try it with Ibsen, the Ring Cycle or Peter Rabbit – it throws a whole new light on them!

AFTERTHOUGHTS

A colleague of ours stresses the need for underpinning case study answers with academic theory by saying: 'You have to pin the tent of theory into the groundsheet of reality.' An Irish friend of ours puts it rather more prosaically: 'If you can't back up what you're saying then you've got no arse in your trousers . . . .'

'I've always been interested in people, but I've never liked them . . . .'
W. Somerset Maugham (1949)

3 Approaches to Organisation and Management

CASE STUDY

A woman's place is in her own business

A big crop of entrepreneurs springs up in eastern Germany

When the Berlin Wall fell, Cornelia Pfaff exploited her new-found freedom by opening a boutique in the east German city of Erfurt. Women jammed in to snatch up the latest in West German fashions. Six years later, the 38-year-old Pfaff runs a chain of five stores with 21 employees, and plans to expand to nearby cities. 'It was supposed to just be for fun,' she says. 'But I did it with so much love, it has become a success.'

Companies started by women are becoming important players in the burgeoning service sector in eastern Germany. With unemployment among women around 20 per cent in eastern Germany, female entrepreneurship is surging. More than half of self-employed professionals such as doctors, architects, and lawyers are female. Nearly a third of all businesses launched in eastern Germany since 1990 were founded by women, compared with 21 per cent in western Germany. Altogether, economists estimate, the 150 000 new female-run companies in eastern Germany have created about 1 million jobs and contribute about $15 billion to Germany's annual gross domestic product. Some are key additions to the *Mittelstand* – the small and medium-size manufacturing companies that make up Germany's economic backbone.

Necessity forced many east German women into business. As the region's old-line industries stumbled and folded after reunification, women were hit especially hard. Layoffs in factories in the textile and electronics industries and in agriculture put more than 750 000 women out of work. Compared with western Germany, where 38 per cent of women work, 94 per cent of eastern Germany's adult women had worked before reunification. While many held menial jobs, others built up careers as administrators, economists, and physicians. When the wall came down, women borrowed money under scores of government-sponsored programmes designed to kick-start growth in eastern Germany.

Take Käte Lindner. Under the old regime, she was economic director for a collective of 21 state-owned packaging companies in the southern part of eastern Germany. 'Women were equipped with management skills,' says the 59-year-old grandmother. Just months after the wall fell, she managed to purchase from the still-extant East German government what remained of the *Mittelstand* boxmaking company her grandfather had started in the village of Mühlau in 1909. After buying new machinery and replacing the rundown former dance hall that served as a production facility, Lindner now employs 72 people and produces glossy packaging for such clients as CompuServe Inc. and *Reader's Digest*. Sales have quadrupled since 1991, to $3.5 million.

Not all female-run companies are so bent on expansion. Researchers who study new business growth in Germany say that companies run by women develop more slowly than those managed by men. One reason is that the profit motive isn't as strong among women entrepreneurs. According to government surveys, women cite earning profits as a fourth or fifth reason for setting up their own companies, after their desire to be self-sufficient and develop their own ideas. Male entrepreneurs cite profits as the No. 1 motive.

Laid-back approach

Gunhild Haase, for example, is content to see her kitchen-design and installation company grow at a modest 2 per cent annual rate. 'I don't want to immediately make a huge profit,' says the former optical engineer, who set up her business in two houses she bought in the cobblestoned city of Jena in 1992. She makes sales calls in her eight-year-old Mercedes and employs just five people, two more than when she started. 'I'm happy with my business. It's exactly as I imagined it,' she says.

To be sure, such a laid-back approach means that the female-owned *Mittelstand* and service sector of eastern Germany will hardly be able to absorb the region's 1.3 million surplus workers on their own. In addition to small service companies, the region needs to create more manufacturing jobs in order to bolster employment, economists say. Nevertheless, the explosion in female-owned businesses has provided an important cushion against devastating joblessness – and has emerged as a surprising consequence of communism's collapse.

Activity brief

1 Why is it that companies started by women are becoming increasingly important players in European economies (and not only in the burgeoning service sector in eastern Germany – see also Application 1 on pp. 17–18)?

2 Whereas male entrepreneurs cite profit as the number one motive, the profit motive is not as strong among women entrepreneurs (according to this case). Comment on this statement.

3 Does your role model of a good manager fit the idea of equal opportunities for men and women in the management ranks in organisations?

4 What competences and characteristics does a successful entrepreneur need? Are these different for male and female entrepreneurs?

Sources: Reprinted from 18 March 1996 issue of *Business Week* by special permission, copyright © 1996 by The McGraw-Hill Companies, Inc. Questions quoted from Keuning, D. (1998), *Management: A Contemporary Approach*, FT Pitman Publishing.

ACTIVITY

Using the example on p. 53 of Mullins as a model, develop a programme using scientific management techniques for a simple household task such as:

- mowing a lawn;
- cooking a simple meal (e.g. spaghetti bolognese);
- bathing a small child;
- tidying a bedroom.

DEBATE

'Anyone who teaches management and anyone of even moderate intellect and experience who is subjected to such teaching, soon becomes aware that the theories used are often of limited scientific validity in terms of the explanations or predictions which they offer. At best they are partial; applied in the wrong way, without understanding of the necessary complementary caveats and provisos, they may even be misleading.' (*Lee and Lawrence, 1985*)

Starting points

For

- The research studies are not only inconsistent but also contradictory – nothing can be gained from 'meddling' in this way.
- Social behaviour is, for the most part, genetically determined. We would do better to study sociobiology rather than psychology and sociology.

Against

- Research by psychologists, sociologists and anthropologists has enabled considerable progress to be made in being able to explain and predict people's behaviour.
- Admittedly, understanding human behaviour is not as simple as understanding the behaviour of a chemical, but any attempt to do so should be welcomed.

Further reading

Lorsch, J. W. (ed.) (1987), *Handbook of Organizational Behavior*, Prentice Hall.

Mullins, L. J. (1987), 'The Organisation and the Individual', *Administrator*, 7 (4), April, 11–14.

Whyte, W. F. (1987), 'From Human Relations to Organizational Behavior: Reflections on the Changing Scene', *Industrial and Labor Relations Review*, July, 487–500.

ASSIGNMENT

'Many modern franchise operations such as tyre/exhaust centres and fast-food restaurants are organised directly along with principles of scientific management – in fact this "old-fashioned" view of management is the key to their success!'

- By visiting a local franchise operation, interviewing managers and staff, and observing their activities, consider the extent to which the management techniques currently in operation make use of scientific management.
- In 1500 words write a report which explains how useful scientific management can be in a modern organisation. What are its strengths and limitations? How have its methods been adapted or built upon in the organisation which you observed?
- Try to support your arguments with evidence which you have observed or gathered.

APPLICATION 1

Women's progress in the business world has been likened to the advance of the next ice age. There are few clear signs of a thaw.

The newest, and most controversial, reason cited for giving women a break is a change in management culture. Women in management used to be criticised for their inability to behave like men in the corporate world, but now management gurus such a Peter Drucker, Tom Peters and Robert Waterman are saying that corporate cultures must move towards a style that in the old days would have been thought of as typically feminine. The buzzwords are co-operative leadership, teamwork, an emphasis on quality, intuitive problem-solving and light control.

A major EU study showed that in 1987 women made up 4 per cent of middle management in the Netherlands and Ireland, 7 per cent in Belgium, 8 per cent in Denmark, West Germany and Italy, and 9 per cent in France. The proportion of women in top management was even lower – less than 3 per cent everywhere except in France, which headed the European league table at 7 per cent.

Yet women across Europe account for between 36 per cent and 48 per cent of the labour force. There is ample evidence that most of them are no longer content with what the Germans call the three Ks – *Kinder, Küche, Kirche* (children, kitchen and church). Many are looking for managerial opportunities; few are getting them.

When male bosses are pressed on the question of unequal promotion chances for female managers they will usually admit, slightly shamefacedly, that it has 'something to do with babies'. They mean that women's careers are liable to be interrupted, at least temporarily, by childbirth and child care. It is this expectation, as much as the fact itself, that will affect promotion prospects. Some of the most high-powered women in business get round the problem by remaining childless, or even husbandless, but if that solution were widely adopted the population would plummet.

One solution to the problem of combining job and family is part-time work. But in many employers' eyes management is a full-time and continuous job that is incompatible with divided attention. Women, both in management and in lower-grade jobs, have taken the hint: most women workers are employed full-time, says the OECD.

If academic qualifications were the main key to Europe's boardrooms, women would be entering in droves. The large gap between numbers of male and female university graduates in the 1940s and 1950s has narrowed dramatically in most European countries over the past few decades. Women now make up more than 40 per cent of graduates in business, economics and law, although they remain severely underrepresented in engineering and natural sciences.

In a few European countries – Germany, Italy, the UK – governments have mandated some form of positive discrimination within public administrations, but there are few sanctions for non-compliance.

In a survey covering 500 000 employees, one in every three companies in the European Community was found to be discriminating in favour of female employees and searching out women candidates to fill top jobs. More than two-fifths of companies were providing general management training specifically for female staff to help them crash their way through the 'glass ceiling' on their promotion prospects.

If promotion is not coming their way, corporate life proves too inflexible for their needs or unemployment looms, women are increasingly setting up their own companies. In Germany a third of all new business start-ups involve female entrepreneurs; their total number has risen to 600 000. Several European governments, including the Netherlands and Sweden, have introduced policies to encourage women entrepreneurs.

Is all this enough to make a real difference?

Source: *International Management*, March 1992. © Reed Business Information Limited.

APPLICATION 2

A new generation takes the spotlight

FT

Long before the guru as entertainer-cum-evangelist was born with Tom Peters in the 1980s, management ideas were genuinely changing the nature of business.

Peter Drucker recognised post-industrialism and coined the phrase 'knowledge worker' as early as 1969. The quality revolution led by the late W. E. Deming and Joseph Juran is so embedded that it now seems extraordinary that manufacturing should ever have run on a principle of inspection for errors instead of designing errors out of the process.

Even the largely discredited 'scientific management' purveyed by Frederick Winslow Taylor in the 1900s, which gave rise to work study and time and motion, partly survives in re-engineering.

The work done in reaction to Taylorism 30–60 years ago by the behavioural psychologists Elton Mayo, Frederick Herzberg, Abraham Maslow and Douglas McGregor underpins today's human resources theories such as empowerment and self-managed teams.

But what of more recent luminaries? When I first compiled my guide to the gurus in 1991, Gary Hamel was virtually unknown outside the lecture room. His rise to stardom, along with Mike Hammer's has been the most marked among the new entrants in the updated edition of the book.

The quiet, academic C. K. Prahalad, co-author with Hamel of the hugely influential *Competing for the Future* (1994), is respected as a cerebral powerhouse, but the book's ideas of core competencies and strategic foresight are now heavily associated with Professor Hamel, who runs his own lucrative consultancy, Strategos Inc, outside San Francisco and can command lecture fees in Britain of £20 000 a time.

The differing fame levels of bestselling co-authors is a familiar phenomenon in the guru business, often attributable to temperamental differences. The pair behind business re-engineering also went different ways after *Reengineering the Corporation* hit the bestseller lists in 1993, with James Champy of Computer Sciences Corporation (CSC) concentrating on his business career while Michael Hammer, a personality of tank-like force on the platform, left his academic berth at Massachusetts Institute of Technology for the global guru circuit.

Other new entries in the revised edition include Robert Kaplan and David Norton, who developed the Balanced Business Scorecard. They are not global celebrity gurus, but their concept of measuring non-financial performance has spread extensively through business organisations.

Peter Senge popularised the 'learning organisation' which, using knowledge and shared resource, is informing almost every other management discipline as well as spawning phenomena such as 'corporate universities'.

Finally, John P. Kotter of Harvard, formerly classified as a 'lesser guru', has achieved 'greater guru' status following a string of respected books on leadership and culture in organisations.

Source: Carol Kennedy, *Financial Times*, 17 April 1998.

4 The Nature of Organisations

CASE STUDY

Cleaning up in Poland

FT

Stephen and Kerry-Jane Martin spent three weeks travelling around Poland investigating the possibility of starting up a furniture importing business to the UK.

But it was their growing pile of washing that provided the inspiration for their first business venture together. Kerry-Jane searched for the nearest launderette but could find nothing resembling a Western one, even though many people lived in huge tower blocks with little space or money for their own washing machines.

The couple saw their opportunity. Five years on, they run six dry-cleaning shops, have eight agents and several industrial contracts, and takings last year reached £294 789.

Stephen, 40, a former commodity broker and management consultant, had been made redundant in March, 1991, from his job as director of a Midlands-based management consultancy. Kerry-Jane, 30, worked as a political lobbyist but the two were keen to work together on their own ventures.

A friend who had gone to Poland with a school party returned full of enthusiasm and recommended a visit.

Stephen remembered: 'We went out with the idea of buying a product, such as furniture, and importing it into the UK as a nice, simple business venture. But so many of the things we looked at were just too badly made.

'After we had the launderette idea, a contact we knew carried out a survey for us of 1000 people in Lodz, Poland's second city, and the response was very positive.

'It seemed a terrific plan and we thought we were going to be millionaires in three years,' he said wryly.

They returned to England and approached the chief executive of the commodity company Stephen had worked for and he agreed to invest in their idea.

The couple set up a Dutch holding company with £100 000 capital, 90 per cent from their investor and 10 per cent from their savings, and called it East European Holdings. This became the parent company of their Polish limited liability company Luxomat, of which they are both directors. Once in Poland, the company provided them with a rented house in Warsaw, a car, flights home and a basic salary.

Stephen said: 'We learnt about the launderette business as fast as we could and bought the best equipment from Belgium and America. We gave up our rented house in England and returned to Poland with our two dogs in September 1991.

We took on a full-time assistant/translator and found premises in Warsaw in a very good tower block area where there were 250 000 people living on top of each other.

'This building was going to be the first Western-style launderette in Poland and we wanted it to be our super flagship which we would then replicate all round Poland.'

It was opened in June 1992 by the Irish ambassador and featured on television. During the first week, they offered a special deal and the local people were very enthusiastic. 'It was all music to our ears,' said Kerry-Jane. The couple had an office in the basement, just under the water pipes. They began their second week expecting to hear water gushing through them – but they heard not a drip. The launderette stayed empty.

'We discovered just how family-minded the Poles are. They often have a mother or grandmother at home during the day to do the washing, and are distrustful of outsiders. So the idea of sitting around in a launderette with a lot of strangers did not appeal.'

Luckily, the couple had also bought a small dry-cleaning machine and ironing table and, bit by bit, demand took off.

So, the two set about restructuring the business, concentrating on the dry cleaning. They bought new dry-cleaning equipment and retrained their staff. It was a difficult time. 'The cash flow was so bad at times we had to take money out on our credit cards to pay the staff bill.'

They found a factory to use as a central processing plant. It now services their six shops and agents, all in Warsaw and its outskirts. It also does the dry cleaning for several industrial contracts with embassies, the armed forces, restaurants and hairdressers. Luxomat now has a staff of 35.

The couple were determined the shops would stand out as modern, efficient and competitive. But marketing was a problem as they did not want to appear just another foreign organisation looking for a quick profit. However, their Polish manager convinced them it was important the shops had a Western cachet and so the shop signs now announce they are The British Dry Cleaners. 'The difficulty is, the people expect a superior service because it is Western but do not expect to pay more than for using their old local service which left their clothes smelling of old cabbages,' Stephen said.

Turnover for their first two quarters' trading in 1992 was £15 669. The following year, takings reached £85 500. Turnover doubled to £174 181 in 1994 and again in 1995 to £294 789. Takings in the first two quarters of 1996 reached £141 156. Operating profits are about 20 per cent. They say they now need to open more shops and look at the opportunities in other cities.

There is a very strong labour code and little is done to help employers

The couple, who have a daughter Venetia, nearly two, and a second baby due in October, lived in Poland until last Christmas when they felt their general manager was ready to take responsibility for the shops.

Kerry-Jane spends between two and three days there every six weeks and is in weekly telephone contact. They are now living in the Cotswolds after spending three months in France to 'clear their heads of Poland'. The two found working in Poland very frustrating at times. Stephen said: 'The people are very money- and commercially-minded with plenty of entrepreneurial spirit but everyone is struggling against the state. There is also very strong labour code and little is done to help employers.

'Many problems arise from the Poles' habit of non-co-operation with each other. In government offices and utilities, they still treat the consumer like a supplicant who should, in many cases, be obstructed.

'In business, a contract is readily discarded if the terms no longer suit and employees have a low sense of personal responsibility for their work or conduct. All this stems from having been an enclosed society. Things have improved in the past five years but only in the upper echelons of the capital's business community.'

Wages are low – the average salary of the laundry staff is £175 a month – but the company has to pay a further 68 per cent of that amount on top to cover tax and social security. It means the company's average monthly staffing bill is about £10 000.

'Our rents are also high – an average of about £1900 a month – and we have to get everything from the chemicals and bags to cover the clothes to the tagging guns and safety pins from abroad,' Stephen said.

'The bureaucracy is a complete nightmare. Getting permission to open an outlet at one of the city's supermarkets took written permission from 14 different authorities.

'We even had to get permission from a major and a captain in the army. They had no idea why but, aided by a gift of a bottle of vodka each, they said "fine".'

The couple are now looking for new ventures. 'We were asked to set up something in Lithuania but this time we want to do something in Britain or in Western Europe,' they say.

Activity brief

1 Does the growth rate in this case follow a 'standard pattern'? Are the founders looking to achieve too fast a rate of growth?

2 What specific problems were complicating the take-off phase in Poland as a result of it having been a rather 'enclosed' society?

3 What managerial and other arrangements should the couple make when delegating responsibility for their shops to their general manager?

Sources: Financial Times Weekend, 28–29 September 1996. Questions quoted from Keuning, D. (1998), *Management: A Contemporary Approach*, FT Pitman Publishing.

ACTIVITY

1 Make a list, either individually or with others, of as many organisations you can think of not specifically mentioned in Chapter 4 of Mullins (for example, a tennis club, an art gallery, an amateur theatre society, a children's play group, an orchestra, a farm, a public house darts league, a natural childbirth association, etc.).

2 Test this list against the criteria established in Mullins (Chapter 4) for identifying an organisation. For example: do they share the 'common factors' (pp. 88–9); or the 'basic components' (pp. 93–4); can they be classified according to one of the theories presented (pp. 89–93); may we think of them as 'open systems'?

3 Look at the six characteristics that constitute a group (Mullins, Chapter 13, p. 452) and consider whether they would be better classified as groups rather than organisations.

This activity should help you revise Chapter 4 in Mullins and sharpen your understanding of the concept of the organisation by means of contrast (compare Mullins, pp. 381–2, on external factors that increase attention).

DEBATE

'The study of the development of organisation theory has no practical relevance for today's managers.'

Starting points

For

- It provides frameworks and models for managers to measure and assess performance. The 'best' or most suitable aspects from the approaches can be taken and applied to specific organisational issues.
- It is only by looking to the past that we can set the present in its correct context and attempt to predict the future.

Against

- Many of the approaches are now outdated and do not apply to the 'modern' organisation. For example, scientific management is synonymous with 'work study' rather than with current TQM thinking.
- There are too many models and they are too confusingly interrelated to provide a coherent approach to practical application.

Further reading

Etzioni, A. (1986), *Modern Organisations*, Prentice Hall.

Perrow, C. (1986), *Complex Organisations: A Critical Essay*, Random House.

Stewart, R. (1986), *The Reality of Management*, Pan Books.

ASSIGNMENT

In order to complete this assignment you will need to finish the Activity on pp. 22–23 first. Choose one organisation from the list you made in the Activity and, using techniques such as reading publicity material, interviewing, work shadowing and so on, investigate an example of one of them in your area (a local museum, a community care unit, a pub quiz league, a live music club, etc.).

In 1000–1200 words, write up your findings in the form of a case study to support either Chapter 4 or Chapter 5 of Mullins. To do this successfully you will need to emphasise those aspects of your chosen organisation which illustrate analyses in the selected chapter. It is unlikely, however, that you will be able to 'cover' all aspects of the chapter.

Now complete your case study by designing three questions or activities which would help a student get the most out of studying it.

APPLICATION

Innovation and risk taking that breaks free of bureaucracy FT

Norma Redfearn's working life seems to be the managerial equivalent of Dr Dolittle's famous pushmi-pullyu, the animal that faced in two directions at once: she is a public sector entrepreneur.

At first sight the idea of public sector entrepreneurship seems a contradiction. The public sector is made up of large, often slow-moving bureaucracies. Managers are often seen as no more than administrators, implementing policies decided by politicians. They operate within tight rules, designed to protect public money against fraud, which inhibit risk taking and innovation.

Yet there is much more entrepreneurship in the public sector than many people realise and if the public sector is to deliver the ambitious social goals set by the government, we will need a great deal more of it. Take Mrs Redfearn as an example.

When she became head teacher at West Walker primary school in Newcastle in 1986, she took over a school in a state of near collapse. About three-quarters of the children had free school meals. Most of the parents were unemployed single mothers. Only a few of the school's 18 classrooms were occupied.

In a decade Mrs Redfearn and the parents have transformed the school. She realised that to educate her pupils, she had to educate their families. To involve the parents, the school had to become more than classrooms – and was turned into a catalyst for community renewal.

The school's attendance record is now in the 90 per cent range. Scores in national tests are improving. And it is home to a thriving adult education centre with a lively cafe providing breakfast for 60 children and lunch for parents doing courses. Parents who met while building a nature garden formed a housing association, which has built 70 homes opposite the school.

Mrs Redfearn realised that to revive her school she had to be more than a head teacher; she had to be a civic entrepreneur. Civic entrepreneurship is vital to meet demands from clients for better services, politicians for greater effectiveness and taxpayers for more value for money.

We do not need to further restructure or rationalise the public sector, but must revive and revitalise it. A spirit of entrepreneurship, creating social capital in pursuit of social value, is vital. We need not only more output from the public sector, but better outcomes. Not more arrest warrants issued and hospital beds filled, but less crime and better health. The question is not only how big or small the state should be, but what skills it needs. Civic entrepreneurship is vital. At the grass roots of the public sector, a generation is emerging frustrated by bureaucracy and prepared to take risks to create new ways of delivering services.

Like entrepreneurs in other walks of life, they are ambitious, visionary, rule breakers and risk takers. Often great story-tellers and lateral thinkers, they are quick to seize on opportunities. Yet entrepreneurship in the public sector takes a different form.

Civic entrepreneurship is about political renewal as well as managerial change. Public organisations cannot be revitalised unless they renew their sense of purpose. Entrepreneurship requires risk taking.

In the public sector managing those risks requires political skill and leadership. That is why straight business entrepreneurship will not work in the public sector: business entrepreneurs are not good at managing political risks or winning public legitimacy for change.

In the private sector there is a myth of entrepreneur as hero. Civic entrepreneurship is collaborative, because creating more effective services usually means working across boundaries between professions and organisations. Mrs Redfearn realised that her school would only be revived if she was interested in what her pupils were eating, the quality of the homes they came from and the environment they played in.

The good news is that there is a lot more entrepreneurship in the public sector than people think. The bad news is that there is nowhere near enough. What would it take to create a more entrepreneurial public sector? First, the government needs to finance more risk taking and innovation, for instance by creating an innovation fund. The public sector needs its own venture capitalists.

Second, the government needs to reward and recognise innovation, for instance by allowing innovative organisations to keep a share of savings they generate or by creating a new Queen's Award for Excellence. Third, the public sector needs a better system to disseminate innovation. Each Whitehall department could have a Lesson's Learned Unit, dedicated to promulgating good ideas, modelled on the highly effective unit run by the US Army.

Fourth, entrepreneurship in the public sector is virtually impossible without political leadership. Reform to local government, for instance through directly elected mayors, should be aimed, in part, at promoting innovation.

Fifth, the public sector needs to develop a cadre of public sector managers, trained, motivated and rewarded to act as civic entrepreneurs.

The public sector remains central to British society. It can become a source of energy, creating social value and social capital rather than consuming it, but only if more of our head teachers, police officers and doctors are encouraged to become civic entrepreneurs.

Source: Charles Leadbeater, *Financial Times*, 28 April 1998.

5 Organisational Goals and Objectives

CASE STUDY

Holier-than-thou-bank's ethical audit

FT

The Co-operative Bank has for years annoyed its competitors with its holier-than-thou advertisements and its marketing campaigns designed to put rival banks on the spot as financiers of death and destruction. But when the bank publishes its financial results today it will also be putting its ethical claims up for scrutiny, with the publication of its first 'partnership report', covering relationships with staff, customers, suppliers and the wider community.

The results, audited by Richard Evans of a group called Ethics etc, will provide some ammunition for those who have dismissed the Co-op's ethical and ecological claims as marketing gimmicks.

Customers who rushed to sign up for the bank's biodegradable credit card, launched with much trumpeting last year, for example, will be disappointed that the Co-op failed to recycle a single can, tin or piece of aluminium last year.

'NatWest recycles more cans than we do, although we are better on plastic cups. We were so busy developing biodegradable credit cards and ecologically sound fire systems that we lost sight of it,' confesses Paul Monaghan, who ran the partnership team for the bank.

The bank also draws only 1.8 per cent of its staff from ethnic minorities, when they make up 3.9 per cent of the population in the north-west of England, the Co-op's home region. Only 20 per cent of its middle managers and 8 per cent of senior managers are women, where other businesses involved in the Opportunity 2000 equal opportunities scheme score 31 per cent and 17 per cent in these tiers.

Overall, however, the Co-op Bank believes its partnership audit has produced a ringing endorsement of its ethical and ecological stance. Questionnaires found, for example, that 89 per cent of staff said they were proud to be employed by the bank; that 67 per cent of current account customers said they were very satisfied with the service, and a further 26 per cent quite satisfied; and that all of its suppliers rated it as very or quite prompt in paying its bills.

Perhaps most importantly for the Co-op's credibility, the audit concludes that the bank follows through on commitment not to finance the arms trade, oppressive regimes, exploitative factory farming, the fur trade, blood sports or businesses that use animals for testing cosmetics. 'Fox hunts do get turned away – and yes, they do apply,' says Simon Williams, head of corporate affairs.

Mr Evans reviewed the procedures for implementing the bank's ethical policy and checked decisions taken on new customers. 'I am satisfied, from reviewing a random sample of cases referred by the screening process to the ethical policy unit, that the ethical policy in all cases overrides any consideration of economic advantage to the bank,' he says.

The main reasons for turning away business are environmental damage and inadequate animal welfare, such as battery farming.

Environmental audits are making headway among several large businesses, including banks such as NatWest. But the Co-op report is broader, seeking to test the extent to which the bank delivers value to its partners and lives up to its social responsibilities, as well as meeting the goals of its ecological mission statement.

The group of partners, too, is defined somewhat more broadly than most companies define their stakeholders. Besides obvious groups such as shareholders – only one, the Co-operative Wholesale Society, in the bank's case – customers and staff, the bank also includes staff's families, and 'past and future generations of co-operators'.

If the Co-op denies that its social and ethical positioning is just a marketing gimmick, Mr Williams insists that it is not altruism, either. 'We are not seeing this as philanthropy or do-goodism or a marketing ploy. There is a deep-rooted belief that there is a business purpose to this – that if we do all these things, better profits will result.'

Source: George Graham, *Financial Times*, 15 April 1998.

Activity brief

1 How realistic do you think 'ethical management' policies are in today's business climate?

2 Are customers really influenced by a company's ethical policies or are they far more interested in price and performance?

3 Are society's ethical values changing?

4 Are ethical considerations more or less influential on businesses than they used to be?

ACTIVITY

For a work or social organisation with which you are familiar, carry out a SWOT analysis (see Mullins, pp. 131–2), identifying its strategic strengths, weaknesses, opportunities and threats.

Write a report of approximately 1000 words:

1 Presenting each of the four areas of strengths, weaknesses, opportunities and threats in turn.

2 Identifying the opportunities and risks for the future of the organisation which are highlighted by the SWOT analysis.

DEBATE

'Profit maximisation is the only criterion by which organisational effectiveness can be judged.'

Starting points

For

- It is the only criterion which can be applied to any organisation and which, therefore, can allow for direct comparison.
- At the end of the day, profit must be any organisation's guiding principle. Without it, there would be neither organisation nor any of the so-called soft objectives.

Against

- Whilst all organisations need to make a profit in order to survive, there is a difference between this and 'maximisation'. The statement implies that this should take precedence over any other issues such as people development, social responsibility, and so forth.
- The statement implies a return to Taylorism. Profit is not the *only* criterion on which effectiveness can be judged and should be considered alongside other, more qualitative measures as well.

Further reading

Drucker, P. F. (1989), *The Practice of Management*, Heinemann.

Roddick, A. (1991), *Body and Soul*, Ebury Press.

ASSIGNMENT

1 Select three organisations with which you are familiar, trying none the less to get a good range of types (school, bank, toiletries factory, ferry port, employment agency, town council, etc.).

2 Using Fig. 4.7 in Mullins (p. 102) as a prompt, establish which elements in the environment of your three organisations have most influenced their behaviour. This could be information technology at the bank leading to unemployment, customer self-service, extended range of products on offer, such as financial advice at the counter, and so on. In a school the environment might include government policy over the last decade or so in Britain: local management of schools, national curriculum, profiling, national testing, examination league tables, parents' charter, and so on. Notice though, that Mullins draws a distinction between 'impersonal' contingencies which the theorists have concentrated on and others such as cultural ones and, in this case, those resulting from 'power factors' (see Mullins, pp. 569–70).

3 Invent a diagram to show how the behaviour of just *one* of your three organisations is contingent on those environmental factors. There are many kinds of diagram (Venn, flow charts, systems maps, rich pictures, matrices, company charts, etc.) a number of which are used in Mullins (e.g. pp. 18, 363, 436 and 506).

4 Make a list of other variables that may have impinged upon the behaviour which your diagram has suggested is contingent on environmental factors. Remember, simple causal relationships between structure and performance have been queried (see Mullins, p. 569).

APPLICATION 1

'Stakeholders' hope to lift ailing company

FT

A German businessman who was one of Labour's leading industrial advisers before the general election is putting his 'stakeholding' theories into practice with a £2m rescue plan of an ailing mail order company in Liverpool.

Bob Bischof, best known for his corporate turnround skills in the lift-truck industry and in former communist Europe, is putting more than £100 000 into McIntyre & King, a privately-owned company that last year was technically insolvent.

He has introduced 'stakeholders' in the form of the Department of Trade and Industry, Liverpool city council and the Bank of Scotland which have guaranteed funds for the project. He also plans to involve McIntyre's 500-strong workforce in regular 'team meetings' to increase commitment to the company.

Mr Bischof has become chairman of McIntyre after taking a 27.5 per cent stake. Other investments have come from individuals plus 3i, the venture capital group, which has put up £550 000 for a 30 per cent stake. McIntyre is planning to invest nearly £1m in the next year on new telecommunications, computer and mail-handling equipment to participate in the fast growing field of 'direct' mail order, in which consumers place orders for goods such as petcare products or women's clothing using the telephone or the Internet.

He plans to increase the company's workforce to 850 by 2001, raising annual sales 50 per cent to £15m. This will depend on McIntyre increasing its 40 or so customers, which are mainly retailers and other businesses with specific product lines that want to use mail order and direct delivery techniques to get to the consumer.

'We are going to turn the company into a one-stop shop for home shopping with businesses around Europe,' said Mr Bischof, who has lived in the UK for almost all the past 30 years. He expects to push up McIntyre's non-UK sales from 15 per cent to 30 per cent by 2001. The company plans soon to start invoicing in euros.

Before Labour came to power, he advised it on industrial strategy, particularly on ways to tap German experience in involving workers and private and public sector agencies in promoting industrial growth. 'This is one way to put my ideas into practice,' said Mr Bischof, who is writing a book about his industrial strategies.

He previously worked for Jungheinrich, the German lift-truck company. In 1994 he became chairman of Boss, formerly Lancer Boss, the UK company Jungheinrich bought after it went into receivership.

He has also worked for the German and US governments in turning round formerly state-owned companies in east Germany and Slovakia.

The DTI is among the groups to have put money into Mr Bischof's new company through a £500 000 business assistance grant, while the Bank of Scotland has lent £750 000.

Source: Peter Marsh, *Financial Times*, 27 April 1998.

APPLICATION 2

Respected, but short on excellence

FT

The definition of excellence in companies will always be partly subjective. But there is one measure which is, within its narrow limits, purely objective: how far a company has created value for its owners, in the form of increased dividends and a rising share price.

This question was touched on in a recent survey, but in an indirect way. Respondents were asked which European company was best placed to provide maximum long-term value to shareholders. Put that way, the question is one of forward-looking opinion, rather than a bald appeal to the record.

The difference is subtle, but important. Shareholders naturally prefer to emphasise past share price performance, since it leaves less room for excuses on the part of underperforming managers. And in Europe, it is often argued, shareholders tend to occupy a less important place in the scheme of things than in the US.

The typical survey respondent was the chief executive of a large European corporation. Most of those executives would probably work on longer planning horizons than five years. Many, one suspects, would regard the shareholders' interest as only one component – sometimes a minor one – in a much larger whole.

This touches on a wider debate. It is a cliché to say that continental European companies place more emphasis on stakeholder relationships – suppliers, bankers, employees – than do their competitors in the US and UK. It is also a cliché to accuse the US–UK approach of resulting in a short-term attitude to business and investment.

But the debate is shifting ground. The recent ousting of Carlo de Benedetti as head of Olivetti, for instance, bears some of the hallmarks of a shareholders' revolt.

Equally, it is notable that the survey respondents named General Electric of the US as their favourite company worldwide. Jack Welch, GE's chairman, is certainly a long-term strategist. But he is also an explicit champion of shareholder value.

Indeed, he has said that rewarding his managers in stock – as GE increasingly does – is an important way of channelling their competitive instincts into working for the good of the corporation as a whole. European managers plainly admire Mr Welch's results. It might also pay them to emulate his methods.

Source: Financial Times, 18 September 1996.

APPLICATION 3

A social worker being interviewed for a managerial post was asked what she thought her main task as a manager would be. 'To keep my team happy,' she replied. The panel unanimously struck her off the list of possibles.

But was she so far from the truth?

Librarians may be heard complaining that people disturb the books on the shelves, university lecturers say how nice it is in the vacation when the students are not in college, and in Britain it has been rumoured that hospitals have been turning away patients who are too sick. These reactions are not surprising if quality (and therefore remuneration and advancement) in these professions is to be measured in terms of short waiting lists, research output and – who knows, one day – clean books? If a charity for the blind specialises in training clients to be more independent, it would be natural enough to select people who are not so very blind, for they would produce better outcome statistics.

Who, then, are the true clients of the organisation?

In a university is it the students, or the agencies that pay their fees, their grant authorities, their parents? Or is it the omnipresent taxpayer? Or the government, or the research councils, or the loans agencies and banks that lure needy students, their affluent customers of the future, with free offers? Or is it the lecturers with their interesting, reasonably paid, secure jobs? Are they the 'prime beneficiaries'? (See Mullins, p. 98.)

Managers need to know not only *what* an organisation is for (to produce bicycles or trained nurses, etc.) but also *who* it is for. The organisation is not only an open system sending useful outputs into the environment, but also a homeostatic one concerned for its own survival. The two should ideally be complementary, but sometimes they get out of kilter, and then librarians, lecturers, charity workers and the like seem to put the customer far from first.

'Organisations exist in order to achieve objectives and to provide satisfaction for their members' (Mullins, p. 88). That social worker was at least half right.

APPLICATION 4

You can still find pockets of English people (in bowling clubs and other such bastions of tradition) who think that French plumbing stinks, metaphorically and literally. But the *pissoir*, the male urinal open to public gaze and sniff, gave way long ago to the high-tech loo. And its inventor, that backward nation France, soon began exporting this sweet-smelling, self-disinfecting, musical lavatory to as many countries as could afford such luxurious latrines. France also exports its space rockets, air traffic control and field communication systems, Exocets, nuclear-produced electricity, digital telephones, fibre optics, and the fastest train in the world.

One of the most remarkable of this stream of technological successes appeared in the 1980s when the state postal and telephone company distributed free, in place of the phone directory, millions of dedicated computer terminals, *minitels*, connected to the nation's telephone network. This telematic system provides the whole country with access to data banks (including a nationwide telephone directory), interpersonal communication by electronic mail and notice boards, and commercial transactional facilities. Businesses rushed to avail themselves of this immediate and interactive access to a vast network of potential customers, and services available include: teleshopping, telebanking, educational back-up for pupils revising for exams, research and reservation facilities in libraries, booking restaurants, trains, theatre tickets, buying and selling wares such as shares, placing bets, and so on. There is notably the *minitel rose* where lonely hearts, singles, pleasure-seekers and the like are served by all manner of ingenious agencies.

No French organisation can afford to neglect the opportunities offered by this remarkable technological system, which provides new work for hardware manufacturers, maintenance technicians, data input typists, games inventors and manufacturers, graphics designers, and so on and so on.

APPLICATION 5

Much has been written over the years about how an organisation should treat its employees. The Quaker factory-owners of the nineteenth century built housing for their employees, American and Japanese corporations in the twentieth century provide crèches for employees' children and expensive work-out areas to alleviate executive stress. As we approach the millennium, companies are urged to be more caring both towards their staff and the environment: 'printed on recycled paper' and 'not tested on animals' have become *de rigueur*. Indeed, The Body Shop founder, Anita Roddick, when announcing plans recently to open an 'alternative business school' for the twenty-first century, said, 'All that . . . stuff about the only responsibility of business being to the shareholder's pocket can be dumped' – *her* school will challenge traditional theories and get students to look beyond shareholders at issues of animal, human and environmental rights. We have seen the paternalism of the human relations school not only going full circle but off at a tangent.

However, an interesting comment on paternalism as the perceived 'duty' of the employer is given by Ricardo Semler in his book, *Maverick!* (1993). Semler took over the family business, Semco – Brazil's largest marine and food-processing machinery manufacturer – in 1981 and since then has adopted such an unorthodox approach to management that not only is his company the fastest growing in Latin America but he is also much in demand as a public speaker and organisational 'guru'. Semler says that paternalism is 'a dirty word at Semco. We don't want to be a big, happy family. We want to be a successful business. We're only concerned with our employees' performance on the job, not their personal lives. You won't find a running track, swimming pool, or gym at Semco. If our people want to join a health club, that's their business. We do offer health insurance and other benefits, but we ask employees to help manage them. Occasionally, Semco will lend employees money, but only for unpredictable emergencies. Instead of treating employees as children who need looking after, we treat them as adults who are capable of making decisions on the job.'

APPLICATION 6

The word 'bureaucracy' has come a long way since it was originally coined by Weber who used the term to describe a structure which he saw as bringing order and rationality to our lives. Today the word has come to be synonymous with, and used to express our exasperation over, red tape, officialdom and excessive rules and procedures – exemplified, perhaps, in the person we love to hate, the traffic warden. Bureaucrats, like garden weeds, are not only always with us, popping up when you thought you'd finally conquered them but, in these days when 'downsizing' and 'delayering' are trendy buzzwords, actually seem to be increasing. Where are they all coming from? It can't, surely, be from local authorities who, in preparation for their new structures, are trying to lose people? No, this new breed of bureaucrat is coming from further afield – all the way from Brussels, in fact. The last few years have seen a veritable plethora of regulations and directives all apparently aimed at curbing our freedom. The latest EU ruling has halted Mr Spock in his efforts 'to boldly go'. Toys made in China can only be imported if they are 'human-like': Christopher Robin is in, Pooh Bear is out; Postman Pat is OK, his cat isn't; Batman gets the elbow but sidekick Robin is acceptable; and no doubt a subcommittee will be formed to decide if Big Ears is human . . . . At first these were met with exasperated amusement but then amusement was replaced by howls of frustration.

However, whilst the British rail against such an apparent straitjacket, muttering 'I knew this would happen if we went into the EEC' under their collective breath, they attempt to use the rules to win their case: they do what they are told – follow the appeals procedure all the way to Brussels or Strasbourg, wait for two years and are then turned down. Why is it that in the UK we seem to be strangling ourselves in a tangle of regulations when the rest of Europe seems to carry on in spite of, rather than because of? The answer lies in the fact that while Fred in London pours laboriously over his forms, the French, Italians and Dutch all 'know a man who can' – be it a Pierre, a Marco or a Hans. This is not to suggest that a well-greased palm is the key, simply that these countries have become so over-regulated that nobody follows the rules any longer and the resulting lack of recrimination has brought about a freedom of its own.

What happened to Weber's idea of 'technical superiority'? Given that, in some form or another, we *need* bureaucracies, should we work through them (as we do currently) or should we work around them (as everyone else does)? As the French might say, '*C'est la vie*'.

APPLICATION 7

Consider the following e-mail 'conversations' which recently took place:

E-Mail from Karen Meudell to Computer Support: 'Paul, I need to be able to e-mail Tony Callen. Since he's in the School of Languages and therefore not on our local Business School network, what's the easiest and quickest way of finding out his e-mail address?'

Reply from Computer Support to Karen Meudell: 'Hi Karen, the easiest and quickest way to find out the address is to phone him up and ask him . . . .'

Telephone call to Tony Callen: 'Tony, what's your e-mail address?'

Reply from Tony Callen: 'I haven't the faintest idea, I'll have to ring up our Computer Support people and ask them. Once I know I'll let you know – what's your e-mail address?'

Reply from Karen Meudell: 'I don't know, I'll find out from Computer Support and e-mail you back . . . hang about, I can't if I don't know your address . . . I'll write a note and use the internal post – it might be quicker . . . .'

APPLICATION 8

'In 1987 people began to flee to Malawi . . . we fled Mozambique because Renamo and Frelimo were shooting against each other . . . they would shoot people who even looked at them who were only children and women . . . armed bandits arrived one Sunday morning . . . they burned all the houses and killed every family in our area . . . my brothers and my sister were all killed . . . we walked for three days in the shrub . . .

- "Where are you going?"
- "To the Changlambica camp . . . ."
- "You are armed bandits."
- "No, here are our documents, rosaries, crucifix . . . ."

'We were imprisoned for three days . . . but in Malawi the government began to distribute flour, beans, salt, sugar, clothes and soap . . . they built a hospital, a school, a store and wells . . . in that same year I began to study in the first form and now in 1994 I am in the sixth form . . . in the first lesson we received an exercise book and a biro . . . I am very happy to hear the war in Mozambique has ended . . . I would like to be there in my country . . . .'

After independence in 1975, right-wing guerillas began undermining the pro-Soviet government in Mozambique. The resultant civil war saw hundreds of thousands killed. Over a million took refuge in Malawi, and many more in other neighbouring states.

Compositions like the ones the above extracts – from Changlambica camp – are taken from are being collected from all over the world by Martin Smalley at The Body Shop with a view to publishing them to sell for charity. Save The Children are closely associated with this venture. The idea was conceived under the scheme that organisation operates whereby employees may use company time to work on projects of social worth.

'Some organisations extend the range of social responsibilities . . . to the needs of developing countries' (Mullins, p. 138).

APPLICATION 9

A look at the future . . .

The following is an extract from an Information Services Strategy Document for a university.

'Telecommunications, broadcasting and publishing technologies are converging. The implications of the convergence for education and entertainment are most significant. As legislation lifts the constraints, the impact of developments in consumer electronics will be immense and is largely unpredictable. However, the convergence will have tremendous implications for the future operation of our higher educational establishments. Any university which fails to take a positive and proactive approach to the new technologies will rapidly become disadvantaged in the marketplace and reside in the second division or even risk becoming absorbed by a more aware institution.

'In the effective university there will be a comprehensive communications network spanning the entire university, and available to every member of staff and every student. On the desk of each member of academic staff will be a personal computer (PC) linked to the network, or at very least an access point for the connection of a portable PC. A similar facility will be available to the great majority of support staff. In general the computer will become "an information access device" first, and a "computer" as a secondary role.

'Students should have their own low-cost portable PCs and have access to the network at a variety of points (e.g. the library, seminar rooms, laboratories, halls of residence and even in the "bed sits" in the town).

'The network will provide a range of information and communication services, available to a common standard at every access point. These will include: electronic mail; a standardised "bulletin board" providing administrative information; commonly available teaching and learning materials; library services; and access to off-campus networked materials and services. The network will also offer the opportunity to interwork nationally and globally with industry and commerce, which in turn could generate new commercial revenue streams to augment university funds.

'For a university whose buildings are dispersed the consequent changes in working practice would be massive and beneficial. The IT revolution, long heralded, is available at last at reasonable cost to transform the working practices of the University. A sound Information Services Strategy, properly implemented with strong corporate leadership and coordination would usher this university into a position of institutional leadership within the UK and Europe.'

With thanks to Jim Brookes, University of Portsmouth.

AFTERTHOUGHTS

'Excessive forethought and too great solicitude for the future are often productive of misfortune; for the affairs of the world are subject to so many accidents that seldom do things turn out as even the wisest predicted; and whoever refuses to take advantage of present good from fear of future danger, provided the danger be not certain and near, often discovers to his annoyance and disgrace that he has lost opportunities full of profit and glory, from dread of dangers which have turned out to be wholly imaginary.'

Francesco Guicciardini (1483–1540): Storia d'Italia

Alan, taking his usual Sunday pilgrimage to the DIY Superstore, was pleased to find that, unlike their competitors, they had the exact item that he needed. On approaching the cashier he was told, 'I'm sorry but I can't sell that to you because the computer is telling the till that we're out of stock'. Unable to believe what he was hearing he replied, 'How can you be out of stock when I'm holding three of them in my hand?' The answer was, 'I'm sorry but the computer thinks we're out of stock and and it won't read the bar code'. Alan said, 'Well if I'm holding three non-existent items you won't arrest me for shoplifting if I walk out of the door with them, will you?' The reply was, 'I think I'd better call a supervisor . . . .'

'The world community can continue to pursue the arms race and build ever-larger and more deadly weapons, or it can shift and move deliberately and urgently towards the provision of the basic needs of our global family. It cannot do both. Either we invest in arms and death, or we invest in life and the future development of the people of the world.'
Cardinal Basil Hume

6 The Nature of Management

CASE STUDY

Great expectations and hard times: A tale of two managers

The following case study is based on research carried out by Dr Colin Hales and Michael Nightingale for the Hotel and Catering Institutional Management Association. The research used depth interviews with the managers' role sets and the managers themselves, together with structured observation of the managers' work.

Alex

Alex is the manager of a busy unit of a family restaurant chain owned by a large food, drink and leisure company which has shown steady growth over the past twenty years. The restaurant, situated beside a main road, is open daily and offers a standard low-price fixed menu of popular dishes and waitress service for up to 150 people. The site also offers washroom facilities, a small shop and a children's play area. All areas of work in the restaurant – cooking, service, cleaning/maintenance, billing and record keeping – are standardised and codified in detailed operating manuals. Alex, who has worked for the company for the past five years, is 34, married, educated to HND level, and has switched careers from retail to catering management. He works shifts with two (variable) days off in seven. He has a deputy manager, restaurant manager and chef reporting to him directly and he, in turn, reports to an area manager.

A number of people, therefore, have expectations about what Alex *ought* to be doing in his job: his immediate boss, senior line and head office managers, his deputy manager, other staff in the unit, the restaurant's customers and, of course, Alex himself. Despite some differences, there is considerable agreement among these expectations and, indeed, many of them are explicitly communicated in such things as company regulations, operating manuals, standard forms and controls.

Broadly speaking, Alex is expected to deal with eight key areas:

1 *Staffing* Ensuring adequate staffing levels, recruiting/selecting staff (waitresses and cooks), conducting training, allocating duties, organising rotas and holidays, dealing with grievances and keeping staff records.
2 *Premises/equipment* Making sure that they are kept clean and well maintained.
3 *Materials* Controlling stock, ordering goods and checking deliveries.

4 *Money* Controlling costs, controlling cash and completing financial returns.
5 *Customers* Liaising with customers, monitoring customer satisfaction with the service and dealing with customer requests and complaints.
6 *Operations* Organising, monitoring and checking work.
7 *Quality* Ensuring that company product and service standards are maintained.
8 *Business performance* Meeting sales/profit targets, developing promotions and new business ideas, and making the business grow.

Predictably, Alex's managers emphasise the 'money', 'customers', 'quality' and 'business performance' aspects of the job, whilst his staff place more emphasis on 'staffing', 'materials' and day-to-day 'operations' matters. Alex himself acknowledges that these are what his job is about, with two notable exceptions: first, he does not believe that it is his job to train his staff; and second, he does not see it as his responsibility to develop new business for the restaurant.

In terms of how he spends his time, Alex concentrates on maintaining the provision of a standard service by ensuring that the restaurant has an adequate supply of staff, materials and equipment and by monitoring the operational performance of the restaurant, using standard control procedures. The key *tasks* which occupy most of his time are:

- Ordering/controlling materials.
- Controlling money (cash receipts and expenditure).
- Monitoring operational performance.
- Maintaining company quality standards.
- Planning and maintaining staff levels.

This means that, in terms of *activities*, Alex concentrates on the following matters (in descending order of time spent):

1 Cashing-up (emptying the till, counting the takings) and putting them in bags to take to the bank).
2 Stocktaking (day-to-day checks plus a full stocktake lasting five hours on a Sunday evening).
3 Ordering goods (completing order forms and telephoning for goods which run out unexpectedly, and checking deliveries).
4 Talking to customers at the till and dealing with customers' requests or complaints.
5 Helping out in areas of operational work (cooking, moving stock, working the till, cleaning, making minor repairs to equipment and, occasionally, serving in the restaurant).
6 Drawing up staff rotas, allocating duties and recording time sheets.
7 Checking the quality of food and service by observing staff at work.

There are two activities which, in view of other people's expectations of him, are conspicuously absent from Alex's work: first, training (except for the occasional cursory instruction to an employee on how to do something, usually in response to an employee request); and secondly, any kind of 'entrepreneurial' activity such as local advertising, offering special promotions or generating new business ideas.

This absence of entrepreneurial activity is not surprising, however, given the number of rules and procedures within which Alex has to work. Such things as menus and prices, methods of food preparation and presentation, restaurant decor/furniture and nominated suppliers of materials are all determined by head office. The only area of choice available to Alex is where to purchase fresh vegetables.

Yet much of what Alex does is chosen, rather than imposed. For example, he chooses to carry out stocktaking and cashing-up himself rather than delegating them and he is quite happy – indeed, rather enjoys – working the till, replacing light bulbs and broken toilet seats, and cooking at the griddle. On the other hand, he is content to exercise indirect 'paper' control over the restaurant, leaving the more direct management of staff to his deputies.

This is reflected in the manner in which Alex does his job. He spends most of his time at his desk in a small, windowless office, away from the restaurant. For the remainder of the time, he is operating the till in the restaurant, working in the stockroom, or is out, paying in takings to the local bank. About a third of his time is spent on various forms of paperwork: completing weekly trading reports, records of takings, ledgerbook, staff time sheets and stock records, and checking delivery notes, price lists, invoices, and so on. About a sixth of his time is spent helping out on operational tasks. The remaining time is spent in some form of interaction with others. A small proportion of these contacts are scheduled meetings – usually in the form of regular meetings with the area manager to discuss day-to-day issues or, less frequently, with the regional manager. The remaining contacts are either telephone conversations, usually with suppliers about orders and deliveries, or unscheduled meetings, which are many, varied, generally short-lived and are usually initiated by someone else (either a member of staff or a customer). These unscheduled meetings are mainly either brief exchanges with customers as they pay their bill or they are interruptions from staff – requests for information or assistance – during paperwork. It is not unusual, for example, for Alex to be interrupted during completion of the weekly trading report by a cook asking for help in opening a can of fruit cocktail.

Alex, therefore, tends to be much more attuned to expectations which are either immediate – that is, they come from face-to-face contact with his staff or his immediate boss – or specific – that is, they are explicitly stated in regulations and manuals. He is much less aware of the more general expectations of senior managers in the company or of customers. Therefore, he tends to do the things he *must* do, rather than exploring what he *could* do. As a result, his job is predominantly one of routine paperwork and 'helping out'.

Rose

Rose is the manager of a domestic services unit responsible for the cleaning and housekeeping of a large National Health hospital in the Midlands. In common with other hospitals, it is undergoing considerable changes in funding and structure. Most relevant here is the move towards 'contracting out' ancillary services such as cleaning, laundry and catering through a process of competitive tendering in which existing in-house services, such as domestic services, are invited to participate. The provision of domestic services, however, continues to be subject to stringent regulations, imposed by the health authority, relating to hygiene standards. The domestic services unit is strongly unionised and staff are fearful of, and opposed to, the impending changes.

Rose, who has worked in hospital domestic services for seven years, is 29, single and educated to HND level. She reports directly to the hospital administrator and has six supervisors reporting to her, each in charge of cleaning in a particular area of the hospital (a group of wards, for example).

A very diverse set of people have expectations about what Rose *ought* to be doing in her job: her immediate boss (the hospital administrator), other senior managers (such as personnel), her immediate subordinates (the supervisors), the domestic staff of the hospital, trade union representatives, the nursing and medical staff, and the patients. Therefore, she is subject to different and conflicting pressures, not only from 'above' and 'below', but also from three different areas within the hospital – administration, domestic services and health care – each with its own distinct culture. Because it is a time of change and uncertainty, there are many new and ambiguous expectations emerging in addition to those currently expressed more explicitly in hospital regulations.

In broad terms, Rose is *expected* to work on seven key areas:

1 *Staffing* On a day-to-day basis, this means ensuring adequate staffing levels, recruiting and selecting domestic staff, conducting training, allocating duties, organising shifts and holidays, dealing with grievances, and keeping staff records. In the longer term, however, it means managing, or reconciling, the administrators' requirements – that the domestic services unit become more efficient and competitive through changes in work practices and possible redundancies – with the staff and union expectations that their jobs remain secure. These long-term expectations also colour, and make more difficult, short-term issues such as allocating duties, recruiting new staff and dealing with grievances. They also give rise to ongoing industrial relations work, meeting and negotiating with trade union representatives.

2 *Premises/equipment* Making sure that all surface areas of the hospital and linen are kept scrupulously clean.

3 *Information* Explaining existing and new regulations and policy, and offering technical advice when required.

4 *Operations* Organising, directing and monitoring the work of domestic staff.

5 *'Client' liaison* Liaising with nursing and medical staff.

6 *Quality* Negotiating and reconciling the competing and often ambiguous standards of service quality defined by nursing, medical, domestic and administrative staff and ensuring that these negotiated standards are met.

7 *Self* Being knowledgeable, acting as a source of information and advice and being involved in the process of change within the hospital.

Therefore, although there is general agreement about the *areas* of work which make up Rose's job, there is considerable disagreement over *what* she should be trying to achieve in these areas. Rose not only recognises these areas as central to her job but also recognises that the job is 'political' in that she must manage these conflicts.

Because of this she perceives her job as having clear priorities and, consequently, sees certain tasks, such as staff induction, training and development and acting as a technical adviser, as less important, at least for the present.

Rose, therefore, spends her time trying to bring about an increasingly efficient and effective cleaning service to the satisfaction of both administrative and nursing/medical staff. This means that she has a preoccupation with day-to-day staffing matters and long-term staffing issues. The key *tasks* which occupy most of her time are:

- Planning and ensuring adequate levels of staffing in the short term.
- Maintaining good industrial relations.
- Ensuring and maintaining standards of cleanliness.
- Controlling the cost of the domestic services function.
- Bringing about a lower level of staffing in the long term through the restructuring of work.

She is, therefore, mainly engaged on the following activities (in descending order of time spent):

1 Organising staff duties, rotas and holidays.

2 Dealing with staff grievances.

3 Checking work quality and hygiene standards.

4 Negotiating with union representatives and handling disputes.

5 Identifying the need for equipment repairs and new materials.

6 Discussing organisational policy changes for staff.

Contrary to others' expectations, but consistent with Rose's own priorities, three activities are absent: first, staff training; second, acting as a general technical adviser; and third, general liaison with nursing and medical staff. In the prevailing atmosphere of crisis and uncertainty, in which staffing and industrial relations issues are to the fore, Rose sees these other activities as unaffordable luxuries.

Indeed, the climate of change has made Rose's job less clearly defined than before. Under these circumstances, although the restructuring issue is *what* must preoccupy her, Rose has considerable choice about *how* she handles it. She chooses to make the job people-oriented and 'political', trying to reconcile competing interests, ameliorating the impact of change on domestic staff, and fighting for the integrity and continued existence of the domestic services unit within the hospital. This means that her approach is proactive and highly involved in hospital matters.

This is reflected in the manner in which Rose does her job. She spends a significant amount of her time out of the office, either at meetings or touring the hospital, speaking to domestics, nurses or administrative staff and checking the progress and quality of work. Indeed, interactions of one kind or another take up most of Rose's time. Many of these are scheduled and time-consuming committee meetings, policy meetings or negotiations, involving a wide variety of people (administrators, the personnel department, trade union representatives and medical staff). In addition, Rose also spends much of her time on more fleeting unscheduled meetings or conversations – with domestic, nursing and administrative staff. Many of these are instigated by Rose herself, seeking out people to obtain or give information, to deal with problems and to request or give assistance. Paperwork takes up relatively little of her time and is largely concerned with staff/personnel matters. Telephone calls are mainly internal, again predominantly about staff-related matters.

Rose's mobile, proactive involvement in the hospital reflects her general awareness of the politics of the organisation. She defines her job not only in terms of the more formal demands of her superiors and the medical staff but also in terms of the more ambiguous expectations of her supervisors and staff. Out of this uncertainty she has created the kind of job which she feels she *ought* to do: the proactive, personalised management of a key political issue.

Activity brief

1 Compare and contrast the two jobs in terms of:

(a) Mintzberg's 'managerial roles';
(b) Stewart's 'demands, constraints and choices' model.

How useful are these frameworks for pointing up the similarities and differences between the two jobs?

2 How far and in what ways are the two managers influenced by:

(a) the internal environment of the organisation; and
(b) the external environment?

3 How far can the similarities and differences between the two jobs be explained by the fact that they are both in the service sector but one is in the private sector whilst the other is in the public sector?

4 Which of the two managers is the more effective? Give your reasons, indicating in particular how you define 'effective'. What other evidence, if any, would you require in order to judge the managers' effectiveness?

Case study provided by Dr Colin Hales, University of Surrey.

ACTIVITY

This activity is a time management exercise. Read the text below and then, in small groups, answer the questions at the end.

Suzanne Potts has been an area sales manager for Page Fashions in the south-west for the last six months and is an energetic manager who, prior to her promotion, had been with the company for five years as a store manager. Page Fashions have both stand-alone high-street shops and also shop-in-shops in many of the large department stores.

She believes that she manages her time effectively but recognises that sometimes distractions prevent her from accomplishing what she considers to be the most important aspects of her job. Suzanne generally likes to do some informal planning of what she thinks must be achieved each day.

On Monday evening Suzanne was relaxing at home, thinking about some of the things she knew needed to be done the next day. In her mind she prepared her schedule for the following day.

Planned schedule

AM Check progress of new manager at shop-in-shop, Badgers, Bournemouth.

10.00 Appointment with David Douglas, store director, Badgers, Bournemouth.

PM Follow-up customer care training, Page stand-alone shop, Bournemouth and complete an area managers' sales and branch administration checklist.
Ring regional sales director to discuss arrangements for appraisal next week.
Ring Jane Pearson, recruitment officer, about vacancies in the area.

Actual schedule

8.30 Arrives at Page shop, Bournemouth, has a cup of coffee and discusses the recently received new range with the manager.

9.00 Leaves to walk to Badgers across the precinct.

9.05 Arrives at Badgers to talk to Sarah Brooks, the new manager. However, Sarah has an appointment with personnel at 9.15 to discuss the customer service training sessions organised by Badgers and had expected to see Suzanne after her appointment with Mr Douglas.

9.15 Suzanne notices the department is looking untidy and starts to remerchandise it. The part-timer assists and gets extra stock from the stockroom to fill up the department. Suzanne is pleased to be able to serve two customers who each buy a complete outfit.

9.45 The manager returns, joins in the remerchandising and helps the part-timer to put the stock on the correct hangers.

9.50 The Page shop, Exeter, rings Suzanne with an urgent query concerning the banking. They appear to be missing £10 from the cash register and the manager suspects a member of staff, although she does not have any evidence.

10.00 Suzanne makes a note to ring the personnel department for information concerning the member of staff and some guidance concerning the correct procedures. She leaves the floor after checking that she has made a note of all the problems associated with the query.

10.05 Suzanne arrives late for her appointment with Mr Douglas. His secretary has just put through a telephone call and asks Suzanne to sit and wait.

10.15 Mr Douglas greets Suzanne and apologises for keeping her waiting. They discuss the plans for resiting the department and the schedule previously discussed. As an additional point, he is concerned about the size of the deliveries and the amount of stockroom space that seems to be needed. Suzanne agrees to look into the problem.

11.00 Suzanne has a quick coffee in the customer restaurant and uses the time to make some notes concerning her meeting with Mr Douglas.

11.20 She returns to the department. Sarah and her part-timer have completed the remerchandising. There are one or two changes which Suzanne feels that she needs to make and which she briefly discusses with Sarah.

11.45 Sarah asks if she can talk to Suzanne about a personal problem. She needs to take some holiday to try to sort out an argument she has had with her landlord which may involve her moving out of her present accommodation. They discuss the issue at length on the shop floor and Suzanne agrees that Sarah can take two days' holiday the following week.

12.20 Suzanne leaves to go back to the stand-alone shop. On the way to the shop she buys some sandwiches and a drink from Marks & Spencer.

12.45 When she arrives at the shop, the manager is at lunch. Suzanne eats her sandwiches and then sits in the office and makes her phone calls to head office.

1.00 Jane Pearson, recruitment officer, is interviewing, so Suzanne leaves a message for her to ring back. The merchandise department checks the deliveries and allocation for Badgers and it appears that they are only marginally larger than in the previous year, but they agree to check the details and ring back.

1.15 Anne, the manager, returns from lunch and Suzanne starts to talk to her about the customer care programme. Debbie, the deputy, comes into the office to say that there is a problem with the cash register and they all go out on to the shop floor. Suzanne realises that it is a problem with the audit roll and spends five minutes fixing it. While they are out on the floor a customer complaint appears to be getting heated and Suzanne steps in to sort it out.

1.45 Suzanne returns to the office to ring her sales director concerning her appraisal next week. They discuss the format and Suzanne agrees to prepare some notes beforehand. She does this straight away while it is fresh in her mind.

2.00 The training manager rings to discuss Suzanne's nominations for the next New Manager Induction Course. They also discuss Suzanne's recommendations for an area trainer for the south-west region.

2.10 Suzanne continues her discussion with Anne about the customer care training. She then spends fifteen minutes talking to the sales assistants about their comments on the package.

2.25 The merchandise department ring Suzanne back to confirm the information regarding Badgers.

2.30 Suzanne starts to complete an area manager's report on the stand-alone branch. The report is designed to cover all aspects of the sales and general administration of the branch.

2.35 Jane Pearson returns Suzanne's call and Suzanne asks if she can ring her back because the information she requires is up in the office. She continues with her check of the branch.

3.30 Suzanne moves some fixtures because they appear to be out of line. She asks Anne to tidy the accessories fixture which looks untidy.

3.45 Suzanne and Anne have a cup of tea and discuss Anne's forthcoming wedding.

4.05 Suzanne phones Jane Pearson to discuss staff vacancies.

4.20 She decides to do a full administration check with Anne. There are a number of queries outstanding which Suzanne tries to sort out.

5.25 Anne goes down to the shop floor to ensure that the cashing-up is done properly and to tidy the shop before closing.

5.40 Suzanne agrees with Anne to continue with the administration check on her next visit. She has completed the area manager's report on the shop floor and stockroom, and hands it to Anne. There are a number of critical points which Suzanne asks Anne to put right.

5.45 Suzanne leaves to go home.

6.00 On her way home, Suzanne makes a mental note to write to Mr Douglas about the stock problem and the reply from the merchandise department.

Questions

1 How effective has Suzanne's day been?

2 What has she achieved?

3 What impression has she created with each of the people she has visited?

4 Has any time been wasted? If so, how much and on what?

5 What work is outstanding?

6 What advice would you give to Suzanne?

Activity contributed by Jackie Rainford, Common Sense Training Ltd.

DEBATE

'Someone with poor social skills can never become a good manager . . . you can't make a silk purse out of a sow's ear.'

Starting points

For

- Some people just don't understand what makes other people 'tick' and always put their foot in it.
- Getting on well with other people is an essential part of a manager's job.
- People with poor social skills often don't understand the impact they have on other people – so they don't see the problem.

Against

- People can learn to change their behaviour and become more skilful at handling other people.
- Organisations are made up of all sorts of people: if one person has poor social skills, others can make up for them.
- Systematic appraisal will help managers to see their deficiencies more accurately.

Further reading

Drucker, P. F. (1989), *The Practice of Management*, Heinemann.

Mintzberg, H. (1973), *The Nature of Managerial Work*, Harper and Row.

Pedler, M., Burgoyne, J. and Boydell, T. (1994), *A Manager's Guide to Self-Development*, 3rd edn, McGraw-Hill.

ASSIGNMENT

In not more than 1500 words, critically evaluate the statement: 'There is no difference between "management" in the public and private sectors.'

You need to consider areas such as:

- approaches to planning and forecasting;
- how approaches to customers vary;
- what/who are the key influencers of strategy;
- what their approach to allocating resources and making profits is;
- the levels of freedom and constraints in the way they handle their employees;
- how publicly accountable they are for their actions.

Further reading

Bourn, J. (1979), *Management in Central and Local Government*, Pitman.

Mullins, L. J. (1999), *Management and Organisational Behaviour*, 5th edn, FT Pitman Publishing, 178–81.

Assignment adapted from Meudell, K. and Callen, T. (1996), *Management and Organisational Behaviour: A Student Workbook*, 2nd edition, Pitman, pp. 203–4.

APPLICATION 1

One of the authors was involved in a customer care initiative in a company who had (rightly) decided that the ethos of customer care should pervade the whole organisation. The board of directors were to receive the first tranche of training and it would then cascade throughout the company.

The trainer decided to use the same activity throughout all the courses, which involved participants in constructing a parachute-type contraption that, when filled with a fresh egg, would enable the egg to be dropped from a given height and land unbroken. Participants were given forty minutes to complete their task. The following happened.

1 At the end of the allotted time, the board of directors were still arguing about who was going to do what. The production director (who was an engineering graduate) poured cold water on any idea that was suggested, quoting laws of physics, stress and aerodynamics; the managing director had taken the role of chairman but no one was following his lead; the personnel director was trying, in vain, to act as a gatekeeper; the finance director had switched off completely and was reading a newspaper; and the marketing director was more concerned with the look of the finished article than whether it could do the job.
2 A second group was made up of canteen assistants, cleaners and general maintenance workers. Halfway through the exercise the trainer went up to the group to see how they were doing, expecting them to ask for further time. Not only had they completed the task but they had even tried out a prototype. When asked how they did it so quickly, one member of the group replied: 'Well we all decided who was going to do what and then we got on with it.' Looking a bit guilty, she added: 'And it helped that Freda had done something similar before, so she was a sort of adviser.'

The moral of this story? Things go much more smoothly when you can agree on what's got to be done and who's going to do it. In this case it also helped that a previous situation and solution could be transferred to a new situation – but don't forget that what has worked in the past may not *always* work in the future.

APPLICATION 2

Mary is a well-qualified, widely experienced, highly professional nurse in her early fifties. She has worked within the National Health Service for the whole of her career, holding the post of 'Sister' for many years.

Sweeping and fundamental changes have been, and still are, taking place within the service. Imposed from the very top, these are cultural as well as organisational and financial. Control by 'market forces', the formulation and implementation of a Patients' Charter, together with stated objectives and measurable targets are all part of these changes. Management responsibilities which once concerned only the topmost levels are now devolved down through the organisation to unit level and include responsibility for budgeting, purchasing, staff appraisal, cost control, feasibility studies and the compilation of various statistical and management reports.

Until recently, Mary's role, one of 'team leader' for a specific aspect of health care, was very much a 'hands-on' appointment, working with a close-knit team of professionals. Over a very short period of time her role and job title were changed to 'manager' although no training or development were given to enable Mary to cope with this change, other than a dramatic increase in the requirement to attend meetings.

Although she seems to cope as well as anyone in the new situation, Mary believes and insists that she is a professional nurse and *not a manager!* She regrets the move away from her traditional role towards increasing managerial responsibilities and activities. She is particularly competent at team-building, able easily to develop and maintain interpersonal relationships. Her senior manager considers that she is carrying out her new duties and responsibilities well.

There are many implications for both present and future managerial and organisational effectiveness in this situation: the questions raised are many and varied.

- Can such changes be imposed automatically from the top, as in this situation, with a high guarantee of success?
- What skills (if any) are transferable between the technical and managerial role needs, and what are the implications for future individual and team motivation and relationships?
- How should training and development be viewed in this type of situation?
- What are the moral and ethical implications of arbitrarily changing a job which the job holder finds satisfying and rewarding into one which is considerably less so?

Provided by David Callas, Development Consultants.

APPLICATION 3

In his book *The Age of Unreason* (1989), Charles Handy describes managers of the future as 'portfolio people' who will simultaneously have a variety of paid and unpaid jobs rather than the generally accepted career/job pattern of today.

Even post-recession this may sound a little implausible for some people but the market for 'executive temps' or 'interim managers' is a growing one (*Management Today*, May 1994). Originating in the Netherlands as their answer to restrictive employment legislation, the concept spread first to the USA and has now reached British shores.

The reasons for using these near-board-level people are many and varied: when an organisation needs specific skills to start up, turnaround or close a department, division or subsidiary; when specialist skills are needed for a short time only or for a fill-in post between a senior person leaving and a new person being appointed. The agencies who specialise in this growing breed of 'leased manager' appear to be somewhat élitist in their approach. They stress the difference between *their* temps and the growing band of freelance consultants as one of commitment to both providing solutions *and* implementing them.

Is this the way forward for both organisations and surplus-to-requirements full-time executives in the future? What is the difference (if any) between this élite band and Handy's concept of the 'shamrock' organisation?

APPLICATION 4

David was a managing director who believed firmly in the art of delegation – so much so that by 11.30 every morning his desk was free of post except for one or two letters to dictate to his secretary. Now in case you've misunderstood, David didn't see *all* the company's post and pass it out accordingly, this was his *own* post. Thus everyone else also had their own little piles – plus, by 11.45 each morning, most of David's as well. If, during the day, calls came in to him or problems arose, they also would be delegated. If he was able to find the appropriate person at their desk, the delegated duty would probably be passed over by phone. If a manager rashly left their desk they would return to find a Post-it note stuck to it. One person came back from a week's holiday to find not only the entire desk covered in Post-it notes but also half the wall . . . .

David never followed up to see if the job had been done, he made the assumption that you would get on with it – he didn't even necessarily require you to report back when it was completed.

Was this too good to be true: the manager who delegated according to all the rules in the textbooks and who then, secure in the knowledge that the work would be done, takes the afternoon off? Or was there more here than meets the eye? What about perception, personality, motivation and control? You see, you cannot just look at one aspect of 'managing' in isolation without considering all the other variables as well.

APPLICATION 5

The Oast House Theatre has been recently restored. The original Kentish oast house has been converted to a studio theatre and artists' workshops, while a new extension has been added on to house the main theatre, cafeteria and bars.

The money to convert the theatre came mostly from government and EU grants, donations and fund-raising events. Its organisation structure is not particularly unusual: there is a board of management made up of local dignitaries, patrons of the Arts and some well-known names from the world of theatre and entertainment. Their job is to oversee the strategy of the Oast House and to use their network of contacts to raise both money and public awareness. Reporting to the board of management is the Oast House director and reporting to him are a cook and a part-time administration assistant. These last three are the only people at the Oast House who are currently paid for their labours, although it should be said that they all frequently work over and above their paid hours.

All other 'employees' from cafeteria assistants to bar staff and box office are volunteers who give their services free. They do so for a variety of reasons: some because they genuinely want to see the Oast House as a working theatre; some younger ones because they are doing drama or stage management courses; some because it provides an opportunity to socialise and get out of the house; and some for all of these reasons.

Can you see how 'managing' these people is very different from managing paid employees? Anything resembling an autocratic style, they'll be off like a shot and there's nothing anyone can do about it. On the other hand, it's very necessary to present the Oast House as a professional organisation and high standards have to be maintained. The theatre director has to walk a very narrow tightrope between these requirements and ensuring that everybody's individual motivations and aspirations are met, at least in part.

AFTERTHOUGHTS

'People ask the difference between a leader and a boss . . . . The leader works in the open, and the boss in covert. The leader leads, and the boss drives.'
Theodore Roosevelt (speech, New York, 24 October 1910)

'If nurses and teachers are trained but doctors and children are educated, where do managers come from?'
Val Marchant (1994)

'The really efficient laborer will be found not to crowd his day with work, but will saunter to his task surrounding by a wide halo of ease and leisure.'
Henry Thoreau (Journal 1841)

AND FINALLY ...*

Mark was the personnel manager for an engineering company. One day, faced with a particularly difficult industrial relations problem, he gave up trying to find a solution, left it all on his desk and walked over to the window to look out.

Lost in thought, he didn't hear his boss come in until he walked over and tapped him on the shoulder. Startled, Mark turned round and somewhat guiltily said, 'Sorry, I know I've got this union problem to sort out – I was just thinking about it.' His boss replied, 'Thinking is as much a part of management as doing things,' and walked out.

Mark said many years later that he had never forgotten his boss's comment – too often we associate management only with activity. Perhaps Mark's boss had read Mullins?

*With thanks to Brian Sutcliffe for the original idea.

7 Managerial Behaviour and Effectiveness

CASE STUDY

Effective management: Hard news or soft sell?

In this case study you will be introduced to two managers, Harold Plumb and Ian McCullem, both of who work for the same small company, Timothy Willis Ltd. Having made their acquaintance you will be asked to make an assessment of their behaviour and effectiveness as managers; but first, let's tell you a little more about the company which employs them.

Timothy Willis Ltd

Founded in the last quarter of the nineteenth century, the company is a weekly newspaper publisher and 'jobbing' printer located in an essentially rural part of north-east Scotland. Family owned (by the Willises) since it was established, the current managing director is a member of the fifth generation to have a direct involvement in the running of the business, succeeding to the post upon her mother's retirement some five years ago. The family has a high profile in the community, supporting local causes and charities, and often using 'the power of the press' to publicise important issues.

The company was established by Timothy Willis to realise his dream of becoming a newspaper publisher. Although never becoming a 'media baron' he was successful in launching a weekly paper, the *North East News* or 'the *NEN*' as it is affectionately known to generations of both readers and company employees. The paper has flourished over the years: its circulation steadily rising to a current level of 18 000 copies a week in an area where the total population (excluding sheep and grouse!) is around 65 000. It has no serious competition, the only other paper in the area being a monthly 'freesheet'. This has attracted *some* advertising revenue, but *NEN* remains a financially sound and profitable publication.

Timothy was a shrewd enough businessman to realise that publishing a weekly newspaper would not occupy the time of all his production staff for the whole week. So, in common with many other similarly sized newspaper companies, he established a printing business which would utilise equipment and employee time when newspaper production was completed for the week. However, printing work has been generally regarded as the 'poor relation' at the company, a view that was certainly reflected in the Willis family attitudes. The new managing director appears, though, to be taking a different approach and is looking at ways to improve the effectiveness and efficiency of this part of the business.

The company employs thirty-one staff organised into four departments each with a manager who reports to the managing director. The editorial department is headed by Ian McCullem and has six journalists and a photographer while the production department, the responsibility of Harold Plumb, employs fourteen staff. The administrative support to the company's operations is in the hands of the office manager and her team of four employees. In addition there is a small team of three advertising staff, including the sales manager.

Many of the staff are long-serving employees, some of who have been with the company for all their working lives. Labour turnover is very low. The only leavers tend to be women in the office roles who choose to start a family and younger journalists who move to further their careers. A trade union is recognised for production workers and a different one for journalists, but both rarely get involved in company matters. The style of the company, perhaps not surprisingly given its family ownership, is paternalistic, although with the last two managing directors being women, 'maternalistic' has been suggested as a better metaphor.

Ian McCullem and the editorial department

Born and bred locally, Ian McCullem is in his mid thirties and has been a journalist all his working life having joined the *NEN* after finishing his college course in journalism some fifteen years ago. He progressed rapidly through the grades of reporter and took over as editor of the paper four years ago when the then incumbent decided to vacate the position. Ian's predecessor is still employed by the company as a journalist but there has been no sign of this causing any difficulties in working relationships. Ian is highly regarded by his fellow journalists and in the community as a whole.

Under his stewardship the paper has maintained its strong readership loyalty despite making a number of changes of which the Willis family were initially unsure. However, all have proved to be a success and as a result Ian suffers from very little proprietorial interference in the way he manages the editorial side of the business. Very early on in his post as editor, he abandoned the paper's tradition of having classified advertisements on the front page, replacing them with news stories. He also introduced changes which affected the work of a number of the journalists. Three of the reporters were given responsibility for particular parts of the news carried by the *NEN*: motoring, sport and farming, the latter being a chief topic of interest amongst the readership. Each of these reporters now compiles the material for these sections, often writing much of the copy themselves but where necessary seeking assistance from colleagues. Ian's policy is to confirm with each of these reporters at the start of the week the number of pages they intend to provide and to leave them to get on with the work, only checking the final material a few hours before the paper is to be printed. He has, however, made it clear to these journalists that he is always available for advice and guidance should they need it. Although quite regular in the beginning, such requests have declined over time.

Although effectively working autonomously on their respective pages, these journalists are still expected to contribute to the rest of the paper. In particular, Ian holds a regular meeting with the whole editorial team at the beginning of the week to identify likely newsworthy stories. These are discussed and responsibility for their coverage determined. Usually this is through personal choice but Ian reserves the right to allocate reporters to particular stories if necessary. This rarely happens since the involvement in the decision-making process usually leads to staff volunteering for jobs even if their preference is for another story.

Most of the editorial staff are in their twenties and the *NEN* is often their first job after leaving college. The company has been able usually to recruit locally: only one of the last four appointments has come from outside the area. However, working for the paper is rarely seen as a lifetime occupation for journalists who, as indicated earlier, move to other organisations as part of their career development. For example, one left three years ago to join an evening paper in the south of Scotland, while the most recent leaver resigned a few months ago to join a local independent radio station as a news journalist. Recognising the reality of this situation, Ian sees part of his responsibility to be development of journalistic careers and the paper is becoming recognised as a place to go to obtain a good 'on-job' training.

Harold Plumb and the production department

Harold is also a local man, in his late forties, who joined Timothy Willis Ltd over twenty years ago as a typesetter – an employee who types material provided by reporters or advertising staff ready for it to be transferred for printing. He took up the position of production manager almost fifteen years ago following the enforced retirement, on ill-health grounds, of the then general manager and a reallocation of duties amongst the management team. Moving straight from the shop floor into a management role was something of a shock for him, particularly as he was offered no training and very limited guidance from the company on what was expected of him.

Harold has three sections in the production department for which he is responsible: typesetting, where the seven operators sit at computer stations inputting advertising and editorial copy for the newspaper; the print floor, which has three machines each with its own operator producing work for the 'jobbing print' side of the business; and finishing, where completed print jobs are trimmed, if necessary, glued, and wrapped ready for despatch to customers. The typesetting department also sets material for the printing machines but this work has to be fitted in around the demands of the paper, which is given priority.

About the time of Harold's promotion, the company was going through what amounted to one of the most significant changes in its history. Until the end of the 1970s the paper had been produced by what is known as the 'hot metal' method. This method was considered to be slow and inefficient, and produced poorer quality newspapers than that available from newer, computer-based technology. A substantial investment was therefore made by the company in updating its production operations. However, Willis was unable to afford a new printing machine capable of producing the *NEN* and since this time, printing of the paper has been subcontracted to a printer about thirty miles away.

The changes in technology meant that some typesetters, particularly the older ones, were unable to adapt to the new work and, in line with the company's paternalistic approach, were given jobs in the finishing department rather than being required to take redundancy. However, some of the remaining typesetters are quite slow at the work and the department is not as efficient as it could be.

The 'jobbing' print work is also a cause for concern. New print machines were also purchased at the same time but no formal training was given to the operators. The majority of the work is 'short-run' jobs from the local area including parish magazines, advertising posters, personal and business stationery and business documents. This means that the printers spend much of their time cleaning the machines after one job and getting ready for the next with a comparatively short time actually printing.

Harold is not a printer by trade and is unable to give much help even if he were asked. This is unlikely as the printers seem to have little respect for him. Morale throughout the production department is low but nowhere lower than on the print floor. The operators hardly speak to, and refuse to help, each other. All are concerned with 'protecting their own back'. Each of them at one time or another has been threatened by Harold with the sack if they 'don't pull their socks up'; this despite the fact that only the managing director has the authority in the company to dismiss an employee. When faced with problems, Harold's preferred style is to shout and 'bawl out' the employee and even, on more than one occasion, to threaten physical violence.

However, there have been no voluntary leavers amongst production employees, partly due, it is supposed, to the limited job opportunities locally, certainly ones that pay as well as Timothy Willis.

The managing director has become increasingly concerned at the poor utilisation of employee and machine time and the financial losses that the print side are incurring. When she has broached this to Harold his response has been to blame this on the laziness of the staff. The MD is less than convinced since there appears to very little planning of work and jobs are allocated to machines apparently at the last minute.

The company has also received a number of complaints from print customers about late delivery of work and missed deadlines despite their having received an assurance from Harold that their work would be completed on time. One or two have also remarked on Harold's rudeness to them both on the telephone and face to face. There are now a number of other print companies becoming established in the area, who appear to be cheaper and more reliable than Timothy Willis, and a loss of customers could damage the company's profitability and lead to job losses.

Activity brief

1 Utilising the exposition in Mullins (pp. 208–11) of Theory X and Theory Y, and the Leadership Grid, how would you characterise the differences in approach Harold and Ian take to people and management? How effective does each appear to be as a manager?

2 What are the variables, both personal and organisational, that may have influenced the pattern of management displayed by Ian and Harold? (You may find Likert's analysis of management in Chapter 7 of Mullins a useful starting point for answering this question.)

Case study provided by Derek Adam-Smith, University of Portsmouth.

ACTIVITY: The jigsaw test

Logistics

The group should be divided into three smaller groups: Organisation A, Organisation B and Observer group. The composition of each organisation is as follows:

A customer
A distributor
A development manager
Development staff
A chairman
A production manager
Production workers

Whilst each organisation is identical in terms of work roles, Organisation A has a supportive climate with management and subordinates working together to sustain the business, and Organisation B has an authoritarian climate, with management and subordinates working apart.

Materials required

- 5 m of fishing line (40–50 lb breaking strain).
- A supply of medium-sized paper clips.
- A supply of A4 laser copier paper (80–100 grams weight).

Task

Each organisation must select their own roles from their respective team members. Your task is divided into phases 1–3 below.

Phase 1: Innovation (10 minutes)

Rules

- *Organisation A* The subordinates must *respect* management directives, leadership and decision-making. Management must *support* both each other and their workforce.
- *Organisation B* The subordinates *must not* advise management. Management must *control* the workforce using their authority and power.

Task

You are to produce a product to your customer which is a simple paper dart. Each paper dart must be delivered to the customer over a distance of four metres, unassisted, using only the materials supplied. Your objectives for this phase, therefore, are:

1 To design the paper dart.

2 To construct the transport system for product delivery.

You will *not* be allowed to proceed to the next phase until you have achieved these objectives – the organiser's decision is final!

You should collect from the organiser a 5 m length of fishing line, a supply of paper clips, and some A4 paper.

Phase 2: Manufacturing (20 minutes)

Rules

- *Organisation A* Subordinates are *empowered* to control the manufacturing process and improve efficiency. Management are to analyse workforce behaviour, *advise and support* the workforce. (NB: Management will be entitled to a 50 per cent share-out of the total profits made during the manufacturing phase.)
- *Organisation B* Subordinates are *not empowered* to control the manufacturing process or to improve efficiency but only to *respond* to management directives. Management must *control* the manufacturing process; decisions made by the chairman are final. (NB: Subordinates will be entitled to a 50 per cent share-out of the total profits made during the manufacturing phase.)

Task

The key objective during this phase is to deliver as many paper darts as possible to the customer within the time allowed. Each paper dart successfully received by the customer wins the organisation a profit of £100 000. Management in both teams must record the number of successfully received paper darts.

Each team member is to take their place according to the layout shown in Fig. 7.1. The constructed transport system must separate management from the workforce. The following are the tasks for each section of the organisation:

- *Development* To create a model paper dart and pass it to Production together with an additional sheet of A4 paper. The department then continues to resource production.
- *Production* To receive the model dart from Development and replicate it. The finished product is passed to Distribution. The department then repeats the manufacturing process.
- *Distribution* To receive the dart from Production and attach the paper dart to the transport system for despatch. Each paper dart is detached by the customer.

Phase 3: Share-out (10 minutes)

The management of both teams calculate the total profit gained during their manufacturing phase. Each chairman will then allocate 50 per cent of the profits to those entitled to receive them.

Phase 4: Plenary session

This should be led by the Observer group using the questions below. They should also present their perceptions as to the *nature* and *performance* of both organisations.

Organisation A

1 What behaviours emerged when innovation became a joint effort between management and subordinates (motivation vs roles)?

2 Did management experience a greater accessibility to the attitudes of their empowered workforce (attitude vs influence)?

3 Did management experience any dilution of leadership identity, power or influence as a result of working with an empowered workforce (self-perception vs power-redistribution)?

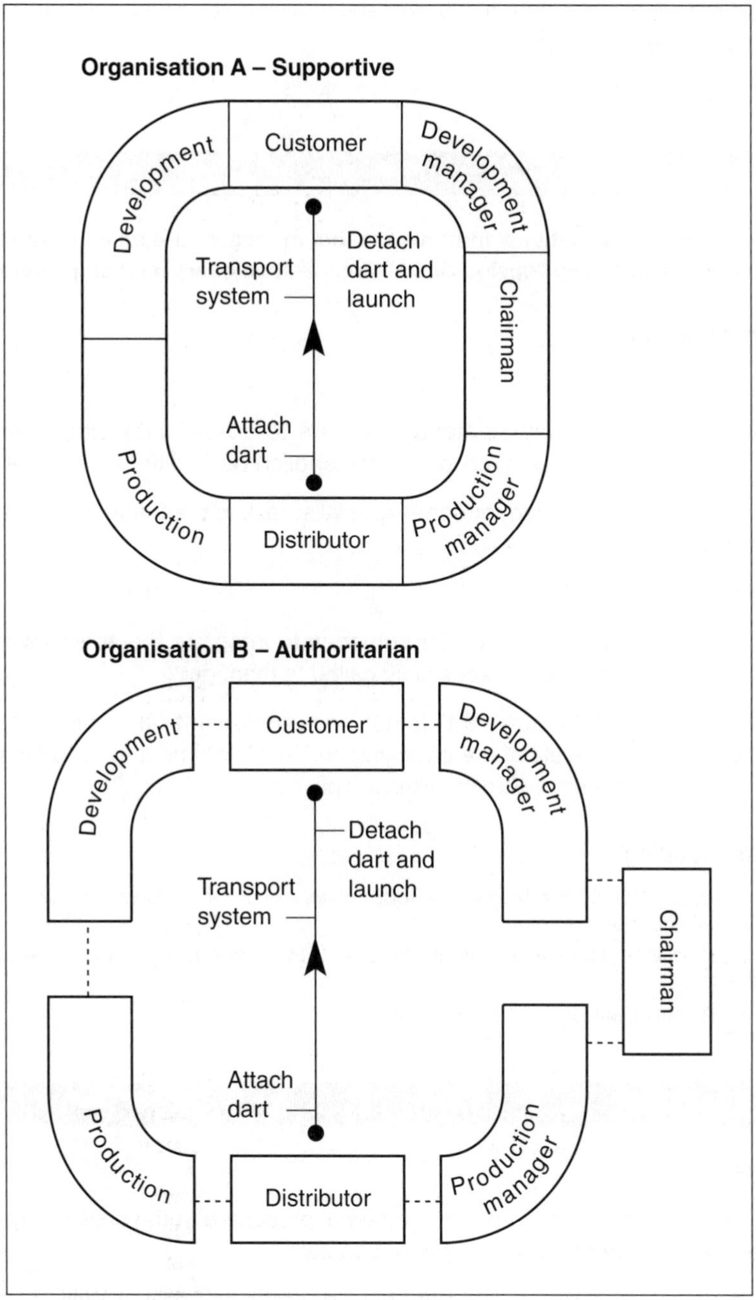

Fig. 7.1 Team layout for Organisations A and B

Organisation B

1 What perceptions were experienced by the subordinates when their management controlled innovation (perception vs leadership)?

2 Did the subordinate workforce react to the unequal distribution of management authority (conflict vs authority)?

3 Did management favour a subordinate, challenge an equal or desire the role of chairman (power vs politics)?

Activity provided by Nick Cox.

DEBATE

'The modern organisational form means that managers are an unnecessary luxury. They have been replaced by "upside-down" organisation charts and empowered employees.'

Starting points

For

- At the end of the day all managers do is to co-ordinate. Empowered employees don't need the degree of co-ordination applied by traditional managers.
- If managers are needed for some specialist task in the future, they can be 'bought in' or 'leased' as necessary.

Against

- There will always be a need for someone to integrate the activities of the business, even if that person isn't necessarily called 'a manager'.
- Mullins says: '"Management" is not homogenous. It takes place in different ways and at different levels of the organisation.' The statement for debate implies that it is only present at senior levels: this is simply not true.

Further reading

Mintzberg, H. (1990), 'The Manager's Job: Folklore and Fact', *Harvard Business Review Classic*, March–April, 163–76.

Semler, R. (1989), 'Managing without Managers', *Harvard Business Review*, September–October, 76–84.

Stewart, R. (1976), *Managers and Their Jobs*, Macmillan.

ASSIGNMENT 1

Context

This assignment is based upon the material presented in the case study in this chapter, 'Effective management: Hard news or soft sell?'

You have been asked by the managing director of Timothy Willis Ltd to apply your understanding of organisational behaviour theory to the problems she is facing in the production department of the company.

Task

Prepare a report for the managing director which:

1 Identifies the factors which you believe are important in explaining Harold Plumb's approach to the management of his staff.

2 Provides reasoned recommendations on the action she might take to improve the productivity and morale in the production department.

The report is expected to be between 1500 and 2000 words in length.

Alternatively

Make a short, individual or group, seminar presentation on the matters requested in the task making the assumption that the tutor and rest of the seminar group are the managing director and key members of the Willis family.

Assignment provided by Derek Adam-Smith, University of Portsmouth.

ASSIGNMENT 2

Mullins (pp. 178–81) discusses the differences and similarities between public and private sector organisations.

Imagine that you are a management consultant who has been brought in by a public sector organisation to advise on either:

- the change to privatisation; or
- a management buy-out.

Task

Write a paper for the senior management team outlining the changes which will be needed in, for example, management style, culture and organisation structure, and give suggestions as to how these might be achieved.

APPLICATION 1

The hotel and catering industry relies to a very large extent on the employment of casual staff to cover seasonal peaks and troughs in its business. This is particularly true of the banqueting and conference department where labour demand can fluctuate rapidly – sometimes in a matter of hours, particularly if a 'Dinner and Dance' originally booked for 200 guests suddenly increases to 250 during the afternoon of the event. In operational terms that means finding space for at least another five or six tables and conjuring up five or so extra casual staff at short notice.

In general terms, these casuals (or 'black and whites' as they are sometimes known after their usual uniform) consist of two main types: catering students who are trying to pay off their overdrafts under the guise of 'gaining valuable industrial experience' and mature women who have been doing the job for years and whose main motivation appears to be to satisfy social rather than monetary needs. It is this latter 'breed' who give rise to the second nickname: 'ducks' (as in, presumably, 'Hello, ducks, how are you?').

One of our Hotel and Catering Management students had, during his industrial placement year, been given the job of banqueting supervisor and, halfway through the training, it fell to one of the authors to visit the student to discuss progress etc. On arrival, the lecturer was greeted by Tom, the student, with the words: 'Can you find me another placement, I'm sick of this one. I'm not getting anywhere and nobody takes any notice of me.' Further questioning revealed some interesting comments from Tom including: 'I'm trying to change the whole department and drag them into the twentieth century. The older women won't listen to anything I say and go off and do their own thing; you need to follow the young kids around all the time otherwise they'll just skive off.'

Now let's try and apply this to a leadership theory by using House's Path Goal Theory. This is the one which is linked to Expectancy Theory of Motivation and which says that leader behaviour should depend on the personal characteristics of the subordinates in terms of how much they will look at Tom's behaviour as a source of satisfying their own needs together with how routine and structured the task is.

In this case the task (laying up, waiting on and clearing down tables) is highly structured and certainly routine; the personal characteristics of the staff and their needs have been recognised by Tom. He should, therefore, adopt a style which is more participative than directive: sell and share rather than tell and do. In this way also, Tom will have a greater chance of success at driving through any changes he might want to make.

APPLICATION 2

Kathryn Kennedy has recently been appointed as the faculty administration officer for the faculty of the Built Environment at Midshires University. (See full case in Chapter 12.) In this particular job, she reports to the dean and is responsible for all administration from managing a large budget to devising exam timetables to initiating administrative policies and procedures.

The academics at the Built Environment faculty see their main role(s) as teaching and/or researching – anything else has a very low priority on their list. However, whether they like it or not (and most of them don't) they are also required to undertake some form of administration. This can range from managing a very large course to being a schools liaison officer.

As well as all the other changes which have happened since Midshires became a 'new' university, academic staff have also had changes to their employment contracts which have affected, among other things, their holiday entitlement. Previously some teaching staff had been known to disappear on the last day of term never to be seen again until the first day of the next term; what happened in between, whether it was genuine holiday leave, study or research time was usually left to an informal, *ad hoc* agreement between each lecturer and their individual head of department. The new contract changes require that some degree of formality is introduced in the form of . . . shock! horror! . . . a 'holiday request form'! (Those of you, dear readers, who are practising managers in the 'real world' are probably raising a quizzical eyebrow at this stage: you have to remember that, to most academics, the words 'administration' and 'control' are synonymous and, when used in conjunction with the term 'management', are akin to the equivalent of a mental and creative straitjacket.)

The design and implementation of this system fell to Kathryn as one of her first big jobs. Tackling it with relish, she designed a form for academics to complete which detailed start and finish of the proposed holiday, number of days actually taken, number of days remaining, a holiday emergency contact number and various signatures for authorisation, including her own. The distribution of a sample form was accompanied by a four-page, closely typed document on the procedure itself.

After a three-month period had gone by, Kathryn was lunching in the Staff Bar one day when her opposite number from Engineering passed by. 'Hi, Kathryn, how're you getting on?' he said. 'Still enjoying the job?' 'No,' replied Kathryn, 'in fact I'm thinking of leaving. Trying to manage academics is like trying to herd cats – on principle they all go in opposite directions to the one you want. Take this holiday form business – no one sends one in and they've all "lost" the procedure I sent out. When I query them on it they all look blank and either say "What form?" or "I don't understand it – *you* sort it out".'

Let's look at Hersey and Blanchard's Model of Situational Leadership for this one. Kathryn's group's readiness level was one of 'able but unwilling' to perform the task. They therefore need to be allowed to share ideas and participate in decision-making so that they feel a greater sense of 'ownership' – a much more participative approach than Kathryn had taken. Perhaps if she had taken note of people's views, explained what was happening and invited suggestions she would have got a more positive outcome. (OK, we're not hiding behind rose-tinted glasses here, we know that, given the 'nature of the beast' she would never have achieved *total* success but it would have been a starting point for her to build on.)

Unfortunately Kathryn hadn't heard of Laurie Mullins (now *he* would have gone along with her ideas because he's that sort of guy . . .) and was last heard of heading for the Job Centre, having locked a lecturer in the stationery cupboard after he had forgotten to sign a requisition form . . . .

APPLICATION 3

Attribution theory can be applied to leadership as well as to perception. It deals with how people make sense of relationships: when something happens, there is a natural tendency for someone to attribute it to something. In the context of leadership, the theory simply says that leadership is an attribution they give to other people.

Using attribution theory, researchers have found that people characterise leaders with traits such as intelligence, an outgoing personality, aggressiveness, strong verbal skills, understanding and industriousness, who are consistent, committed and unwavering in their decision-making and goal-setting (Lord, DeVader and Alliger, 1986). Research shows that a 'heroic' leader is perceived as being someone who takes up a cause which is difficult or unpopular and who, through determination and persistence, succeeds (Staw and Ross, 1980).

How does attribution theory affect our perception of Tony Blair? Would it change if he were to show himself to be more ruthless, authoritative and even immoral?

APPLICATION 4

Organisation Yin and Yang

A rather different view of leadership has been provided by Anita Roddick, founder and managing director of the hugely successful Body Shop chain. She suggests that leaders should have both flair and a sense of fun, and should not adopt a 'holier than thou' attitude reinforced by artificial status, elevated titles, allocated parking spaces or separate dining rooms. Indeed, leaders should be entrepreneurs who create new rules, discard stereotypes and succeed for themselves. It is this high need for personal achievement, for a person she describes as 'marching to a different drumbeat', who is essentially an outsider with a total belief in what they are doing, that characterises a successful leader.

A further point she stresses is the need for organisations to stress both masculine and feminine values, whereas currently too much emphasis is placed on male-dominated culture that not only sets up hurdles for women but also results in hierarchical structures based on authority.

How appropriate is this style of leadership to running, for example, the civil service? Is it only appropriate for an entrepreneurial business?

8 The Nature of Leadership

CASE STUDY

I want a leadership team not a management team

FT

Keith Henry, 52, has been chief executive of National Power, the UK's biggest generator, since 1995. He was previously chief executive of Brown & Root, the international engineering contractor. He joined Brown & Root in 1971 and became managing director of Brown & Root Vickers in 1987 and managing director of Brown & Root Marine in 1989.

'I am very informal as a person. I don't like hierarchy and I don't like status. I wander around in my pullover. I sit in the canteen. I hate the term executive. The terms executive and manager imply status. I don't want managers, I want leaders. Soon after I arrived, I said that, as we were moving into a new era, we would have a leadership team not a management team. By Stock Exchange rules you have to have the term chief executive, but I don't particularly enjoy it.

'My background is construction and project management. I worked at Brown & Root where your assets really were your people. Your life is spent pulling teams together. If you are installing an oil platform, it is a 24-hour task. It can get extremely rough. Everything you do has to be as part of a team. If you come from a construction background you have to be good with people. It is a skill you pick up. I enjoy being with the average worker. I like spending time on the shop floor finding out what people are thinking. We have employee briefings. The first Monday of every month is open house. The first 25 people who e-mail my office are free to come. I speak and then there are questions and answers. The word gets out that I am a human being. Once people get over an initial nervousness, the questions they ask are very valid.

'I am an engineer. I come from a line of engineers. One thing that comes from that is that I plan. I can create bar charts and 3D drawings in my head. I can do that a lot better than creating a balance sheet. If we don't plan, we don't produce electricity. It is a very hands-on, practical company.

'A phrase I use a lot is partnership. In the oil industry when prices were falling and profits were cut to the bone, the different players got together to work out how we could pool our resources, rather than arguing over contracts. Partnership is about accepting that we are human beings, that we are trying to do a good job. Co-operation works better than conflict. Carrot works better than stick.

'I am away two weeks in four. People who do a lot of international travel are pretty good at grabbing sleep and knowing which flights are worth taking. It is just practice. I only ever take hand luggage. That means if a flight is delayed at Bangkok, I can slip up a corridor and get on to an aircraft belonging to a different airline. If I ever checked bags in, I would never get them back.

'I have spent my life on international projects. I have built up expertise. You get an instinct for when things are going to happen. There are a lot of cultural factors. You have to be very pragmatic about when to walk away from deals. You have to know in which countries you are expected to horse trade. The other question is: do they have the resources to do it? They all want new power stations, but can they afford it? I sometimes talk about these issues over a beer with like-minded colleagues from the oil and gas industry. We are all taking long-term views of the same markets. It is a good way of finding out what is going on.

'I never take a decision just on my own. I spend a lot of time talking to colleagues. We have a leadership team meeting every Monday between 12 p.m. and 5 p.m. Looking at any plan there are several options. I am a methodical thinker, so if plan A will not work, I have to be ready with plan B. Organisational decisions are most difficult. They are very seldom black and white. But I don't worry about decisions. The chances are you can't solve things by worrying. If I worried about everything, I would be a nervous wreck.'

Source: Vanessa Houlder, *Financial Times*, 5 January 1998.

Activity brief

1 What would you see as the characteristics of a 'leadership team' as opposed to a 'management team'?

2 What do you think Keith Henry means by being 'good with people'?

3 How do you think that working for international organisations has affected Keith Henry's style of leadership?

4 Should leaders 'worry' about their organisational decisions?

ACTIVITY

Either

1 Working in small groups, design and record a ten-minute video with the title 'The essence of leadership'. Present your completed video to the rest of the class and lead a discussion at the end of the programme.

or

2 Taking the role of a 'shock jock' on Chatterbox AM Talk Radio, plan and present a thirty-minute 'phone-in' on the subject of 'all political leaders are corrupt'. Role-play the programme remembering that, because you are on the telephone, you shouldn't be able to see your contributors, i.e. the rest of the group (we suggest that you turn your back to the audience).

At the end of the 'programme' discuss the following issues with the rest of the group:
- what conclusion (if any) was reached?
- what problems or difficulties did you find in managing this activity?

DEBATE 1

'Leaders are born to be so: it is impossible to train a person to become a leader.'

Starting points

For

- A glance at the world's great leaders shows that they have one thing in common: charisma. This cannot be instilled into a person through a training course, you either have it or you don't.
- The skills associated with leadership can be trained (delegating, influencing, etc.) but the underlying 'leadership personality' must be there to start with; how else can you explain such leaders as Ghandi, Thatcher, Hitler or Churchill?

Against

- The question is only concerned with charismatic leadership: most organisational leaders do not need this ideological approach to be good 'solid' leaders.
- Given this comment, the nature of a leader can, therefore, be broken down into attributes and skills which can be given and/or improved through training.

Further reading

Caulkin, A. (1993), 'The Lust for Leadership', *Management Today*, November, 38–43.

McElroy, J. C. (1982), 'A Typology of Attribution Leadership Research', *Academy of Management Review*, July, 413–17.

Meindel, J. R. and Ehrlich, S. B. (1987), 'The Romance of Leadership and the Evaluation of Organizational Performance', *Academy of Management Journal*, March, 91–109.

Roddick, A. (1991), *Body and Soul*, Ebury Press.

DEBATE 2

'Organisational success depends on the qualities of its leaders.'

Starting points

For

- The organisation/environment-fit equation is important: leaders need to be able to have strategic vision, to anticipate change, to look for and take advantage of opportunities, to motivate their followers.
- Leadership is an integrating activity ensuring organisational co-ordination and control through the ability to make rapid and decisive decisions which are not constrained by bureaucratic policies and procedures.

Against

- Leadership behaviour is constrained by the demands, pressures and boundaries imposed by others. There is not as much unilateral power vested in the leader as is usually perceived.

- Many factors affecting organisational success are outside the leader's control: labour markets, economics, legislation, etc.

Further reading

Jennings, E. E. (1961), 'The Anatomy of Leadership', *Management of Personnel Quarterly*, 1 (1), Autumn, 2.

Kellerman, B. (1984), *Leadership: Multidisciplinary Perspectives*, Prentice Hall.

Kotter, J. P. (1990), 'What Leaders Really Do', *Harvard Business Review*, May–June, 103.

Smith, J. E., Carson, K. P. and Alexander, R. A. (1984), 'Leadership: It Can Make a Difference', *Academy of Management Journal*, December, 765–76.

ASSIGNMENT 1

When emphasising transferable skills, employers often say that they are looking for leadership qualities in their recruits. In not more than 300 words describe an event in your life which could be used to illustrate this quality in yourself and which you could use in an interview or on a CV.

ASSIGNMENT 2

Take any two of the leadership theories or models and apply them to a leader, either in the workplace or a public figure in whom you're interested. You should bear in mind the following:

- You will need to research thoroughly the theories and choose two which appeal to you.
- Look at your chosen leader as objectively as possible, identifying situations and incidents which mark them out as a leader. (If you have chosen a public figure you may need to do some library research at this point.)
- Using your two chosen models, lay them like a template on your leader and see how good the 'fit' is.
- What conclusions can you draw? Does the leader you have chosen 'fit' the models you have selected? Why or why not?

Your assignment can be either written up (in not more than 2000 words) and/or presented to the rest of the group.

APPLICATION 1

It's Stardate 23 30 21 and the Starship *Enterprise* is still 'boldly going' its merry way through outer space. All is peace and calm on the bridge: Ohura has managed to find the galactic frequency for One FM; Spock is tuned to 'Intergalactic Test Match Special'; Mr Sulu is midway through *The Hitchhiker's Guide to the Galaxy* (revised edition) and Captain Kirk is surreptitiously practising his sardonic eyebrow lift and wry smile. He knows that his crew are self-motivated, enjoy their job and are happy to work together as a team, contributing to the smooth running of the *Enterprise* – a typical Theory Y approach, in fact.

Suddenly Ohura loses Zoe Ball and in her right ear she picks up a message delivered in a flat Bawston nasal twang: 'Now let's go through this keyhole and see what we have . . . .'

'Captain,' she says urgently, 'prepare for possible invaders: starboard bow' (why do they never appear on the port bow – are they all right-handed?). All eyes turn to the huge plexiglass awareness panel as, floating into view, comes Loyd Grossman and a team of invited panellists. 'Activate shields, phasers on stun and ahead Warp Factor 12,' barks Kirk. 'Aaaw, Captain, I canna get that much power out of the old girl so quickly,' complains Scotty. 'I'm not asking you, Mr Scott,' replies Kirk, 'I'm telling you. Now get on with it.' The SS *Enterprise* streaks off leaving our hapless quiz show host floating in space.

What happened to our Theory Y leader? Nothing, really, except that he became a Theory X leader when the situation demanded it. If you were on board a Boeing 747 midway across the Atlantic with two engines on fire, what type of leader would *you* prefer at the controls: Theory Y or Theory X?

(It's leadership, Jim, but not as you may have thought about it . . . .)

APPLICATION 2

Lessons in leadership

FT

It is 24 years since I turned up at the gates of the British Army's regular commissions board at Westbury in Wiltshire to undergo three days of assessment that sought to determine my qualities for leadership. If I did possess such qualities, the board failed to find them.

On the application form I had listed sport and listening to music among my hobbies. 'What's your handicap?' asked one interviewer. I had no idea what he was talking about. A round of pitch-and-putt at the local municipal park had been the nearest I had come to a game of golf. Neither had I heard of Handel's *Messiah*. On the other hand the interviewer was not too hot on the Rolling Stones.

The experience left me with an abiding respect for anyone capable of impressing the selectors sufficiently to make the grade. So it was with a sense of nostalgia that I found myself listening to a lecture at the Royal Society for the Arts in London this week delivered by Lieutenant General John Deverell, deputy commander-in-chief, land command, addressing the question: can you teach leadership?

It is a thorny question, asked so many times before and, as with many human qualities, the answer seems far from clear cut, entangled in the long-running debate about nature versus nurture.

But the general had a reasonable stab at it. As a Sandhurst cadet he attended lectures by John Adair who went on to be Britain's first university professor of leadership studies. At that time Mr Adair was teaching a leadership model that called for a balancing of task, team and individual where the leader was expected to subordinate some of his individual freedom for the good of the group.

What seems unclear is how strongly such practices might prevail today when what Lt Gen Deverell called 'old-fashioned concepts' such as duty, service, example and motivation are, he suggested, diminishing in civilian life. But it was not until the general introduced ideas from Greek philosophy – the Socratic paradox of goodness and knowledge – that he reached the nub of the question. Socrates argued that knowledge could be taught and agreed and that acts of goodness could be recognised, but that goodness itself could not be defined. What could not be defined, he said, could not be taught. Detractors such as Protagoras, a fellow intellectual said goodness might be defined as respect for others and a sense of justice – qualities, he said, that were essential for human survival. Some possessed such qualities to different degrees but all, he maintained, had the capacity to improve. He felt sure that goodness could be taught. Plato pondered on the purity of this approach, pointing out that Protagoras derived a healthy income in tuition fees from his conclusion. Consultancy was alive and kicking even then.

Even so, the general came down on the side of the consultants. Leadership, he believed, could be taught. Beyond this companies might ask themselves what kind of leadership should be taught. This kind of debate is becoming central to the administration of companies because it focuses not just upon technical abilities in leadership but upon values.

Not least among these is the moral foundation of leadership, which Lt Gen Deverell said had become an important element of military instruction in today's army. This is understandable when soldiers with a particular national allegiance may find themselves in complex situations while wearing the blue berets of the United Nations. But moral and ethical considerations are also becoming increasingly pertinent in corporate leadership. Issues such as exploitation of sweat-shop labour in supplier countries, product safety and environmental responsibility are all growing concerns for companies seeking to establish strong corporate values. It is no longer acceptable for either the military or people in business to say 'ours is not to reason why' except, perhaps, when struggling with their golf swings.

Executive pay

One notable aspect of the RSA discussion on leadership was the absence of any mention of pay. It was not surprising, therefore, when reading a new report on long-term incentives in large UK companies produced by New Bridge Street Consultants that the report had no mention of leadership. But in the pay-speak that is making a science of executive remuneration, there were plenty of references to performance, re-enforcing the notion that pay and performance are strongly linked.

What is highlighted in the report is that the performance measures of executive share option schemes are to some extent governed by fashion. While the most popular target remains for earnings per share growth to exceed that of the Retail Prices Index by at least 2 per cent a year, the graph here shows that there was a trend in 1997, resulting from institutional pressure, to stiffen the test to 3 per cent ahead of RPI.

In spite of the Greenbury report the nest-feathering of executives in big public companies continues almost unabated. Executive share option schemes were present in 78 per cent of FTSE 100 companies in 1997 compared with 81 per cent in 1996. The word across the FTSE appears to be that after the initial fuss about fat cats and share options, the coast is clear once again.

Students of such schemes will find a wealth of data in the report, which also looks at long-term incentive plans.

Source: Richard Donkin, *Financial Times*, 11 March 1998.

APPLICATION 3

'Learning through doing' dominates

FT

Business leadership development has been one of the big growth areas for management schools during the past decade but there appears to be growing scepticism about the more traditional approaches to the subject not only within business but in the schools themselves.

Part of the problem has been in arriving at a consensus of what is meant by leadership, whether it should be distinguished as something separate from management, whether it comprises definable traits and whether it has changed over the years.

Many of the current theories have a family tree rooted in post-war studies that initially concentrated on military leadership skills. This military link was promoted by people like Field Marshall Sir William Slim who shortly after the end of the war gave a lecture to managers in the UK on 'management through leadership', arguing that the principles of military leadership could be used in business.

Hitherto the notion that leaders were born not made had tended to prevail in society but Sir William's observations suggested that there could be transferable leadership skills. The idea was developed by people such as John Adair, the UK's first professor of leadership who incorporated them into his Action Centre Learning model, initially adopted at Sandhurst, the British Army's officer training college.

Mr Adair was among a number of academics, including Warren Bennis and John Kotter in the US, who distinguished between leadership and management. Management, he argued, involved administration and control, features not necessarily present in leadership.

Warren Bennis defined the most important ingredient of business leadership as the need to provide a guiding vision. He also identified the need for leaders to demonstrate passion, integrity, curiosity and daring. But can such qualities be instilled into people or are they innate? Ruth Tait, head of PA Consulting Group's search and selection business, who interviewed a series of business leaders for her 1995 book *Roads to the Top*, found difficulty drawing together a set of common attributes although she found that many of the executives had some childhood experience of adversity that gave them their drive.

'What distinguished most of them, however, was cross functional experience and responsibility early in their careers,' she says. She found that while management education was regarded as helpful it was stressed far less than the learning they achieved from experience.

Her observations about early responsibility are confirmed by David Norburn, director of Imperial College Management School, London, who carried out a detailed study of directors of large companies in the UK and the US, looking for the factors that distinguish the more successful of them from the less successful.

'I can tell you it has nothing to do with potty training, child sibling positioning or types of education. Statistically two features come shouting through – the experiences that they get in their formative years between the ages of 25 and 35 and international exposure,' says Prof Norburn. The most crucial formative influences on business leaders, he found, were inter-company moves exposing young managers to early responsibilities. if you get sent off to Borneo to be in charge of some petrol pumps you have to understand pricing, delivery systems, logistics, cash flow and working in a different setting. In effect you are a mini-managing director,' he says. 'But a company must have an underpinning of acceptance of failure when it stretches people beyond their previous experience.' These findings raise questions about the effectiveness of the classroom approach to leadership development. Prof Norburn is an advocate of managers with senior executive potential taking on non-executive roles.

'A lot of the business schools are teaching history. I would like to see more emphasis on simulations and projects where people can be stretched.' One area, he says, where business schools can help is providing an environment for risk-free experimentation.

'Companies need to encourage the maverick in people so that they are working one deviation away from their area of comfort. If this happens in school and it goes wrong there it will not hurt the company financially.'

Andrew Kakabadse, professor of International Management Development at Cranfield School of Management, agrees that leadership development needs to go beyond the classroom. 'The most likely and unlikely people can reach senior positions. There are no common traits in terms of personality but there are abilities that can be developed and working in the organisational context can be particularly effective,' he says.

This emphasis on context is also stressed by Nigel Nicholson, a professor at London Business School. 'What makes a good leader does depend very much on what kind of organisation you are in and the role you play in that organisation. Charismatic leaders, for example, come into their own when people are in a state of crisis but they can overstay their welcome when calm is restored and a different kind of leader is required.'

It should be noted that the nature versus nurture debate is still simmering beneath the varying approaches to leadership development. Meanwhile, learning through doing appears to be in the ascendancy.

Source: Richard Donkin, *Financial Times*, 20 April 1998.

APPLICATION 4

Fizz is a leadership factor

What makes a bad boss? Dogmatism, inflexibility and 'inspiring fear' are the three worst characteristics, according to research published by the UK's Industrial Society.

The ability to delegate, trust employees to do the job with minimal supervision, and actively encourage employee initiative are among the most highly prized attributes, found a survey of 1000 employees conducted for this study. All three were rated above the 'ability to provide direction' or 'take decisions'.

The belief that a boss's primary role is to closely supervise his or her workforce is outmoded, unpopular and ultimately counter-productive, says the society.

The research finds that more than 80 per cent of those identified by employees as having genuine leadership ability are not in positions of formal authority.

'Too many bosses still equate delegation with abnegation,' says Mahen Tampoe, consultant to the Industrial Society, 'and may actively hold back the development of their employees either because they fear they will lose authority and status among their workforce or because they secretly doubt the strength of their own abilities.

'But in today's business environment, where structures are far flatter and where employees are often highly skilled and highly intelligent, it is crucial to give people their heads and allow them to make, and take responsibility for, their own decisions.'

Mr Tampoe notes that in more traditionally run companies there is a marked resistance to the notion that managers and workers should work together and pool ideas to achieve their common objectives.

'Too little autonomy at work causes stress and frustration among workers and wastes the time of management. Like a can of Coke which has to be opened to release the bubbles, workers have to be empowered to demonstrate their fizz, too.'

Source: Virginia Matthews, *Financial Times*, 26 January 1998.

9 Individual Differences

CASE STUDY

All the world's a stage ...

Organisational behaviour has much in common with theatre. Hamlet has already made an appearance in this book, after all. And although we tend to quote him regularly enough ('To be, or not to be', 'Alas, poor Yorick', 'perchance to dream', 'brevity is the soul of wit' etc.) it is when he says 'the play's the thing' or 'God has given you one face and you make yourselves another' that Shakespeare is analysing aspects of human personality that interest the student of OB.

Mullins makes it clear that, like Hamlet, people can 'put an antic disposition on' when he remarks that 'in a selection situation candidates may indeed consider the "type" of personality they wish to fake'. The point is that certain psychometric tests may be susceptible to manipulation by those being tested rather than the testers. Fears that such tests may now be used to identify suitable candidates for redundancy (for example, at Anglia Water in 1994) exacerbate the situation. Other anxieties include the concern that personality tests have no predictive validity for job suitability; that some tests discriminate between races and genders; and that when bought 'off the shelf' they are often unfit for the purpose. In short, they might be said to be 'more honoured in the breach than in the observance' (*Hamlet*, Act 1, iv).

Actors, of course, exert control over their personalities for a living. Anthony Hopkins, knighted in 1992 after more than twenty years at the top of his profession, highlighted this control in a succession of character parts having split personalities. Amongst the more celebrated were the ventriloquist in *Magic* who was taken over by his dummy, the actor in *Kean* who confused acting with life, and the killer in *Silence of the Lambs*.

Sociological role theory (see, for example P. Berger, *Invitation to Sociology*) asserts that we are all actors in the sense we select from a set of scripts depending on which audience we are playing to at any given time: interviewer, professor, lover, etc. Shakespeare wrote famous lines about role theory:

> . . . All the world's a stage
> And all the men and women merely players;
> They have their exits and their entrances
> And one man in his time plays many parts.
>
> (*As You Like It*)

For the individual this phenomenon can raise issues of identity. If we are a set of roles, which one is the real us, for instance? G. H. Mead's theory (see Mullins, p. 308) could indicate one answer: the I (a sort of casting director) chooses the me (the appropriate role), or as Mullins puts it 'the concept of role focuses on aspects of behaviour existing independently of an individual's personality' (p. 473). Anthony Hopkins exemplifies this distinction clearly. Roger Lewis in *Stage People* (1989) presents Hopkins as a hard-working, level-headed man whose job is to play roles. He does have personal characteristics of course: 'I've always been a little self-involved, private, a loner' (p. 289), a man who, despite his accent and origins, is far from being the stereotypical Welshman: 'I've never been interested in rugby; I can't sing . . . and I cannot speak Welsh' (p. 287). And though, just as Richard Burton did in *Under Milk Wood*, he too has finally done a performance of Dylan Thomas, and does come from the same part of Wales, he has managed to avoid the trap of alcohol and has had the quality career that Burton never achieved. Hopkins, then, is a family man who loves his job and works very hard at it. Not really material for the gossip columns though anyone with as high a profile as this will be someone's target, to wit the rather bitchy item (*Sunday Times*, 26 September 1993) implying he was two-faced about his knighthood, when claiming that, while he was not interested in it, his wife was. 'Frailty thy name is woman' is one of Hamlet's less endearing observations.

An idiographic view (see Mullins, p. 305) allows the possibility of individuals shaping their personality to some extent. Such manipulation has clearly benefited sportsmen, politicians and businessmen; and it is a must for spies, as Anthony Hopkins reminded us in his *Blunt* (1986). But actors, except perhaps when making adverts, are involved in relatively innocent make-believe in which the audience participates. Role-playing is routinely used in therapy, of course, and an actor can escape from shyness by hiding behind the mask of assumed personalities. But if that seems like running away from problems, it does take a certain kind of courage to let go of one's personality: 'I am always trying to conquer my cowardice', said Hopkins. In his career, many of his parts have been a long way from his own quiet and private personality. Thinking of Lear, he said 'I've been lucky to have been offered monsters', but in 1990, of course, his role in *Silence of the Lambs* topped them all. One columnist claimed the actor had to dine facing the wall in restaurants because people would back away from him if they saw his face. So, it is perhaps ironical that just as a politician might climb the ladder of power through dissembling, so the mild-mannered Hopkins won an Oscar for playing the most vile of all his creations, a psychologist who is also a serial killer who eats his victims.

Films seem to have abandoned the convention of bringing baddies to book. Hannibal the Cannibal is preparing to carry on killing and eating at the end of the film. And if Oxford University final exams in English Literature in 1994 are anything to go by, Shakespeare himself might follow the fashion. One question demanded, 'Make out a positive case for the witches in *Macbeth,*' and apologies were sought in other questions for Malvolio, Claudius, Goneril and Regan. True, a British cabinet secretary achieved Hamlet's quotability when he invented the phrase 'being economical with the truth'. But, clearly, controlling the personality can and does have some undesirable outcomes in public life. Hamlet, though, advises us to be philosophical about such imperfections: 'Use every man after his desert, and who shall 'scape whipping?'

Activity brief

1 How does the paradox of an actor showing off on stage because he is fundamentally shy seem reminiscent of Eysenck's introvert/extrovert continuum?

2 The acting profession is often perceived as having many homosexuals in it. Ingenious explanations for this include the idea that, being generally childless, they choose creative work to compensate; that being skilled at disguise ('in the closet') they are well prepared for the job; that, without the responsibilities of raising a family they are more prone to 'play' than other adults. On the basis of this argument, or any other, can you think of any other profession homosexuals might be suited for? Or is this to take stereotyping too far?

3 Hopkins has said 'We are all of us stuck with the same personalities', but Mullins suggests in his Fig. 9.1 (p. 303) that, though our personalities are given in the nomothetic sense, we none the less do change them by adopting roles, and that our life experiences can change them too. What anecdotal evidence does the above case provide for either of these views? You might like to try them out on your own character by talking through with a friend how roles you adopt affect your personality. Does your experience support the nomothetic or the idiographic approach?

ACTIVITY 1

In groups of three (one candidate, one interviewer and one observer), role-play interviews for the following jobs:

- a commission in the armed forces;
- a secondary school teacher;
- a TV researcher;
- a personal secretary;
- a graduate management trainee in a bank.

Discuss any assumption made about personality in terms of the theories you have studied. Discuss their applicability or otherwise to the job in question.

ACTIVITY 2: You are what you write

Introduction

Graphology is the technique of interpreting personality traits from analysis of movements in handwriting. Its use in Europe is widespread, particularly in France and Switzerland where over 75 per cent of companies use this technique to assist in personnel selection. However, in Britain graphology has been the subject of much controversy and scepticism, although the number of businesses using it currently is growing.

Handwriting evolves and develops from the rigid style we were first taught at school. It is the differences from the 'copybook' model that the graphologist studies in detail and to which he or she assigns interpretations. Each of the particular handwriting movements may affect and modify interpretations of the next handwriting movement, and so subtleties of character emerge. Professional graphologists undergo a minimum of three years' training to understand and interpret the nuances of handwriting analysis and to reach The British Institute of Graphologists' qualification standards.

It is very difficult to change one's handwriting without losing its natural spontaneity, its rhythm and speed. Many handwriting movements are unconscious and the writer may not be aware that he or she may be forming a particular letter or stroke quite differently to someone else. To become aware of the differences between styles, try copying a sentence or two of someone else's handwriting. Even if you manage a convincing copy, the concentration required to do this can be very high. Imagine trying to fill in a whole application form in someone else's handwriting.

The following short self-administered test was designed for sessions to help individuals who were facing job change, either through choice or redundancy, to help them focus on their 'selling points' and to home in on particular areas where they would do well. It gives a superficial glimpse of some of the positive aspects that can be gleaned from handwriting, without going deeply into the modifying or contradictory factors in handwriting that can alter interpretations.

Task

Write a letter applying for a job and spell out your good points. Then try out the following test on yourself, or on a colleague. Does it work? You be the judge. (Some guidance notes as to how the test should be interpreted are given in an Appendix on pp. 221–5.)

Look at a sample of your handwriting and use the examples as a guide.

1 Is the middle zone of your writing (a, c, e, m, n, o, r, s, u, v, w) measuring from top to bottom
(a) large – over 4 mm high;
(b) small – under 3 mm high; or
(c) mixed?

See Fig. 9.1.

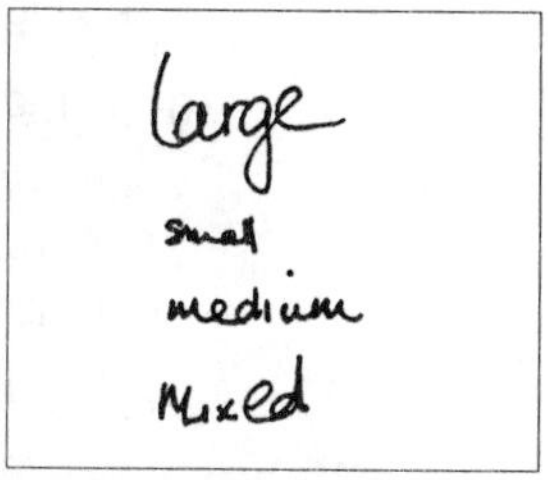

Fig. 9.1 Size of writing

2 Are the letters in the words
(a) all joined up;
(b) all disconnected; or
(c) a mixture?

See Fig. 9.2.

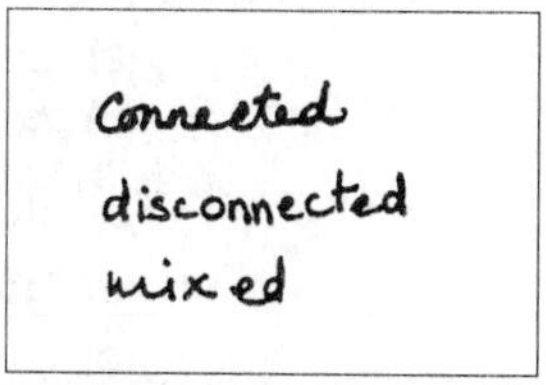

Fig. 9.2 Letter connections

3 Is the shape of your writing
(a) loopy; or
(b) loopless?

4 Is your writing
(a) rounded;
(b angular;
(c) stretched; or
(d) mixed?

See Fig. 9.3.

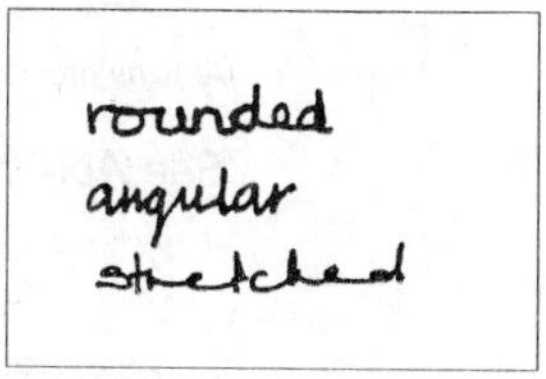

Fig. 9.3 Overall shape of writing

5 Are your m's and n's
  (a) humped;
  (b) angular;
  (c) pointed; or
  (d) mixed?

6 Are your left and right margins
  (a) about equal;
  (b) wider on the left; or
  (c) wider on the right?

7 When you write 'I am', is the capital 'I'
  (a) as large as the other capitals;
  (b) larger than the other capitals; or
  (c) smaller than the other capitals?

8 Is your signature
  (a) larger than your writing;
  (b) smaller than your writing; or
  (c) the same size as your writing?

9 Are the words in your writing
  (a) fairly close together;
  (b) fairly wide apart; or
  (c) a mixture?

  See Fig. 9.4.

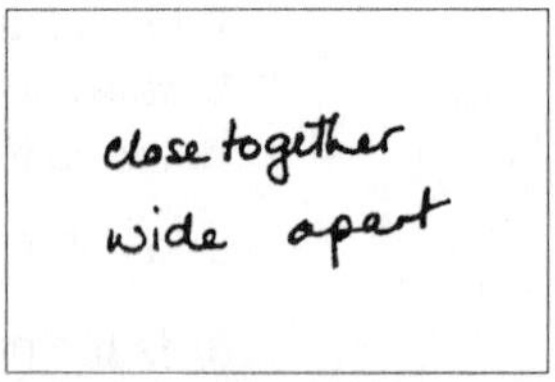

Fig. 9.4 Spacing in writing

10 Is the slant of your writing
  (a) vertical;
  (b) right;
  (c) left; or
  (d) mixed?

  See Fig. 9.5.

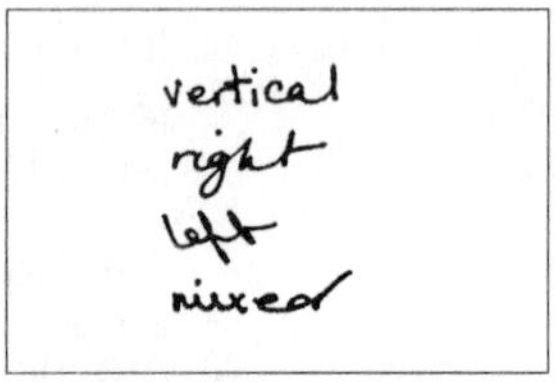

Fig. 9.5 Slant in writing

11 Is every letter
  (a) clear and easy to read; or
  (b) some letters skimmed over, but generally legible?

12 Are the lines in your letter
  (a) going up;
  (b) going down;
  (c) forming an arc; or
  (d) horizontal?

Activity provided by CB Graphology Consultants, Chandlers Ford, Hampshire.

See Appendix for a full explanation of how to interpret your results.

DEBATE 1

'Interviews are preferable to psychometric tests in the recruitment process.'

Starting points

For

- Everyone uses interviews for selection – it is so universally accepted that candidates would be suspicious of any firm not doing so.
- The value of tests is questionable (see Mullins, pp. 747–8).

Against

- Interviewers are generally untrained, reliant on their intuition and, like everyone else, subject to perceptual errors.
- If an interviewer's time etc. is costed, selection tests are much cheaper than interviews and enable an objective comparison to be made between candidates.

Further reading

Bertram, D. (1991), 'Addressing the Abuse of Personality Tests', *Personnel Management*, April, 34–9.

Fletcher, C. (1991), 'Personality Tests: The Great Debate', *Personnel Management*, September, 38–42.

Goodworth, C. T. (1993), *Effective Interviewing for Employment Selection*, Business Books.

Mullins, L. J. (1999), *Management and Organisational Behaviour*, 5th edn, FT Pitman Publishing, 747–53.

DEBATE 2

'Freud's personality theories are of no use to the organisation.'

Starting points

For

- Freud's id, ego and superego are hypotheses that cannot be tested.
- Dreams and Freudian slips are glimpses only of the subconscious. We cannot, and should not, delve into them when considering employees for promotion, transfer, training, and so forth.

Against

- Freud was trying to understand the whole human being rather than individual personality traits, attitudes or any other little fragments of a person.
- Freud's account of our fundamental drives helps us to understand such organisational behaviour as power struggles, attitudes to leaders and conflict.

Further reading

Eysenck, H. J. (1972), 'The Experimental Study of Freudian Concepts', *Bulletin of the British Psychological Society*, 25, 261–7.

Kline, P. (1972), *Fact and Fantasy in Freudian Theory*, Methuen.

Mullins, L. J. (1999), *Management and Organisational Behaviour*, 5th edn, FT Pitman Publishing, 309–11.

ASSIGNMENT 1

In order to undertake this assignment, you will first need to complete Activity 2 (pp. 74–6). Using the results from this activity, try to analyse your own and others' handwriting.

Your results can be used as a basis for group discussion and/or written up as a report.

Some discussion points could be:

- How predictive and reliable is graphology as a recruitment tool?
- Whilst graphology is widely and openly used in many European countries, its use in the UK is thought to be more covert. Why is this? What are the implications for, for example, perception and attitudes?

ASSIGNMENT 2

Write a 1500-word report of a survey you have conducted in your organisation to discover any differences between younger and older workers in attitudes held towards work.

This task is probably best done by a small group and you will need to remember the following:

- First, establish in discussion an appropriate hypothesis to examine (e.g. older people value work more highly than younger ones).
- Construct a series of questions which give rise to clear differences between respondents (i.e. where they can reply 'strongly agree' sometimes rather than 'neither agree nor disagree' most of the time).
- Select respondent groups which not only have a certain homogeneity (e.g. one between 18 and 21 and another between 25 and 35) but also a certain representativeness (e.g. a reasonable mix of men and women, doing a range of tasks, etc.).
- Remember, too, that such work is beset by rogue variables: asking questions before lunch might give different results from asking them after, allowing different questioners to adopt non-standard approaches to respondents could confuse outcomes, etc. Try in discussion to spot as many of these potential problems as you can. If you have time it is a good idea to conduct the survey again with the same people but at a later date.

In your report remember clearly to state your hypothesis, the design of the survey, the make-up of the surveyed groups, and the raw results *before* evaluating the findings. It is worth assessing the validity of your work too (What flaws did it have?, How could it be improved next time? etc.).

Alternative surveys could investigate differences between male and female attitudes or between native and foreign workers.

APPLICATION 1

Sunnyside Hotels is a medium-sized group of three-star hotels which annually takes ten to twelve graduates on its management training programme. The programme is a very concentrated one with graduates taking six-month supervisory positions in a variety of functions in a number of hotels. Thus a graduate trainee may work as a reception supervisor in Barrow-in-Furness for one module and then as a restaurant supervisor in Torquay for the next. As well as job competence, this calls for a high degree of flexibility and mental, emotional and physical toughness.

Over the years Sunnyside have found that, on average, only 20 per cent of graduate trainees make it through the training programme to their first junior management appointment. For the company this doesn't represent a good return on their investment and they began to look at their recruitment process. They've decided to institute a series of 'open days' for up to a hundred applicants at selected hotels which will involve presentations on the company and the training scheme together with a personality test which the personnel officer has seen advertised in a training catalogue. All this will happen in the morning and whilst the potential recruits are having a buffet lunch, the personality tests will be scored and, from the results, a short-list drawn up. Successful candidates will go forward to a formal interview in the afternoon from which a final choice will be made.

All seems OK, doesn't it? They've chosen a relatively scientific approach to their recruitment and tried to limit subjectivity. Why, then, did they find no improvement in their retention rates of graduates? Look at Application 2, below, and see the difference.

APPLICATION 2

UK Leisure plc are a broad-based company with interests in hotels, holiday centres and pubs. Like Sunnyside they, too, have problems in recruitment, both in making up short-lists from a first sift of applications and in retaining graduate trainees. Also like Sunnyside they have opted for a 'scientific' approach and have decided to use a psychometric test. However, it is at this juncture that all similarities disappear. UK Leisure are using a test which is validated, approved by the British Psychological Society and is administered and interpreted by a trained consultant. They are also not using it to obtain their first short-list but as *one part* of the final interview process.

Their 'open day' policy is similar to Sunnyside's but final choices are not made at that stage. Instead, a further short-list is drawn up and candidates attend an intensive two-day assessment which includes a series of group and individual exercises, presentations, the personality test and an in-depth interview. It is at this latter event that the results of the test are shared with the candidate who can comment on the interpretation. After all this, the assessors sit down, compare their results from each activity, the test results and the interview, and a final decision is made. It is interesting to note that *their* attrition rate is very low: many of their graduate trainees complete their programme and go on to take up junior management positions.

Can you see the differences in the two approaches to the use of personality testing? Sunnyside used a statistically unproven test and used it as the only basis for selection without sharing the results. UK Leisure used an approved test as *one part* of the whole process and shared results with the candidates, thus giving them the opportunity to comment on the findings.

APPLICATION 3

We have heard much about the subjective, inaccurate nature of the selection interview and yet it still remains one of the most popular methods of recruiting people. In the past, emphasis had been placed on improving the reliability of the selection decision by underpinning it with such instruments as personality tests. Other elements came into vogue for short periods of time including graphology and phrenology. Now there is yet another medium by which companies can determine business and organisational compatibility: astrology.

The California based Triangle Group marketed a computer disk called 'Seer' which, for about £60, would evaluate the compatibility of two people on a rating of 0–30. The owner of Triangle, British-born Peter Mackeonis, declared that the disk calculated the conjunction of planets and stars which astrologers believe determines individual characteristics and patterns of behaviour. Triangle claimed to have signed up Pizza Hut and Motorola as customers (*Sunday Times*, 15 May 1994).

Perhaps in future we will be analysing our teams according to astrological compatibility rather than by Belbin's team types – Mercury rising and the Sun in Leo rather than Completer–Finishers and Plants?

Could this be the *real* dawning of the Age of Aquarius?

APPLICATION 4

It's early morning and the village is just waking up. Shutters are being drawn back, children are being got ready for school and the little harbour is beginning to bustle as the fishing *caïques* return with the day's catch. The only place open on this tiny island is the *kafeneíon* (the local coffee shop) which, at this time in the morning, is full of local workmen watching cartoons on television and drinking coffee before going off to lay a few more bricks on a villa which will bring an ever-increasing number of tourists to this largely undiscovered and poor island. Through the day the men will gather to drink thick Greek coffee or an ouzo, gossip, put the world to rights and single-handedly solve both the Macedonian and the Albanian problems. Sometimes towards evening the local priest will tether his donkey to a nearby olive tree and join them in their leisurely discourse. It is a scene unchanged in Greece for centuries . . . the menfolk traditionally sit together in cosy camaraderie, for this is a male-dominated society. Indeed, on some of the smaller, tourist-free islands not only the *kafeneíon* but also the village *tavérna* would be a male preserve – a place where no self-respecting husband would be seen taking his wife.

The scene now changes to Athens where the *kafeneíon* setting, although urban, is essentially the same . . . except for one crucial difference: the customers of *this kafeneíon* are all women. Fed up with the traditional attitudes of male chauvinism and female exclusion, Athenian women have decided to fight back and have created their own women-only *kafeneíon* where they, too, can discuss politics, books and music and exchange gossip.

Does it always have to be the case that when faced with such a situation, the automatic answer is to apparently apply Newton's Law – for every action there is an equal and opposite reaction? Will we ever successfully *change* attitudes this way or will we merely engender and preserve two opposing attitudes? Is there a case to be made for an integrated male and female *kafeneíon*? Given these two apparently entrenched attitudes, what, if anything, could be done to change them?

APPLICATION 5

Jonathan is the son of a friend of ours. A few years ago he completed a Zoology degree and since that time has been working for the Forestry Commission at a research station which monitors wildlife, plantlife and the environment. Having been unemployed for six months, Jon got this job through a government initiative and, as his friends would say, 'Since then he's been counting moths and greater spotted liverworts for £50.00 a week.' Whilst meant partly in jest, there is also a degree of incomprehension underlying their comments. Friends from his university days are well fixed with their feet on the second rung of the career ladder, most are earning competitive salaries and many have company cars and mortgages. They can't understand Jon's value system and he can't understand theirs. When they ask him, he says, somewhat flippantly, 'I want to save the planet – simple as that!' Underlying this apparently glib reply is a serious assertion – he cares deeply about environmental issues and really does want to do something which will be a useful contribution. That matters far more to him than material gains and comforts.

To this end, Jon has now decided to do a PGCE course so that he can qualify as a secondary school science teacher. He says he realises that at this stage in his career he isn't going to discover a particularly rare breed of lesser spotted fruit fly nor is he set to become a latter day David Attenborough. However, he feels that he can make a mark by trying to impart his knowledge and enthusiasm to young people in the hope that some of it will rub off.

Pleased with his decision, he tells his friends, assuming that their approval would be gained – at last he's on the 'approved' way. 'Oh, Jon,' they all said, 'why on earth do you want to be a teacher – it's poorly paid, career paths are slow and the kids are awful. Haven't you ever watched *Grange Hill*?'

Can you see the differences here not only in attitudes but also in underlying values between Jonathan and his friends? Notice again how the role of perception fits in here in terms of trying to understand other people's attitudes. Looking ahead, you could also look at this scenario in the light of motivation theories – where, for example, do Maslow and Porter and Lawler fit here?

APPLICATION 6

On any Wednesday afternoon during a parliamentary session turn on the television at 2.45 pm and tune to BBC2 for a quick look at Prime Minister's Question Time in *Westminster*. For those of you who normally switch off after *Neighbours*, let us set the scene . . . Imagine a great barn of a place, longer than it is wide with a corridor down the middle and men and women of all ages, dressed in business suits, seated either side. At the top end sits the Speaker, an imposing figure who is dressed as if she's just come off the set of a BBC production of any Dickens novel.

After a certain amount of pomp and ceremonial, the proceedings get off to a relatively leisurely and polite start. People on the left of the corridor stand up to catch the Speaker's eye and are nominated to put a point. The situation is reversed on the right-hand side of the corridor and the point is answered (or not, depending on your political leanings and perception).

Suddenly there is a stirring in the ranks . . . the Prime Minister enters and makes ready to answer apparently impromptu questions. The scene now changes from one of almost mundane sedentariness to one which resembles a cross between the first day of the Harrod's sale and a verbal loose scrum at Twickenham. People pop up and down like hyperactive jack-in-the-boxes in vain attempts to catch the Speaker's eye (watch their facial expressions when they don't . . .). Expressions of agreement or disagreement are manifested in loud cheers or boos and everyone seems intent on scoring points (with self-satisfied expressions if they succeed), temper tantrums occur, and the scene quickly becomes one which resembles *Grange Hill* rather more than the Mother of Parliaments.

You may be asking yourself at this stage whether this has got *anything* to do with personality. Trust us, dear reader, *it has*! Let's look at Freud for this one – remember he said that under stress we regress into habitual ways of responding that worked for us as children. Think about how *you* behaved as a child when you couldn't get your own way – can you see a correlation?

AFTERTHOUGHT

'When white collar people get jobs, they sell not only their time and energy, but also their personalities as well. They sell by the week or the month their smiles and their kindly gestures, and they must practise that prompt repression of resentment and aggression.'
C. Wright Mills (1916–1962)

10 The Nature of Learning

CASE STUDY

The sense of learning

Background

You are a member of the Training Department of Dassan Ltd, a manufacturer of domestic 'white goods'. The company employs some 5000 staff at seven locations spread throughout the country. The company has pursued a policy of decentralisation over the past ten years and each site operates as an autonomous business centre with its own manufacturing, administrative, finance, personnel and sales departments. There is also a small head office located on the west side of London near the M25 where the company's corporate departments are based. In line with the policy of decentralisation, the main functions of these departments are to develop policy within which the business units are required to operate and to provide advice to unit managers should they not have the particular expertise needed to deal with specific problems.

Each unit has its own personnel manager but there is a head office Personnel and Training Department headed by the personnel director. Within this department is a team of six training officers, including yourself, reporting to the training and development manager. The department has a number of functions including identifying the training needs of all employees, recommending appropriate courses to meet these needs and designing and running in-house programmes for staff nominated to attend by their manager. Where there is no in-house course suitable, the department retains brochures of externally run programmes and arranges the booking of staff onto these. In addition the department carries out a regular evaluation of the courses it offers to ensure that they still meet the business objectives of Dassan Ltd and the business units. This work involves close liaison with the personnel and training managers of the business units who are the budget holders for training received by staff within their unit. A significant demand for training results from the annual staff appraisal process which covers both manual and white-collar employees and managers.

The responsibilities of the head office training officers are wide ranging and all are involved in the variety of work carried out by the department. This means that they contribute to corporate training policy, undertake training-needs analysis of groups of employees at a unit and deliver training courses to employees either at head office or, more likely, at one of the business units.

Leading the team

Amongst the portfolio of programmes you and your colleagues have designed and run for staff is a two-day, non-residential course called 'Leading the Team'. This course has been developed for supervisors and first-line managers to enhance their skills and knowledge in order to help them and the groups they supervise become more effective. The objectives of the programme are such that by the end of the course participants should:

- have developed their understanding of the role of the first-line manager/supervisor;
- understand different leadership styles and their application to managing people;
- be able to recognise the symptoms of poor motivation and understand what motivates and demotivates employees;
- have increased the knowledge and skills needed to build an effective team of staff including being able to manage conflict;
- be able to provide counselling to employees who have personal problems which may affect their work performance.

Since the majority of those attending the course will not be used to the 'classroom environment' or being 'lectured to', the programme is designed to be highly participative. The trainer running the course is expected to provide only short teaching inputs and a number of other activities have been designed to facilitate learning. In addition to plenary discussions led by the trainer, these include:

- small group discussions on particular topics, during which the participants are expected to note the key points of their discussions on flipchart paper and report these back to their colleagues in a plenary session;
- individual 'pencil and paper' exercises where the course members complete a questionnaire either by ticking a box to indicate their response to a question or by allocating a score showing the extent to which they agree or disagree with the statement;
- small group activities designed to explore teamwork; for example, the physical task of building a tower out of Lego bricks against specific design criteria;
- watching a video and discussing the learning points contained within it and their application to participants' own work roles;
- short role-play exercises designed to develop interviewing and interpersonal skills.

For some of these activities the trainer will introduce the subject and use viewfoils on an overhead projector or write on the whiteboard, as well as leading a review which may similarly involve noting the points that emerge during the plenary discussions. The training team have also produced a number of handouts to complement the course and relieve the participants of the need to take copious notes.

The issue

Your department has been approached by the general manager of an associated company, Dassan (Applications), with a request to run the 'Leading the Team' course for a group of fifteen of her managers and supervisors. She has written to the corporate training manager stating that she believes the objectives are such that the course will meet the identified training needs of these managers. In addition, two of her current staff attended the course when they worked for your organisation and she has received very positive feedback from them on the course content and the learning methods used.

Dassan (Applications) have developed a range of consumer goods which have been specifically designed to meet the needs of people who are visually impaired. There is a significant demand for the company's products and the associated company is regarded as a market leader in the field. A number of the company's employees are themselves visually impaired and as the general manager's letter requesting the course points out, nine of the fifteen potential participants are visually impaired. Five are described as 'large print users'. This means that they are able to read print provided it is THIS SIZE and are able to see images on a television provided they are able to sit very close to the screen. Of the remainder, four are blind. They are, however, competent braille users and the general manager has stated that she can arrange for all the printed teaching material to be converted to braille provided she receives copies in advance of the start of the course. The blind participants can also take notes during the course, if necessary, using a portable braille writer. This machine needs to be rested on a table since it is too heavy to be placed on someone's lap for any length of time. Obviously, since it produces braille output it cannot be read by anyone not proficient in braille which includes the majority of the other course participants and the team of trainers who might be involved in presenting the course.

Activity brief

The training manager has asked you to plan and deliver this course for Dassan (Applications).

1. What are the particular difficulties you see in presenting this course to the mix of participants from the associated company?
2. How might a knowledge of learning theory be helpful in seeking to ensure that the objectives of the course are met for *all* the participants?
3. What practical steps can be taken by the trainer delivering the course to assist in the learning process?

Case study provided by Derek Adam-Smith, University of Portsmouth.

ACTIVITY 1: Breaking assumptions

For this activity form into small groups of about four people and, if possible, go into separate areas where you cannot overhear the conversations of your colleagues. Each group should be given a bag containing a mixture of letters (those from a Scrabble game are ideal).

Task

Your task is as follows:

- Produce as many four-letter words as you can in a three-minute timed run. The timed run is to commence from the time that the bag is opened.
- There will be three timed runs and you should improve your group's performance on each successive run.
- The results of each run for each group should be written on a board and communicated to the groups before they commence their next run.

ACTIVITY 2: The origami exercise

Materials required

1 Squares of coloured paper.

2 A book on origami (paper folding) with one exercise copied as follows:
   (a) one picture of the completed article and the written instructions;
   (b) one set of written instructions only; and
   (c) the completed origami item only.

Task

The participants should be divided into three groups and then a trainer chosen from each group. It is the trainer's task to train the rest of the group to make the origami item and therefore trainers should be taken on one side, briefed and given a chance to practise first.

- Group 1 is given the finished item and some coloured paper.
- Group 2 is given the picture, written instructions and some paper.
- Group 3 is given the written instructions only and some paper.

DEBATE 1

'You learn more out of class than in.'

Starting points

For

- 'Learning is a feature of all human activity' (Mullins, p. 369). Much more human activity occurs outside class than inside, in consequence so does much more learning.
- A crossword answer comes to you when you are not thinking about it; you can ride the bike today that yesterday you were still falling off. Learning happens unconsciously all the time.

- Experiments with rats in 1930 (Tolman and Holzick) showed them acquiring cognitive maps of their environment in a process of latent or incidental learning while accomplishing other tasks.

Against

- 'Ratology' (generalising about humans on the basis of experiments with rats) is unreliable and the unconscious is undemonstrable.
- Classroom learning is systematically tested and provides distinctions between people (a process that is ingrained in our society). These distinctions are used in job selection procedures. I sincerely hope my next airline pilot or surgeon has had plenty of formal training and is not just trusting to incidental learning.

Further reading

Kolb, D. A. (1985), *Experiential Learning: Experience as the Source of Learning and Development*, Prentice Hall.

McCormack, B. and McCormack, L. (1994), 'Experiential Learning and the Learning Organisation', in *Cases in Organisational Behaviour*, D. Adam-Smith and A. Peacock (eds), Pitman, 280–7.

DEBATE 2

'Measuring learning leads to strife not knowledge.'

Starting points

For

- To help parents and patients learn more about schools and hospitals, the British government began publishing, in the 1990s, league tables purporting to distinguish between the successful and less successful of these institutions. The scheme was widely criticised by medical and teaching organisations. The Bishop of Birmingham publicly preached that patients are people in need of care, not statistics for the accountants to work on. There is no point knowing how long you will have to wait for attention in a hospital if you have no idea of the kind of care you are waiting for. The plumber whose phone rings three times when you call is not *necessarily* less efficient at mending pipes than one whose phone rings twice.

Against

- Measurements give information. Hospital A will see that hospital B is doing better on waiting lists and might try to learn how this is done. Some hospitals really are 'suitable cases for treatment' (*The Times*, 30 June 1994). Refusing information simply because it is incomplete means you will never learn anything.
- If you believe in individual differences (Mullins, Chapter 9), you will know that each person has different perceptions, attitudes and motivations, and therefore that they need different learning programmes and achieve different results.

Further reading

Eysenck, H. J. (1962), *Know Your Own IQ*, Pelican.

Lessem, R. (1991), *Total Quality Learning*, Blackwell, Chapter 5, 1.

Luthans, F. (1992), *Organisational Behaviour*, 6th edn, McGraw-Hill, Chapter 8, 218–31.

ASSIGNMENT 1

In a survey of twelve London boroughs carried out by the London University Institute of Education, so-called ethnic pupils (Black African, Indian, etc.) were found to have begun outstripping their so-called white class-mates in GCSE examinations (*The Times*, 27 June 1994). A Labour MP called for detailed research to investigate this apparent disparity of educational achievements.

Task

Drawing on ideas found in Mullins, Chapter 10, write a 1500-word essay discussing the kinds of factors that would need to be taken into account in embarking on this programme of research work.

ASSIGNMENT 2

'Change has been one of the common features of organisations over the last decade . . . .' (Mullins, p. 369)

Task

Design a learning or training programme for your group or organisation that is appropriate to the situation it finds itself in after a significant period of change. This might have been brought about by the introduction of new technology, a merger, a rapid growth in student numbers, the launch of a new product, privatisation, a new management structure, and so on.

The factors in Fig. 10.1 will all clearly have to be considered as will alternative strategies arising from this analysis. You will probably find yourself having to make decisions about some of the following issues:

taught courses	–	student-led learning
organisation centred	–	partnership with educational institutions
formal teaching	–	on-the-job training
full-time	–	part-time, day release, sandwich
individual learning	–	group work
grading schemes	–	self- or peer appraisal
punishments	–	rewards
lectures	–	seminars
programmed learning	–	incidental learning
knowledge	–	skills

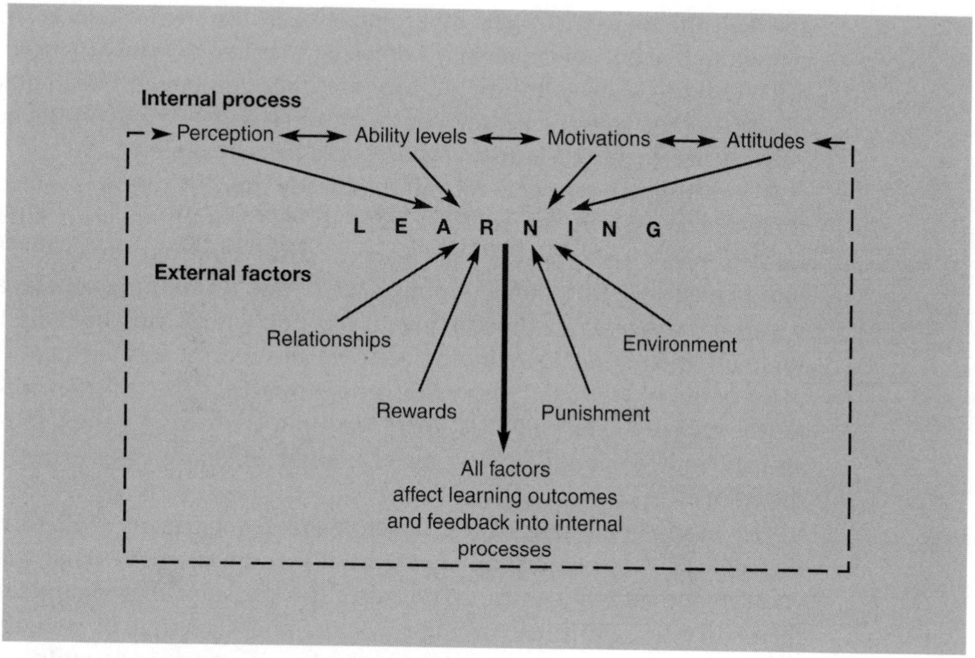

Fig. 10.1 A simplified view of the learning process

Source: Mullins, L. J. (1996), *Management and Organisational Behaviour*, 4th edition, Pitman, Fig. 4.4.

It could be interesting too to attempt a portrait of an 'ideal' teacher (animator, manager, facilitator, counsellor, lecturer?) for the programme. Remember, also, to present, in some detail, the situation the programme is being designed for.

APPLICATION 1

One of the most popular courses promoted by any training organisation is the one usually called 'trainer skills' or 'train the trainer'. Ask any senior manager which course has had most impact on them and the chances are they'll say 'Trainer Skills' rather than 'Advanced Marketing' or 'The business game simulation'.

Why should this be? Why should senior managers remember such a basic course? To try to throw some light on this, let's quickly outline the course programme. First, there would be general introductions – What do you hope to gain from the course? – What problems do you have with training? (Yes, oh cynical reader, we trainers are nothing if not predictable and whilst you're busy doing that, it gives us the chance to work out who the bolshie one in the group is, take a quick trip to the loo, phone the office and work out the next session.) This will be followed by sessions on how people learn, how to structure a training session, some skills work (questioning, listening, etc.) and a demonstration training session by the tutor. Finally comes the chance for delegates to put it all into practice (at least once and hopefully twice or three times) by training another delegate for ten minutes on a fairly simple task like folding a shirt or changing a plug. Because they're very simple tasks, it ought to be easy to train someone . . . not so! Because we do them all the time, we forget to put ourselves in the trainee's shoes and fail to find out enough about their previous knowledge. (If you're not convinced at this stage, ask a child to show you how to do something you haven't been able to master – like setting the video or getting your watch to stop 'bleeping' on the hour – or alternatively try teaching a four-year-old how to tie a shoelace.)

It's only when delegates are put in the situation of training someone that they themselves learn by doing; they learn to find out about prior knowledge, they learn to break assumptions, they learn to make sure that the task is broken down into manageable bits. Some examples we've had on training courses are: changing a motor car wheel and forgetting to put the wheel nuts back on . . . teaching someone to knit without finding out that the trainee was left-handed . . . changing a barrel of real ale without realising either that the task was too complicated for the trainee to absorb or that there was no spare barrel for them to practise on . . . and showing someone how to open a bottle of champagne whilst pointing it at the trainee.

This example illustrates a real casserole of learning theory: Kolb can be applied in that delegates were learning experientially and evaluating what was happening; you can also add in a dash of Thorndike (people learn by trial and error, repeating their successes) and finally a soupçon of Skinner (the trainers were trying to shape their delegates' behaviour to the point where a structured training session would become an automatic response for them).

APPLICATION 2

Imagine yourself at the end of your OB semester – no more 9.15 lectures on Monday mornings, no more frantic copying of other people's notes because 'the night before' and 'the morning after' had merged into a dreadful blur. There's only one hurdle left to jump: 'the exam'.

This year you decide to get organised and allow two whole weeks for revision. Day one dawns and you sit yourself down and open your notes. Two hours later you're still looking at them trying to make sense of pyramids and chessboards with numbers like 1:9 and 9:1 in the squares. Where on earth does it all fit in? You begin to feel like the rat in Skinner's Box except that there isn't a lever to press . . . .

Still waiting for inspiration to strike, you leave it for a while, watch the lunchtime edition of *Neighbours* and pop to the pub for a quick one. The afternoon session isn't any better and again you give up early. You've just settled down to the Six o'clock News when your partner comes in and says: 'If I give a good presentation tomorrow, there's every chance I'll get the promotion I've been wanting, so I'm going to work on it all night. By the way, how's the revision going?' Pause for clap of thunder and 'Blinding Glimpse of the Obvious' . . . was there ever a case of Expectancy Theory in practice? Welcome to the world of insight learning – you've just experienced Gestalt (remember, the whole is more than the sum of the parts?). You've suddenly made the links which have enabled you to see the jigsaw completed.

APPLICATION 3

A different approach to the whole concept of training, learning and educating has been taken by The Body Shop founder, Anita Roddick. The company's training school was started in 1985 because Roddick didn't want staff (or customers for that matter) to stop learning just because they'd started working. Initial courses concentrated on human development and consciousness raising and they've even run a course on management-by-humour.

Roddick feels that education of staff is an important responsibility, particularly since at that time retailing was one of the few growth areas for women. 'Training', however, is a word she professes to dislike, claiming 'that you can train dogs and you can train horses' but the company's aim was to educate people to help them realise their own potential. She claims that the closest the company has ever come to conventional training was a course on customer care, but here again the difference seems to be in the overall approach: employees were told the history of product ingredients, given information and amusing anecdotes to pass on to customers. She says: 'Conventional retailers trained for a sale; we trained for knowledge. They trained with an eye on the balance sheet; we trained with an eye on the soul' (Roddick, 1991).

Given its huge success, this approach has clearly worked for The Body Shop. Could it work for, for example, a high-street fashion retailer? If not, why not? Should it be the responsibility of organisations to train and educate with 'an eye on the soul'? Valid hypothesis or trendy fad?

APPLICATION 4

For many years a popular topic for discussion in Management Studies classes has been 'Are managers born or made?' The existence and growth of manager education and management development supports the hypothesis that, to a very high degree, managers are made.

Wide-ranging changes in the processes of education, training and development and the awarding of qualifications are being forced through the system at an alarming rate. There is an inexorable movement towards National Vocational Qualifications (NVQs) for all levels of achievement in all vocational disciplines, including management.

The making of a manager is a long-term project; 'getting it wrong' has serious and expensive future implications. It would be more appropriate now to consider not *if*, but *how* future managers should be 'made'.

There are claims and counterclaims for the superiority of the two main systems: 'Traditional' management education in centres of further and higher education on the one hand, and vocationally based NVQs on the other.

There are fundamental differences between the two approaches, as Table 10.1 overleaf shows.

In their work on learning, Honey and Mumford identified four preferred learning styles: activist, pragmatist, theorist and reflector. Which are the dominant styles for managers? Which system is more compatible with manager development?

NVQ	Traditional
Based on demonstrating competence	Based on proof of learning
Primarily experiential learning	Primarily teach and test
Candidate-driven (in terms of time scale and speed of learning)	Tutor-driven (in terms of time scale and speed of learning)
Work performance is assessed	Learning and memory are assessed
Assessment based on laid down National Performance Standards with knowledge and understanding as an addition	Assessment based on theoretical knowledge and understanding with performance added in the form of simulations and assignments
Results stated only in terms of 'competent' or 'not competent'	Results expressed in levels of success (pass/merit/distinction)
Uses industrially based assessors and verifiers	Uses academic examiners and moderators

Table 10.1

Quality and credibility are vital in any learning and qualification process. What are the implications for quality control and perceived value of any resultant qualifications associated with the two approaches?

Provided by David Callas, Development Consultants.

APPLICATION 5

'A man should never be ashamed to own he has been in the wrong which is but saying, in other words, that he is wiser today than he was yesterday' (Alexander Pope, 1688–1744). Geoff Armstrong, the Director General of the Institute of Personnel and Development, wrote in the *Independent on Sunday* on 10 July 1994 that his biggest mistake whilst working in industrial relations through the 1960s and 70s was to 'stick so long to the assumptions that had been the basis for people management in the western industrialised countries'. Mr Armstrong changed his views and has been candid and open about the matter. He is now in a position of great influence to perpetuate very different beliefs. However, those of us working in human resource management have at the pinnacle of our profession a man who for twenty years had perpetuated the assumption 'that people came to work to do the least they could get away with doing'.

Ask yourself, which is more commendable – to do something wrong for twenty years and then, in a flash, see the light, change and preach the new gospel or not to have made the mistake in the first place? Is it true that if you say the same thing with conviction for so long, it seems that it must be right and the world believes but if you ask questions, challenge, 'rock boats' and do *not* pretend to be 'right', you gain no credibility and thus no one listens to you?

One single message given repeatedly will become accepted in time, *whether right or wrong*; the 'rightness' will not need to be justified. How do we know whether current practice is, in fact, 'right'? Geoff Armstrong said 'My biggest mistake *in common with others in my field . . .*' – does this excuse it?

Provided by Val Marchant, Ibis Training and Development.

APPLICATION 6

Do students learn or are they taught finance?

In twenty years of teaching finance to university students on non-accounting courses, Jim Logic had come to believe that the tutor made a substantial contribution to student learning and felt that interaction was essential. During the first few years he had believed that the way ahead was to throw a large amount of information at the students during the lecture and ask them to work through questions on the topic before the next session. Fifteen years of working in a financial environment before joining the university had not prepared him for the total lack of numeracy that bedevils many people.

Jim pondered the situation at some length and was struck by the brilliant thought that the way to enable people to learn finance was to interest them in the topic first. Once people became interested in a subject they very quickly learnt about it but the difficulty was to discover which particular aspect of finance they disliked least or enjoyed the most. There were several topics that were found in all basic finance courses and he felt that a scientific approach was called for. Jim chose three basic financial topics and decided to introduce each of his financial courses to the subject using a different topic. Group One would be introduced through the medium of double-entry bookkeeping, Group Two through the profit and loss account, and Group Three through the balance sheet.

Group One started in an encouraging way and several of the students who had good application appeared to understand and enjoy what they were doing. The vast majority, however, were very quickly disaffected with the subject and comments were expressed in loud stage whispers which intimated that the course members were not happy. The more polite comments included 'Why are we doing this?', 'I'm bored to death', 'I wish I'd chosen another course/university' and 'I don't understand what is going on at all'. Jim found that *he* wasn't having a particularly happy time either. Despite his best intentions to the contrary, he found that he was becoming less tolerant as he explained the same minor point for the fifth time. Not only this, but he found his voice was getting louder as he sought to clarify the situation. He reminded himself of the vicar who used to write 'SLAW' at strategic points in his sermons. 'SLAW' meant: 'speak loud: argument weak'! Double-entry bookkeeping did not appear to provide a solution to Jim's problem.

Group Two were initially encouragingly interested in the concept of profit, particularly when it was applied to their favourite football or rugby team. Once this initial interest had worn off, however, and some of the more obscure concepts had been introduced, the group became as disaffected as Group One had been. No amount of cajoling or the introduction of stories about fishermen, men in balloons or women pilots sparked more than a passing interest. The profit and loss account did not offer a great deal of hope.

Group Three were introduced gradually to the balance sheet and Jim was gratified to observe that the initial interest of the students was maintained lecture after lecture; they were able to complete the balance sheet item by item. The two-sided balance sheet was initially used as the learning vehicle as it enabled the students to demonstrate where the resources came from and how they were applied. The interest of the group increased as the size of the balance sheet grew and Jim had a new spring to his step and a twinkle in his eye.

'Pride cometh before the fall!' and the transfer from the two-sided to the narrative form of balance sheet did cause some initial problems, but these were relatively painlessly overcome when the published accounts of companies were produced and discussed. The discussions became quite heated when the accounts of companies for whom the students worked were analysed.

The problem had been resolved: students both learn and are taught finance but they learn it most successfully when the appropriate teaching vehicle is used.

Provided by David Davis, University of Portsmouth.

AFTERTHOUGHTS

This chapter has talked about learning. Under that heading we've encompassed training, education and development. Is there a difference? Yes, and you can display the three words with careful definitions on an overhead slide which you put up on the OHP and then wait while people laboriously copy it down. Unless, that is, you're the student we had once who simply listed all three titles on the whiteboard, prefaced each one with the word 'sex', looked at the seminar group and asked: 'Which one would you want your child to learn in school?'

Despite worldwide record sales of ten million, the Three Tenors, as a result of their contract, only received $500 000 each to sing at the 1990 World Cup Final in Rome. By the time of the 1994 World Cup Final in Los Angeles, Domingo, Pavarotti and Carerras had learned from their mistakes and negotiated a deal reportedly worth a minimum of $4.5 million each.

11 The Process of Perception

CASE STUDY

An interpersonal conflict at Homebuy

Stephanie Barnes had a problem. She was one of the two supervisors of a large team of clerks at the headquarters of Homebuy mail order shopping company. One of the clerks who reported to Stephanie, Martin Warner, was being very disruptive. He seemed to have a grudge against her. On checking her records, Stephanie was surprised to find that his timekeeping was as good as anybody's, and so was his work. But he could be very rude and abrupt towards Stephanie. She found conflict hard to handle at the best of times, and could not understand why Martin apparently disliked her so much. None of the other clerks seemed to find it necessary to behave like that towards her.

As far as Stephanie could see from observing Martin unobtrusively at his desk and in the canteen, he was perfectly civil and friendly to other people. He was however rather cold towards Michael Butcher, who was the other supervisor of Stephanie's grade. Interestingly, Martin seemed to be at his worst when she was trying to check a query about his work. At other times (for example when Stephanie was assigning work or answering a question he asked) he didn't seem so bad.

Things looked different from Martin's point of view. This was the third job he had held since leaving school at the age of 17. In each of the previous two he had had trouble with his supervisor. In his experience, first-line managers were interfering bullies whose main aim was to make their subordinates feel small using all kinds of devious methods. It didn't help that in his first few weeks at Homebuy, Stephanie Barnes had repeatedly checked his work even though the tasks were quite straightforward and did not in his opinion need checking.

She seemed to do it less now, but still more often than he would like, and for all the types of work he handled, even the simple ones. She did not check up on the other clerks so often, and when she checked up on him she would pretend to be giving him a helping hand when she was really snooping. Michael Butler had supervised Martin for a few weeks when Stephanie had been on holiday or ill, but Martin had formed no particular impression of his supervisory style.

After almost a year of this, Stephanie had had enough. She felt that Martin was probably simply an aggressive young man with a chip on his shoulder. Yet somehow it did not all quite add up. Perhaps a quiet chat to show him she was not a threat would help. So Stephanie called Martin into her office. After carefully explaining what she saw as the problem, Stephanie asked Martin whether there was any particular reason why he was such an aggressive person. This provoked an angry response from Martin, so she tried a different tack. She asked him to describe his past experiences with bosses, and his relationships with people more generally. They parted an hour later with Stephanie feeling she had learned a little about Martin and sowed the seeds of a somewhat better relationship.

Activity brief

1 Use attribution theory to predict how Stephanie and Martin might see the causes of each other's behaviour. Are there any special problems which seem to be caused by perceptual distortions?

2 Examine the significance in this case study of:
   (i) expectations based on stereotypes;
   (ii) projection;
   (iii) the 'rusty halo' effect; and
   (iv) self-fulfilling hypotheses.

Source: Adapted from Arnold, J., Cooper, C.L. and Robertson, I.T. (1998), *Work Psychology*, 3rd edition, FT Pitman Publishing.

ACTIVITY 1

Introduction

Recent experiments in social psychology have suggested that:

- happiness makes us more prone to make stereotypical judgements;
- minority members of high-status groups readily stereotype themselves by reference to that group;
- males and females both overestimate their intelligence but it is more usually males who overestimate their physical attractiveness;
- new workers stay longer in organisations if they are referred for the job by current workers than if they enter by different routes, like answering a job advertisement.

These rather simplistic, not to say downright misleading, statements are summaries made of reports found in 1994 issues of two academic reviews, *The Journal of Personality and Social Psychology* and *The Journal of Social Psychology*.

Task

Read and précis one such experiment for yourself, then report back to a discussion group to try to assess the value and shortcomings of the experiments. (For example, how many of them use college students as the subjects of the experiments? Do cultural factors limit the applicability of the findings?)

ACTIVITY 2

Task

Working in groups of four, study the following four items. They give the results of a management assessment exercise completed by Elizabeth (a managing director) and Andy, Steve and Linda (her three senior managers). All scores were given in confidence.

- Item 1 is an explanation of each management skill which is being assessed (see Fig. 11.1).
- Item 2 is an explanation of the rating system to be used (see Fig. 11.2).
- Item 3 contains the results (scores) given by Elizabeth on each of her managers alongside their own self-assessment (see Fig. 11.3).
- Item 4 contains the results (scores) given by Elizabeth as a self-assessment of her own skills alongside those given to her by Andy, Steve and Linda (see Fig. 11.4).

Management skill	*Explanation*
Performance appraisal	The ability to review and rate objectively past performance and to discuss and agree actions/objectives for the coming period.
Performance counselling	The ability to help a subordinate identify, explore and own his/her counselling own performance strengths and weaknesses, reinforcing strengths and correcting weaknesses to achieve or maintain a high level of performance.
Objective setting	The ability to define clear, measurable, challenging but realistic results with deadlines for achievement.
Planning	The ability to define how an objective will be achieved, stating or agreeing who will do what by when and effectively anticipating potential difficulties, but to change and adapt plans when required.
Organising	The ability to make effective use of available resources, set and review priorities, make decisions and take responsibility for them.
Problem-solving	The ability to identify the root cause of a problem to permit effective action.
Decision-making	The ability to choose between various options using sound judgement rather than bias.
Leadership	The ability to achieve results through others, selecting the appropriate style for the situation.
Team-building	To develop the ability of working within a team by individual recognition of styles and strengths and to identify the strengths of team members for maximum effectiveness and efficiency.
Motivation	The ability to create in others a willingness and commitment to achieve the best performance of which they are capable.
Time management	The ability to organise oneself effectively and to maintain an efficient control of time.

Fig. 11.1 Assessment of management skills

Fig. 11.1 continued

Management skill	*Explanation*
Delegation	The ability to identify and overcome difficulties of delegation.
Selection interviewing	The ability to extract effectively the necessary information from a candidate to permit comparison with the job requirements and enable a (later) decision to be made; to interest the candidate in the organisation/job.
Assertiveness	To identify assertiveness as a management skill. To distinguish between assertive and aggressive behaviour and to give and receive criticism in a constructive manner.
Developing staff	The ability to assess development potential effectively to train staff.
Letter and report writing	To enable clear, concise and effective communication in reports and letters.
Leading and participating in meetings	The ability to identify specific results to be achieved, defining the appropriate structure, effectively involving the participants and ensuring that the outcomes are clear and acceptable.
Giving a presentation to inform	The ability to present facts/opinions in a logical and clear way that creates and maintains interest and achieves the level of understanding required.
Giving a presentation to persuade	The ability to present a proposal that highlights benefits to the receiver, proves the case, effectively handles questions and secures approval.
Influencing	The ability successfully to convince others on the same level (or a higher level) to change/negotiate in order to meet his/her own objectives.
Generating options and creative thinking	The ability to generate a wide range of novel options for evaluation.
Managing change	The ability to identify opportunities for improving standards, to plan and organise change, to develop objectives and systems.
Communication skills: • **To/with others**	 The ability to successfully communicate with others and to encourage others to as well.
• **Listening skills**	To demonstrate sound listening skills.
• **Questioning skills**	To identify the varying types of question and which to use in various different situations.

Rating	*Explanation*
1	Rarely displays this skill, if at all.
2	Occasionally displays this skill but considerable development is required.
3	Moderately proficient in this skill but there is still scope for improvement.
4	Displays strength in this skill on some occasions, but not consistently.
5	Displays significant strength in this skill *consistently*.

Fig. 11.2 Rating system for management skills

Management skill	*Andy*		*Steve*		*Linda*	
	A	*B*	*A*	*B*	*A*	*B*
Performance appraisal	4	3	2	3	3	3
Performance counselling	5	3	2	1	4	3
Objective setting	4	3	2	1	4	3
Planning	4	4	3	4	3	2
Organising	4	4	3	4	3	4
Problem-solving	5	4	4	4	4	4
Decision-making	4	4	3	4	4	4
Leadership	4	3	2	4	4	4
Team-building	5	3	3	3	4	4
Motivation	5	3	2	3	4	4
Time management	4	2	2	3	3	3
Delegation	3	3	4	4	3	3
Selection interviewing	4	3	4	4	4	3
Assertiveness	4	3	2	3	4	3
Developing staff	4	3	3	4	4	3
Letter/report writing	3	2	2	4	3	2
Leading/participating in meetings	4	2	3	3	4	3
Giving a presentation to inform	3	2	3	4	3	3
Giving a presentation to persuade	4	2	3	3	3	3

Fig. 11.3 Elizabeth's rating of the others and their own self-assessments

Fig. 11.3 continued

Management skill	*Andy*		*Steve*		*Linda*	
	A	*B*	*A*	*B*	*A*	*B*
Influencing	4	2	4	4	4	4
Generating opinions and creative thinking	5	3	3	3	4	4
Managing change	4	5	2	4	4	4
Communication skills:						
• To/with others	4	3	3	4	4	4
• Listening	4	4	3	5	3	4
• Questioning	4	3	3	4	3	4

Note: A = Elizabeth's rating
B = The manager's self-assessment

Management skill	*Elizabeth*	*Andy*	*Steve*	*Linda*
Performance appraisal	3	4	4	4
Performance counselling	4	4	4	3
Objective setting	4	4	4	4
Planning	4	4	3	4
Organising	4	4	4	4
Problem-solving	4	4	3	4
Decision-making	5	4	4	4
Leadership	4	5	5	5
Team-building	5	5	3	3
Motivation	4	5	5	4
Time management	3	4	2	2
Delegation	3	4	5	4
Selection interviewing	4	2	4	4
Assertiveness	4	4	4	4
Developing staff	4	4	4	3

Fig. 11.4 Elizabeth's self-assessment and the others' rating of Elizabeth

Fig. 11.4 continued

Management skill	*Elizabeth*	*Andy*	*Steve*	*Linda*
Letter/report writing	3	5	4	3
Leading/participating in meetings	4	3	5	4
Giving a presentation to inform	4	4	4	4
Giving a presentation to persuade	4	5	5	4
Influencing	3	5	4	3
Generating opinions and creative thinking	4	5	4	4
Managing change	3	5	4	4
Communication skills: • To/with others • Listening • Questioning	 5 4 4	 5 4 5	 5 4 4	 4 4 4

Discussion questions

1 What differences exist between each person's perception of their own performance and their colleagues' perception of them? Why should this be?

2 What feedback would you, as a consultant, give to the management team?

3 How would you organise this feedback? (e.g. Individually? In what order? All together?)

4 Devise a role-play scenario to act out this feedback session, concluding with an action plan for each of the managers and Elizabeth.

Activity provided by Val Marchant, Ibis Training and Development.

DEBATE 1

'Even knowing about the perceptual process doesn't prevent perceptual errors occurring, especially in an interview situation.'

Starting points

For

- The tendency to, for example, stereotype, is innate and is not only bound to occur but will also predispose us to act in a particular way even though we know that it is wrong. In fact this predisposition occurs even before the interview: we start making judgements as early as the application stage.

- Because perception is such an *individual* process, two or more interviewers will probably have different impressions anyway. A knowledge of the perceptual process can, therefore, be argued to be pointless.

Against

- A knowledge of perceptual errors will assist in an interview situation because the interviewer will make additional efforts to overcome them through use of such techniques as questioning and listening.
- If a knowledge of the perceptual process is pointless then why bother with it? The research experiments show that it happens and we therefore need to know about it not only in order to obtain the best candidate but also to improve our own self-knowledge.

Further reading

McCauley, C., Stitt, C. L. and Segal, M. (1980), 'Stereotyping: From Prejudice to Prediction', *Psychological Bulletin*, January, 195–208.

Wexley, K. N., Yukl, G. A., Kovacs, S. Z. and Sanders, R. E. (1972), 'Importance of Contrast Effects in Employment Interviews', *Journal of Applied Psychology*, 56, 45–8.

DEBATE 2

'There is considerable truth in the commonly held perception that women's motivations and attitudes to work are different to men's.'

Starting points

For

- Women do not perceive themselves as having a 'career for life', rather that a job is only a temporary substitute before starting a family.
- Men are socialised into believing that they should be the ultimate 'breadwinner' and should concentrate their efforts on a 'career for life'.

Against

- Studies concerning this are rare; the proposition, therefore, has not been empirically tested but relies on anecdotal evidence.
- The proposition represents an all-encompassing statement which by its very nature is invalid: both women's and men's attitudes and motivations vary and will change depending on their individual life stage.

Further reading

Alban-Metcalfe, B. (1987), 'Attitudes to Work: Comparison by Gender and Sector of Employment', *The Occupational Psychologist*, 3, December, 8.

Cooper, C. and Davidson, M. (1982), *High Pressure: Working Lives of Women Managers*, Fontana.

Kanter, R. M. (1977), *Men and Women of the Corporation*, Basic Books.

Marshall, J. (1984), *Women Managers: Travellers in a Male World*, Wiley.

ASSIGNMENT 1

Task

Either

1 During a one-week period, review the media (television, radio, advertisements, films, newspapers and magazines) for evidence of traditional male and female stereotypes.

Evaluate the impact and power of these stereotypes *either* in a group discussion *or* as a written report of not more than 1500 words.

or

2 Here is a list of jobs performed in a secondary school:

teacher
child psychologist
governor
caretaker
deputy head
peripatetic music teacher
cook
head teacher
dinner attendant
gardener
secretary
inspector
groundsman
cleaner
maintenance worker
educational welfare officer
non-teaching assistant

Which gender did you intuitively ascribe to each function? Were the people White, Black, handicapped? Did your judgements bear out the theory of stereotyping? How do such judgements match up with reality? (See Mullins, pp. 327–30.)

Contact a local school and check who does these jobs there. Write a 750-word report with the title 'Who works in our schools?' based on two kinds of research approach: case study and statistical. Use the bibliographical evidence given in Mullins (p. 342, notes 73–80) to get you on the trail of appropriate statistical sources. (Notice, incidentally, that bibliographies tend not to identify the gender of the authors.)

ASSIGNMENT 2

Over a six-week period, interview a selected sample of people about their perception of a particular group (e.g. students, personnel managers, trade union officials, disabled people, ex-offenders). Your sample should include representatives from your chosen group.

Prepare a report and/or presentation which evaluates the perceptions of those interviewed and answers the question: 'Do they conform to the "traditional" perceptual errors?'

You will need to:

- devise and, where possible, test a questionnaire or other suitable interview method;
- decide on your sample group and sample size;
- make decisions and arrangements as to how your sample will be interviewed (e.g. by prior appointment or 'on the street', perhaps);

- analyse your results using either a quantitative or qualitative approach;
- evaluate your findings and draw logical conclusions.

APPLICATION 1

Stereotyping and social identity

Stig Kornstadt works in the medical records department of a large hospital. He takes a dim view of doctors: 'The trouble is they are all so arrogant. They walk in here and expect me to find patients' case notes immediately. It's not as simple as that – they could be almost any place in the hospital. They couldn't do their job properly if it wasn't for me, but they seem to forget that. One doctor actually comes in here and threatens to report me if I don't do what he wants right away. Another always finds me in the canteen during my lunch break and makes me come back here for an urgent file she needs. They don't all do things like that, but I bet they would if they thought they could get away with it. And of course I never get invited onto the wards to see what goes on there. I can only remember one doctor being really nice to me – and he had just been promoted! People say they notice doctors being friendly to me sometimes but I can't say I do. So I just do what they ask without wasting my time being pleasant.'

- Go through the section on 'Stereotypes' in Mullins, p. 396, and find as many phenomena as you can which are reflected in this case study. Are there any others? Is there any hope of changing Stig's view of doctors?

Source: Adapted from Arnold J., Cooper, C. L. and Robertson, I. T. (1998), *Work Psychology*, 3rd edition, FT Pitman Publishing.

APPLICATION 2

Expectations and social reality

The manufacturing firm where Brian Hall was personnel officer was looking for a new part-time industrial chaplain for their main factory. One of the local vicars, Peter Hinde, was interested. Brian took him for a thorough tour of the factory, chatting as they went. Brian had previously heard from one of Hinde's parishioners that he could be rather secretive, which was bad news because in his opinion a chaplain needed to be open, honest and sincere. On the way round the factory, he observed that Hinde laughed only occasionally and rarely cracked jokes though when he did they were good ones. He talked to people in an intense way, but not for long. Each time he quickly moved on. Hinde commented a lot to Brian on the people they met on their tour and seemed to feel they were straightforward, open and honest. Especially in the early part of the tour, Hinde did not give much away about his religious beliefs, concentrating instead on *their* lives and points of view. He listened to what they had to stay and never interrupted. Brian asked him some questions about how he handled situations where parishioners wanted him to give more information than he wanted to. After Hinde left, Brian sat in his chair and sighed. Peter Hinde probably wasn't right for the factory. Just his luck! As if he wasn't fed up enough already, having only yesterday been turned down for a promotion that would have meant he could say goodbye to tasks like this.

- What conclusions do you think Brian Hall drew about Peter Hinde as they toured the factory? Why did he come to those conclusions?
- Supposing Brian had got his promotion, and had heard that Peter Hinde was quite open in his dealings with people. How might he then have assessed Hinde's behaviour in the factory?

Source: Arnold, J., Cooper, C. L. and Robertson, I. T. (1998), *Work Psychology*, 3rd edition, FT Pitman Publishing.

APPLICATION 3

A student on one of our part-time management courses had recently changed jobs. Previously she had worked for a large organisation as a training officer where her job had involved writing and delivering a variety of training courses. Her new job was as a training and recruitment manager for a much smaller, less structured organisation. Along with her promotion came a lot more responsibility: she was in charge of a whole department overseeing the analysis of training needs, planning, designing, delivering and evaluating training courses. On top of that, her recruitment 'hat' gave her responsibility for recruiting trainee managers and monitoring their progress.

Two months into her new job, we asked her how she was getting on. 'I think I've made the wrong decision,' she replied. 'The training part of the job is going well but it's the recruitment part that's causing me problems. The area managers have made the assumption that "recruitment" means any recruitment and they've also further assumed that "recruitment" equals "personnel", so I'm being asked all sorts of questions about employment law and dismissal and I don't know anything about it. My one ally in the company has told me that the area managers are beginning to say that my appointment was a waste of time.'

Where does perception fit in here? Can you see how perceptions of one word – in this case 'recruitment' – can mean different things to different people? When our perception doesn't match reality, cognitive dissonance sets in (see Mullins, p. 327) – can you see it in this case? How could it have been avoided?

APPLICATION 4

Consider the following . . .

. . . A housewife looked out of her kitchen window and saw a stranger playing with her neighbour's child outside the house. Alarmed, she was about to call the police when she realised that it was the child's father who had shaved off his beard that morning . . . .

. . . A lecturer was in his university library one day during the vacation and noticed a young woman coming towards him with an expectant look on her face. Assuming that it was a student new to the library he began to ask her if he could be of any assistance and then stopped when he realised it was his sister who lived over 60 miles away . . . .

. . . In the doctor's waiting room, vacantly looking at the child on the chair next to him, John's thoughts were something like this: 'That boy's got a familiar face.

Maybe it's a girl though. It's my Lucy!' Lucy was his daughter. The family's child-minder had a doctor's appointment that day and had brought Lucy with her . . . .

How might a study of theories of perception help explain these real incidents?

APPLICATION 5

We have long attached certain perceptions to certain cars; we perceive that the Reliant Robin owned by Del in the television programme *Only Fools and Horses* is 'right' for him in the same way that the Golf GTi convertible became the required badge of rank for the Yuppies of the 1980s.

The symbolic importance of the company car as a means of perceiving where drivers are placed in their organisation's pecking order was recently highlighted in the television series, 'From A to B, Tales of Modern Motoring'. Details such as metallic paint, alloy wheels and electric windows and sunroof are all important but of crucial significance is the badge on the car – an obligatory 'i' denoting more than an injection engine but also standing for 'important'. One driver said, 'I like to think I'm quite successful because I've got a Rover 600. I sell industrial packaging machines – something with a bit of esteem. Another driver said that when he told his wife that his new company car was a Nissan Sunny 'we both literally sat down and cried . . . going from the BMW down to this, I just wondered what I'd done to deserve it'. He went on to add that when visiting clients he parked it out of sight lest it influenced the day's business.

One of the authors once worked for a company whose sales reps put together a very powerful argument as to why they should be given car telephones (ease of communication, availability, time management etc.). Unfortunately they totally negated all the strengths of their case by adding a final paragraph which said, in essence, 'if we can't have the phones, can we at least have the aerials fitted so that it looks to other sales people as if we have phones?'. . .

If, as it seems, you are judged by what you drive, take a look at the cars parked in your college or company car park – what is your perception of their owners and how accurate is it?

If you're a company car driver, sit in the Honesty Chair: how much do you identify with *your* car? Would you feel devalued if you didn't get another BMW as a replacement? Are *you* influenced by the 'i' factor?

APPLICATION 6

Over the last few years the wearing of a small red ribbon has become increasingly popular and people sporting this emblem can be seen everywhere from provincial high streets to public ceremonies – indeed at some of the latter, notably those conferring film or television awards, it has become *de rigueur*, often being included with the invitation. It is even considered in some circles to be churlish, at the very least, not to be wearing one.

The red ribbon vogue began life in America where it symbolised the red tape surrounding the help and benefits provided for people with AIDS. It is now seen as an emblem for raising awareness of HIV/AIDS, either globally or on a more personal level when it might be worn in memory of a friend who has died of AIDS or an AIDS-related condition.

The wearing of symbolic coloured ribbons is by no means a new phenomenon but, in fact, dates back to the seventeenth century when folk songs of the time record that wearing white ribbons indicated a married woman. They were further popularised during the American Civil War where a yellow ribbon was worn and this was resurrected in memory of those killed or lost in Vietnam and also for hostages in Beirut. Gathering awareness since the inception of the red ribbon we now have a whole rainbow of colours: blue (unborn children), black (for Black people who have died of AIDS) and pink (for breast cancer).

The red ribbon, however, has gone from strength to strength: not only is there now a metal version but limited editions, using precious metals and gemstones, have raised it to the level of designer fashion accessory.

Distasteful as this glamorisation of a dreadful disease may be, at the very minimum awareness *must* be being raised and the AIDS charities *must* be receiving valuable revenue from the sale of ribbons, particularly the expensive versions. Or are they? There is no one specific campaigning organisation behind the red ribbons although in the past their sale has proved to be an effective fund-raiser by AIDS charities. However, it is difficult to copyright a twisted length of red ribbon and, it has been claimed, it is now being incorporated as a fashion accessory rather than a statement of individual attitude: the finale of a recent show by designer Moschino featured dozens of children wearing red ribbons.

- How will the red ribbon be perceived in the next few years?
- How will reading this affect *your* perception of the next person you see who is wearing one?

APPLICATION 7

Consider the following:

You try to be . . .	*You are perceived to be . . .*
Brisk	Brusque
Efficient	Officious
Enquiring	Interfering
Friendly	Familiar
Business-like	Excessively formal
Informative	A know-all
Helpful	Pushy
Brief/concise	Curt
Comprehensive	Verbose

If we seem destined to make these perceptual pitfalls, is there any point in worrying about perception at all?

Provided by Ritchie Stevenson, West Sussex County Council.

APPLICATION 8

It's Saturday evening and Cilla has 'gorralorra' contestants for *Blind Date*. The programme follows its usual format: three people hidden behind a screen and another of the opposite sex on the other side of the screen who poses questions aimed at finding out which of the three will make the perfect blind date partner.

The audience in the studio and at home have the advantage over the hapless contestants, we can at least see what they all look like and we can make our choice based on this. Usually we decide by applying such scientific criteria as 'She looks like Julia Roberts', 'He looks like Patrick Swayze', 'She seems a fun person', or 'He's got a big ego'. In other words we apply our own perceptual criteria based on our attitudes, personalities and assumptions.

The contest is over and the 'winner' walks around the screen to meet his or her blind date . . . next time you watch, look for the expressions on each face – that'll tell you a lot about how perceptual processes work. Watch the programme the following week, hear how the 'date' worked (or didn't) and look again at the role of perception.

APPLICATION 9

A research student of our acquaintance had got to that part of her PhD which involved the actual collection of evidence – a series of semi-structured interviews with various people. She followed all the rules, explained the purpose of the research, how the interview was going to be conducted, and so on, and everything went well. After the interview was over, the respondent asked her about her background. When she replied that her first degree was in psychology, he said, 'I'm really glad that I didn't know that beforehand – I'd have been convinced that not only were there hidden reasons behind your questions but also that you were going to psychoanalyse all my answers.'

- What does this indicate about how we stereotype people?
- Have you ever avoided telling people (such as landlords or bank managers) that you're a student?

AFTERTHOUGHTS

Why does it seem that you only get stopped at Customs when you're wearing a T-shirt and jeans and carrying a backpack and not when you're dressed in a business suit and carrying a briefcase?

'Competence, like truth, beauty and contact lenses, is in the eye of the beholder.'
Dr Laurence J. Peter

12 The Nature of Work Motivation

CASE STUDY

Midshires University: Motivation or abdication?

The organisation

Midshires University is one of the 'new breed' of universities: formerly a successful polytechnic it, like many others, received its new title in June 1992 following changes to government policy. The university has approximately 15 000 students, 75 per cent of whom are full-time. Although the majority of students are studying at undergraduate level, some 20 per cent are registered for postgraduate qualifications either through taught courses or by research.

Like similar organisations, the university, in its polytechnic days, acquired its reputation primarily through the delivery of teaching, with research activities, although important, taking a somewhat second place. Since its change in status, changes in funding have meant that student numbers have escalated and increased competition for research funding has meant that much more emphasis has not only been placed on quantity but also on quality of research delivery and publications. One senior academic was heard to remark 'We've got to make our minds up whether we're a teaching or a research institution. All this "fence sitting" is wrong: not only are we being pulled both ways, we're not being given any additional resources to cope with it. How can I teach fifteen hours a week, supervise projects for twelve final-year students, be an admissions tutor for one of our biggest courses *and* be expected to undertake research work?' These rumblings of discontent were not confined to isolated departments but were apparent throughout the institution.

As with many organisations of a similar size and diversity, its structure is almost guaranteed to create bureaucracy and, to some extent, distance and divisiveness. The administrative core of the organisation (known officially as the senior management structure but unofficially as 'The Centre') is headed up by the vice-chancellor (although the titular head is the chancellor – a well-known industrialist and public figure); underneath him is a deputy vice-chancellor and four pro-vice-chancellors who are each responsible for a specific area (for example, academic affairs). These six, together with the deans of each faculty, form the executive board whose main responsibility is to 'provide corporate leadership'. In addition, there exist administrative support functions such as personnel, marketing, finance, estates and academic registrar.

The academic core of the university is grouped into five faculties: Engineering, Science, Humanities, Built Environment and a Business School. Each faculty is headed up by a dean and subdivided into a number of specialist schools or departments. The hierarchy within each department is loose in nature: although there is a head of department, several principal lecturers, with the remainder being senior lecturers, there is no real emphasis given to job title. Any bureaucracy which exists in the departments is perceived as originating either from 'The Centre' or from department administration staff whose loyalty to the department rather than 'The Centre' is open to debate.

The department

Within the Engineering faculty lies the department of mechanical engineering with some forty staff, most of whom have been at the university for at least eight years and 90 per cent of whom are 'career academics' who have not held posts in commercial organisations. All are male.

The head of department (who is also the Wallace-Price Professor of Engineering) leads the department in a relatively informal and relaxed manner. Like the majority of academics he is an 'ideas' man rather than an administrator and dislikes formal policies and procedures. Frequently heard to remark 'I don't like tying things or people up in red tape, I prefer a democratic approach', he has been accused in the past of inconsistency by his staff, of never treating two people in the same way. However, it is true to say that, in general, academic staff are left to organise their lives as they want within the constraints of their teaching schedule. Their research work is highly respected, several innovative engineering designs have been patented and sold on the open market, and there is a well-established programme of industry collaboration.

Whilst the climate of the department is outwardly relaxed and informal, there is very little interaction among staff, particularly outside working hours. Each academic has his own room, there is no central staff room and many staff work from home, only coming into the department to teach and undertake their administrative duties. Gossip is rife, as is professional jealousy, particularly in terms of gaining research funding.

An increase in student numbers, successful franchise arrangements being made to deliver postgraduate courses in China and the Far East and an attempt to reduce teaching loads has led to the department advertising a vacancy for a senior lecturer. Ideally the preferred candidate will have experience of research work, good external business contacts and will want to travel. As is usual in academic institutions, very little, if any, thought is given to the personality of the successful candidate or to the desirability of them fitting in to the rest of the department.

The candidate

Anne Henderson was one of the first women engineering students at Midshires. Graduating in 1975 with a first class honours degree she immediately continued her studies with an MSc programme, gaining recognition for her work into environmentally friendly car engines, a largely untapped field in those days. On completion of her Masters degree she was offered a post as a research assistant where she could have developed her Masters research and worked towards her doctorate. However she decided that she needed to gain some commercial experience and joined Wallace-Price, a blue-chip engineering consultancy where, apart from a sponsored year out to study for an MBA in the USA, she has remained ever since.

Her tenacity and loyalty to Wallace-Price have paid off and in 1986 she was made a partner in the firm, primarily responsible for bringing in work to the consultancy. With the promotion came various executive privileges including an annual salary of £80 000, a chauffeur-driven car, free use of one of the company-owned London flats, a non-contributory pension scheme, various gold credit cards and first-class air travel. Anne herself would not describe these as benefits, however, but as necessities to enable her to do her job properly. Last year, in order to meet her business target of £2 million of work for Wallace-Price she spent forty weeks overseas, working an average of ninety hours a week. She can't remember the last time that she had a weekend when she was not entertaining clients or travelling but was totally free to indulge herself.

During her time with Wallace-Price she has earned a reputation both as a formidable but honest negotiator and as an innovative engineer, often finding seemingly impossible solutions to problems. Known for her single-minded dedication to her job, she does not suffer fools gladly. She is frequently approached to work for rival firms with promises of even greater privileges and has been the subject of numerous magazine profiles, some concentrating on her work and reputation as a high flier but the majority focusing on her gender.

Her fortieth birthday last year was spent alone in the Emergency Room of a Los Angeles hospital where she had been rushed with a suspected stomach ulcer. Deprived of her portable telephone, fax and computer she had little else to do but to reflect on her life thus far. On her return to health she was working her way through the pile of technical journals which had accumulated during her absence and there she saw the advertisement for Midshires – an institution which had close links with her company and whose Professor of Engineering she knew well. Ignoring the instructions relating to applications she put through a telephone call to the University . . . .

Activity brief

1 Making reference to the appropriate theories, what do you consider to be Anne's main motivating factors? Do you believe that her motivation has *actually* changed on a long-term basis?

2 If you were head of Engineering would you appoint Anne to the position? Why or why not? If you did appoint Anne, how would you motivate her during her first year of employment?

3 A year from appointment, what issues do you imagine might be raised at her annual appraisal and how should they be dealt with?

ACTIVITY: The work/work harder exercise

Either individually, in groups or using a combination of both, list your answers to the following questions:

- What motivates you to work at all?
- What motivates you to work harder?

Can you relate your answers to one or more of the motivation theories?

DEBATE 1

'Money is the only thing that motivates people in the real world – all the theories that abound are redundant when it comes to basic issues.'

Starting points

For

- Money acts as an exchange medium which allows people to 'buy' things which satisfy their needs.
- Money is used as a 'symbolic temperature gauge' by which employees can assess or perceive the organisation's opinion of them.

Against

- There is no guaranteed link between money and higher performance unless it is perceived as a direct and significant reward for performance.
- Motivation is not just about economic rewards, it is also concerned with intrinsic satisfaction and social relationships.

Further reading

Guest, D. (1984), 'What's New in Motivation?', *Personnel Management*, May, 20–3.

Herzberg, F. (1987), 'One More Time – How Do You Motivate Employees?' *Harvard Business Review*, 65, Issue 5, September/October 109–20.

Kovach, K. A. (1987), 'What Motivates Employees? Workers and Supervisors Give Different Answers', *Business Horizons*, September/October, 61.

Locke, E. A. *et al.* (1980), 'The Relative Effectiveness of Four Methods of Motivating Employee Performance', in *Changes in Working Life*, K. D. Duncan, M. M. Gruneberg and D. Wallis (eds), Wiley, 363–83.

Mitchell, T. R. (1982), 'Motivation: New Directions for Theory, Research and Practice', *Academy of Management Review*, 7 (1), January, 80–8.

Sievers, B. (1986), 'Beyond the Surrogate of Motivation', *Organization Studies*, 7 (4), 335–51.

DEBATE 2

'In a recession you can motivate employees to do anything as long as they feel that their job is under threat.'

Starting points

For

- What *actually* motivates at the end of the day is the satisfaction of basic/lower order needs – in other words, Maslow and Alderfer.
- In times of economic crisis managers need to have flexible staff in the organisation – people may have to do the work of two employees and the business is more concerned with staying in business than bothering with ensuring that higher order needs are satisfied.

Against

- How long is the recession likely to last? Organisations which survive are not likely to be the same (in terms of design, culture, etc.) at the end as they were at the beginning. They will need committed and loyal employees and this is not likely to happen if a 'climate of fear' has reigned in the interim.
- Consider McGregor's Theory X and Theory Y: how effective is 'management by fear' likely to be? To enable the organisation to survive it needs employees who are 'singing the same song', in other words who are committed to survival. This will involve flexibility and adaptability (not to mention excellent customer care skills) – qualities which are unlikely to be produced if people are in fear of their jobs and, as a consequence, hate both their jobs and the company.

Further reading

Locke, E. A. (1976), 'The Nature and Causes of Job Satisfaction', in M. D. Dunnette (ed.), *Handbook of Industrial and Organizational Psychology*, Rand McNally, 1297–1349.

Steers, R. M. (1977), 'Antecedents and Outcomes of Organizational Commitment', *Administrative Science Quarterly*, 22, 46–56.

ASSIGNMENT 1

Using *one* of the models of motivation, test it in practice by designing and carrying out a small research study using either work or college colleagues.

You will need to:

- Decide which motivation theory you are going to use.
- Design a questionnaire based on what the theory says.
- Decide on your sample population and your sample size.
- Describe the characteristics of your sample.
- Administer the questionnaires.
- Analyse the results.
- Link your results back to the original theory.
- Decide on your conclusions – for example, did the theory apply to your sample population? If not, why not?
- Decide on your recommendations and how you would implement them.

Your assignment can be written up as a report, presented verbally to the rest of the year, or a combination of both.

ASSIGNMENT 2

An article with the following title appeared in *OB Quarterly*, a behavioural science journal aimed at both academics and practitioners:

At the end of the day, competition is the only thing that motivates – the theories revisited

In *not more* than 2000 words, complete the article as if you were submitting it for publication. You should bear in mind the following:

- Your target audience will be both academics who know the theories in detail and practitioners who probably won't have the same understanding but will have a basic knowledge (in other words, you don't need to redraw Maslow's Pyramid and describe it in detail). The non-academics who read your article will be practising managers and you will therefore need to relate your theoretical arguments to the workplace.
- As with all academic journals, your article will be sent to at least two people with a knowledge of the area in order to obtain their views prior to it being accepted for publication. Your arguments, therefore, must be clear, logical and lead the reader to an obvious conclusion (a one-sentence statement beginning 'Thus it can be seen that . . .' will not only be unacceptable but also indicates that you haven't really thought the issues through).
- Your work must be referenced (for an example of referencing using footnotes, see the final pages of any chapter in Mullins, 'Notes and References'). There is nothing wrong in quoting other authors' views or opinions but at least give them the credit for having stated the point before you did!

APPLICATION 1

One of our students once remarked: 'This business of motivation theory is OK and I understand what they're trying to say but I don't see how I can relate most of it to my job – they just don't work in the real world.' The student was a civil engineer responsible ultimately for the work of up to 200 short-contract labourers involved in a variety of projects including road building, bridge and office block construction. She said, 'I can see where Maslow fits, but at the end of the day all my lot want to do is to earn enough bonus each week to go out on a Friday night, get blitzed and wake up somewhere strange on Sunday morning with a monumental hangover and no memory of the intervening thirty-six hours. Don't tell me that I'm being a harsh judge of them because I see it happening every week and 90 per cent of the time I'm proved right. Where do your airy-fairy process theories fit into that then?'

If, for example, Expectancy Theory is simplified into the proposition that the degree of energy/motivation expended is dependent on the likelihood and attractiveness of an outcome happening, we can translate our student's situation into 'real life' as shown in Fig. 12.1.

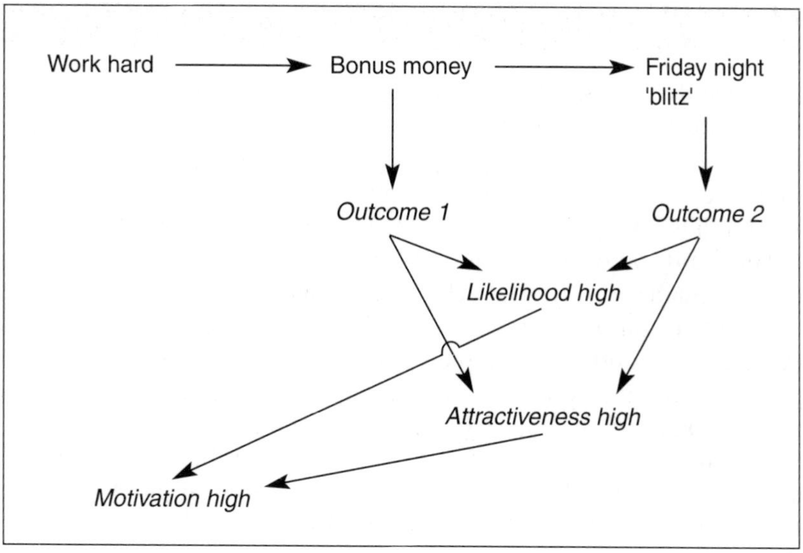

Fig. 12.1 'Real life' analysis of situation

APPLICATION 2

One of the most frequent comments that we receive from students when we return marked assignments is (with varying degrees of politeness): 'I don't understand why you've only given me 52 per cent when I worked myself stupid over this essay – I know that Chris didn't spend half the amount of time in the library that I did, he skipped your 9.15 lecture to write it and you gave him 61 per cent. It isn't fair – if that's all the thanks I get, forget it – I've never liked OB anyway.'

Equally Chris may come to us and say, 'Thanks for my assignment mark, I wasn't sure if I'd taken the right approach – I know a lot of people spent all their time in the library but I thought the question was more concerned with what I thought rather than repeating all the theories word for word. I know that I missed your lecture but I'm really bogged down with assignments at the moment and although I stayed up most of the night I still needed some extra time to put the finishing touches to it.' (All right, we weren't born yesterday but it does sound fairly plausible.) 'I wasn't sure about OB but it's more interesting than I thought.'

For this situation, let's look at Equity Theory and remember that this theory revolves around *perception* of inputs and outputs and the consequences of that perception on individual behaviour. The first student equated time quantity *(inputs)* with an assumed high mark *(outputs)* and used this equation as a comparison with Chris. When it didn't compute, the restoration of equity was achieved by condemning the subject itself – in other words, cognitive distortion.

APPLICATION 3

Increasingly we are told that the traditional organisational configurations which have endured for decades will have to change to meet the challenges of the future. Organisations will be 'leaner and fitter', 'downsized', 'upside down', shamrock-shaped or will even resemble that often neglected plant which graces most office windowsills, the spider plant (see, for example, Handy, 1989, and Morgan, 1993).

The words by which we describe traditional procedures have changed and continue to change: control and delegation are out, empowerment and ownership are in.

The nature of jobs themselves are changing; we have already witnessed an increase in job-sharing and we can look forward to more teleworking via home-based computer workstations. We are told that employees of the future will have not one but several jobs, some paid, some unpaid – they will become 'portfolio people'.

How will the 'manager' of the future (assuming that such a person will still exist) motivate these employees? What roles will, for example, Equity and Expectancy Theory play in these new organisational forms?

APPLICATION 4

In the fifty or so years since Abraham Maslow suggested his theory of individual development and motivation, we have seen the various theories build, develop on each other and finally divide into two schools of thought: content/behaviourist and process/cognitive. With the exception of Maccoby (1988), who suggested that motivation of individuals should be linked to social character types, the last twenty years has seen a scarcity of new approaches.

- Does this mean the end of innovative motivation research as we know it?
- Have we finally exhausted all the possibilities, probabilities and suggestions as to how to get that extra ounce of effort from employees? Is a discussion of 'what's new in motivation' now meaningless?
- How would *you* undertake the next research study into motivation?

APPLICATION 5

You are a first-year student at the Fresher's Ball. You've enjoyed your first week so far and this is a good party. Across the room you see someone who you noticed in your Study Skills lecture and they appear to be on their own, which could be a point in your favour. However, you've also noticed that they're already very popular with other students while you know yourself to be a bit reticent and sensitive, always fearing the 'brush off'. If you ask them for a dance what is the likelihood that they will accept and what is the further likelihood that you may get to see them again?

Can you see where Expectancy Theory comes into play? Think about first- and second-level outcomes, the chance of them happening and their attractiveness – how does this affect your motivation to ask for the dance? (Consider also that there may be an intervening variable coming into the picture here: the DJ may suddenly switch from 'Lady in Red' to 'Guns 'n' Roses' – ask yourself about the timing of the motivational drive.)

APPLICATION 6

As a new second-year student you've had to move out of Halls and into your own accommodation. You have taken great care to team up with like-minded people for a house-share and after many hours of scanning the local newspaper, networking with final-year students and pounding the pavements, you've finally found the perfect place. There are students in the houses on both sides (so noise won't be a problem), there is a take-away and pub within a two-minute walk, the house has central heating, a washing machine, TV, video and telephone and the landlord lives several miles away. Congratulating yourself on your good fortune, you move in and proceed to enjoy your second year away from some of the constraints of the Hall of Residence.

Several weeks go by and your parents pay a 'surprise visit' early one Sunday morning. You proudly give them a grand tour of your new house but to your disappointment your mother remarks on several things: the kitchen in general is dirty and the grill pan in particular has a mixture of toast crumbs and last week's bacon sandwich congealing together; there seems to be an inordinate amount of empty coffee cups and beer cans all over the sitting room; the bathroom has mould on the walls; there is a large burn hole in the settee and there appear to be at least two 'extra' people who have clearly not only just got up but also appear to be somewhat disoriented.

In despair, your mother remarks, 'For goodness sake, how can you live *like* this – it's total squalor. I can't believe that a child of mine has these values.'

Can you see where Goal Theory might apply? Is there a place here also for Maslow? (Think about differing perceptions of what 'basic needs' actually *are*.)

AFTERTHOUGHTS

When asked the question, 'What do you understand by the word "motivation"?', a senior manager within an international manufacturing company said, 'Well, I don't like to give my staff a bollocking every time . . . .'

Provided by Val Marchant, Ibis Training and Development.

Overheard on a train: 'When I first started working I used to dream of the day when I might be earning the salary I'm starving on now . . . .' Eat your heart out Abraham Maslow!

13 The Nature of Work Groups

CASE STUDY

Firing on three cylinders . . .

Lifestyle Cars Ltd, as is general amongst car manufacturers, distributes its vehicles through a series of authorised dealerships all over the UK. In order to successfully qualify for such authorisation, each potential dealership has to undergo rigorous vetting procedures to ensure that Lifestyle's quality standards will be adhered to. Competition for authorised dealerships is always fierce, never more so than when, as with Lifestyle, the products are popular and sell well. Dealers are expected to meet sales and growth targets laid down by the manufacturer – in trade jargon 'to move the metal'. Rewards for success are not just monetary: dealers who are performing well are awarded a variety of other prizes, from holidays to extra deliveries of new models into their showroom. Out-of-date models are obviously not as easy to 'move' and no dealer wants deliveries of these cars when there are new or improved styles.

Once accepted as an authorised dealer, the relationship between dealership and Lifestyle is not always an easy one. The two organisations must live side by side for as long as the contract lasts. Lifestyle have no direct authority over a dealer but indirectly have great power.

To understand this situation more fully, let us look at a typical dealership, Ratchetts Ltd. Founded more than twenty years ago by Alan Ratchett, it has seen steady growth over that time from its humble start as a vehicle repair shop to the present day which sees it as a Lifestyle authorised dealer. Founder Alan Ratchett, managing director of his own company, is also the Lifestyle 'dealer principal'; the organisation chart is shown in Fig. 13.1.

Overlaid on this is the Lifestyle organisation of two regional managers, responsible for either sales or service. Thus the car sales manager reports directly to Alan Ratchett and indirectly to his Lifestyle regional manager who has his own company targets to meet. Equally Ratchett, whilst being managing director of his own company, is also equally accountable to Lifestyle Cars via the two regional managers and *their* bosses. Failure to meet standards and targets set could well result in the loss of the franchise.

It would appear from Fig. 13.1 that the dealership falls naturally into two distinct areas: Sales and After-sales. Even if this were the case, it would not be a welcome division: profit margins on new cars are low and a dealership relies on the after-sales market to engender customer loyalty and boost revenue. However, in the case of Ratchetts, the groups divide even further. Let us look at each section separately.

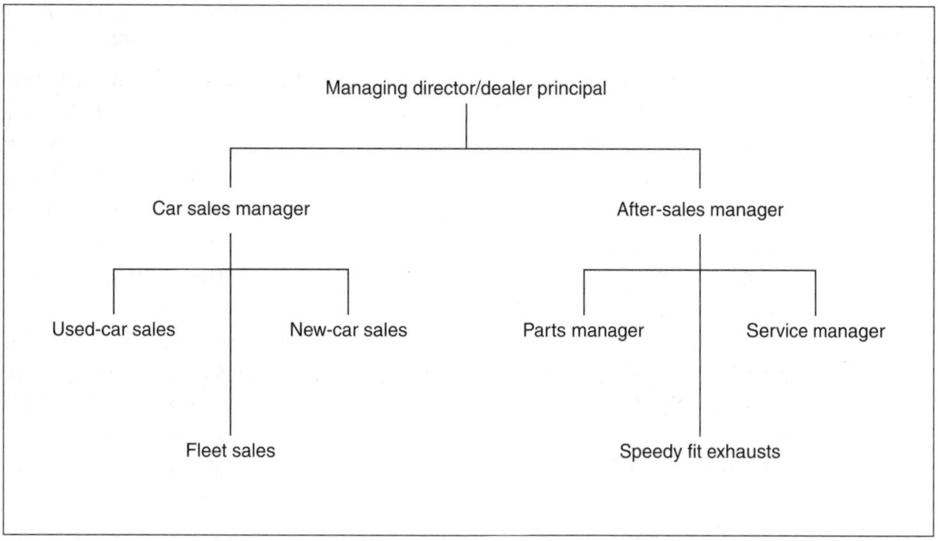

Fig. 13.1 Organisation chart for Ratchetts Ltd

Car sales

The car sales manager is responsible for essentially three separate and distinct areas: new cars, used cars and fleet sales. To take the first two, historically there is always a bigger profit to be made from used cars than from new. 'Used' cars can mean anything from a five-year-old vehicle to one which has only been owned for six months. An unknowing customer, therefore, intending to purchase a brand new car may be successfully 'prospected' by a used-car salesman to buy a six-month-old car before they even get as far as the showroom door. Behind-the-scenes arguments ensue as to the customer's intentions and to whom the commission should go, particularly if the customer has always purchased 'new' before. Similar arguments occur within each team as to who the customer 'belongs' to: comments such as 'She was *my* customer, I talked to her first but Debbie signed her up on my day off – I deserve a percentage' are frequently heard and, in an industry where base salaries are low and made up by commission, are hardly surprising.

Sales techniques can range from the subtle to the not so subtle. Subtle, in that test drives will always take a left-turn route so that the 'prospect' does not feel worried or unsure about how a car will perform if they have to turn right across the traffic. Not so subtle is the use of 'controlled selling' techniques where 'prospects', on a flimsy excuse of taking the used car for a test drive, find themselves minus keys and virtually locked in a room until they sign on the dotted line.

After-sales

This area also tends to fall into two distinct sections: Service and Parts. The Parts department serves two masters: the general public (be it a self-employed motor mechanic or a private car owner intent on doing his own servicing) and the Service department itself. The Parts manager is under increasing pressure to keep his inventory levels as low as possible and is frequently heard on the telephone trying to 'borrow' essential but seldom-used parts from other Lifestyle dealers in the region. The Service technicians are highly trained mechanics who these days have traded in their ring spanners for state-of-the-art computer diagnostics. They are paid by the number of jobs they complete. Taylorism is alive and well in the motor industry: each job has a set time allotted to it and listed in the job book. Therefore if a technician can 'beat the book', not only are they paid for the number of hours that it should have taken but they can also go on to another job. It is not unusual, therefore, for a technician to be paid for seventy-five hours having only physically worked for thirty-nine. Clearly, therefore, there is tension between workshop and Parts: the former don't want to be held up waiting for a part which the department is trying to locate at another dealership.

Against this general background we then have the manufacturer imposing strict controls in all areas from the showroom layout to the procedure for warranty claims. As mentioned, the car industry is a competitive one and Lifestyle have decided to introduce an even greater element of competition by introducing a set of 'customer care principles' against which each dealer will be measured. Ten in total, five for Sales and five for After-sales (but primarily Service), they detail the main stages in a customer transaction and include areas such as 'manner, tone and attitude of the salesman', 'quality of purchase experience' and 'right first time, every time' for Service. Performance against standards will be measured by customer questionnaires and each dealership will be given their results in a monthly league table for the whole region. Lifestyle have decided that each dealer who consistently falls below the region average will lose discounts – a not inconsiderable amount of money over the year.

After the first quarter's figures had been issued, Alan Ratchett called a meeting of all staff and explained the results. Overall they were below the group average in the following areas:

- Customers considered that salesmen were too 'pushy' and they felt that they were abandoned once the deal had been done with them.
- Service department was experiencing a high level of repeat repairs. Further analysis showed that this was partly due to standard of work but also due to the fact that the fault could not be immediately rectified because parts were unavailable and had to be ordered.

All in all, if the dealership were to continue on this slippery slope it stood to lose up to £30 000 in the coming year. Asking each of his managers to come up with some solutions 'PDQ', Alan Ratchett then wandered around the dealership where he overheard the following comments:

- *'I don't know why he's getting at us – the customer care principles don't include Parts.'* (Parts manager)
- *'I hope he's not going to change the payment system unless he's going to double wages. "Beating the book" is the only way I can earn a living wage.'* (Technician)
- *'I try to "move the metal" so that I get my commission and keep Lifestyle happy and now they're saying that I'm too pushy – in this job you have to be, otherwise somebody else gets the deal.'* (New-car salesman)
- *'We'd be a lot better off if Parts got their act together.'* (Workshop supervisor)
- *'We do the best we can and Service lets us down each time.'* (Used-car salesman)
- *'A lot of the problems are due to the Lifestyle warranty procedure – they're just too picky and that's why it seems as if we're getting repeat repairs.'* (Service manager)

Returning to his office Ratchett murmured to himself, 'I just don't know what to do. I read an article recently about "quality circles" but you need a spirit of co-operation for that – this lot aren't even speaking to each other.'

Activity brief

1 Identify reasons for the breakdown in inter-group communications and suggest ways that they might be overcome.

2 Do you consider that the different departments at Ratchetts are groups or teams? Justify your answer.

3 Taking the role of a management consultant, prepare a report for Alan Ratchett as to how things might be improved in his dealership.

ACTIVITY: Working together

Materials required

One box of Polydron material (a building kit available from the Early Learning Centre) for each group. You will need to check and sort the boxes so that each contains identical shapes and colours. The person managing the activity should use one box to create a structure of their choice but should not allow participants to see what has been created until instructed to do so.

Logistics

Divide the participants into groups of four, to a maximum of five groups.

Group briefing

- Each group will be given an identical box of building materials.
- Each group of four will consist of two builders and two architects.
- Architects may visit the structure one at a time. Their role is to communicate the design brief to the builders. They may not draw, record or use their hands to help describe the structure. Their communication with the builders is entirely oral.
- Builders may not visit the structure – their role is to reproduce the structure according to the architects' brief.
- There is no time limit to the completion of this activity.

Discussion points

- What was happening during the activity?
- What were the barriers and blocks to success?
- What worked really well?
- What was happening as the group worked on the task together?

Activity provided by Anne Chivers, Defence Research Agency.

DEBATE

'Individuals will complete a task more effectively and efficiently than a group.'

Starting points

For

- It takes a considerable amount of time to build a group; it *has* to go through the various stages of development until it completes them – if ever.
- There are too many uncertainties surrounding groups – groupthink, risky-shift, and so on – which make them suspect.
- People prefer to be evaluated on their own performance and to be able to see a direct link between their own effort and outcome.

Against

- In a group there is a greater likelihood of creativity in both problem-solving and implementing decisions.
- Behaviour can be controlled more effectively and commitment gained more effectively through the imposition of group norms.
- Groups will happen anyway, so we might as well harness their strengths.

Further reading

Allcorn, S. (1989), 'Understanding Groups at Work', *Personnel,* 66 (8), August, 28–36.

Grayson, D. (1990), 'Self Regulating Work Groups – An Aspect of Organizational Change', ACAS Work Research Unit Occasional Paper No.146, July, HMSO.

ASSIGNMENT

Mullins (Chapter 13) identifies many different kinds of group: formal, informal, defensive, non-defensive, apathetic, strategic, and so on. Working either individually or in small groups use these categories to differentiate any *four* of the groups in the following list, justifying your decisions. Is it possible to use just two categories – social and work groups – to differentiate between these examples? Indicate, if necessary, where the two types overlap within a group.

a semi-professional jazz band	a family
a racing cyclist team	a hikers' club
a yacht club	a section of The Women's Institute
a special events project group	a doctors' partnership in a health centre
a street gang	a class of students
a team of workmen	a submarine crew
an amateur dramatics group	a voluntary or charity organisation

Write up your findings in not more than 2000 words and, if you worked in a small group for this assignment, include a one-page report on how the group worked during the assignment. You may find the following questions helpful for this.

- What type of group were you?
- What roles were taken by individual group members? Were these roles chosen by the individuals or given to them by the rest of the group?
- Who was the leader and did they emerge naturally?
- Did the leadership change? If so, why?
- Did everyone work together or did some opt out? Why?

Try to be as objective and constructive as possible when writing this part of the report. Equally try to be critically analytical about group roles and so forth. Comments such as 'The group worked well together and Matthew did the typing' are not really what is wanted.

APPLICATION 1

One of the groups of students taught by the authors are on a one-year full-time postgraduate management course. In one particular year the group was made up of a wide variety of ages (from 21 to 45), a variety of nationalities, some with no work experience and some with twenty-five years' experience. The group was 70 per cent male.

For their major OB assignment of the year (which carried a 70 per cent weighting towards their final mark), the author decided to set a group assignment which consisted of some research, some analysis, a presentation to a panel of visiting managers and a written report. Normally, at this stage of their studies it would be expected that each group would form naturally but because in this particular year it had been noticed that there was a very definite 'in' group and 'out' group (one academically strong and the other weaker), the lecturer decided to predetermine the groups. Each group comprised a representative sample of gender, nationality, work experience and academic ability because the lecturer thought that this would make things fairer and that the group members would learn more from each other if they were so mixed. Oh, how wrong can you be! There was inter-group and intra-group conflict and rivalry, deputations to the lecturer to change the groups, and complaints about the assignment. Interestingly, although there was no group cohesion towards getting the assignment completed, there was a high degree of cohesion against the common enemy, the lecturer, which continued long after the assignment had been completed.

Can you see how strong the influence of the informal group can be and the problems associated with attempts to break it up?

Can you also see where the power of individual motivation comes into play? It was a final assignment with a high weighting of marks – the drive to succeed was so strong that students didn't want to be associated with others whom they perceived as weaker academically and who might pull down the final mark.

APPLICATION 2

For an example of how informal groups govern individual behaviour, have a look at *Prisoner Cell Block H* (any episode will do – they're all rich in examples). For the purposes of this application we've created a composite scenario.

The scene is set in the prison laundry where tension has been rising. No doubt some of it has to do with those endless blue sheets and overalls but the majority of it is to do with who is to be 'top dog' – the informal leader for the prisoners. Various fights ensue and Bea Smith emerges as victor. From now on the prisoners will take their cue from her and even the warders will take notice (although this occurs in different ways: Miss Ferguson works against Bea, Mrs Morris – representing the 'caring' face of officialdom – tries to work through her). Maybe Bea isn't the staff's idea of the perfect leader but group consensus has voted her in.

Another classic example occurs in the next scene. A prisoner is beaten up (any spurious reason will do) and accuses Bea who is promptly despatched to 'solitary' for forty-eight hours to ponder the error of her ways. The prisoner is beaten up again and warned of the perils of being overaccurate with the truth. The scene cuts to a hospital bed where, when asked 'Who did this to you?', the prisoner replies through suitably swollen lips, 'I didn't see anyone.' Ferguson turns to the Governor and says, 'It sounds like a lesson in "lagging".' 'I don't care,' says the Governor, 'I shall find out who did it.' What chance do *you* think she has against such strong group norms?

14 Group Processes and Behaviour

CASE STUDY

Just another cog in the machine?

Englishmen have been known to behave in a superior way about their cricket: what other country can boast a competitive event of such complexity and which lasts five whole days? 'Le Tour de France', reply the equally smug French, who as good as founded cycling by inventing the penny-farthing in the 1860s.

The Tour can last twenty-four days, involving nearly 200 competitors who endure all kinds of weather from Mediterranean heatwaves to mountain blizzards and cycle nearly 2500 miles, crossing borders into as many as seven countries. Like cricket, its jargon is so impenetrable that books about it need a glossary and the outsider might well be forgiven for thinking that, as in cricket, for hour after hour nothing really happens. When it comes to the Tour, Frenchmen have it in their bones, but the English can find themselves on a sticky wicket. Would *they* know the difference between the yellow, the green and the polka-dot jerseys? Or between the general ranking, the team ranking and the points ranking? The standard stage, the time trial stage and the criterium? What *réel, fictif,* and *village* starts are? Do they understand what an escape is? Or a *domestique?* Or a neutralised section? Yet this is the biggest annual sporting event in the world: it is claimed that twenty million people watch it from the roadside and that nine hundred million in more than 120 countries watch it on television.

The event is clearly extremely complex, involving many interacting groups. The *Société du Tour de France,* a body roughly thirty-strong, connected with a company that publishes two sports papers in France, has to co-ordinate a great variety of groups, all necessary to the operation. There are the local authorities of the towns and counties that host the start of each stage of the race (and who pay tens of thousands of pounds for the privilege), police departments throughout on the route (for shutting off roads, attending to security, etc.), sponsors who make up the huge publicity cavalcade (1500 vehicles) that precedes the cycle race and who cover 60 per cent of the Tour's costs, the hoteliers who will house and feed the Tour at each stage, journalists who need to follow the race with their cameras and microphones in their shared cars and on motor bikes, medical services, the army of stewards, timekeepers and judges, and, of course, the racing teams themselves, usually about twenty, with nine riders each.

Each of these groups are complex in themselves, of course. Just to take the racing teams, they include the cyclists, their manager, their *soigneur* (who looks after the athletes' physical needs, including their daily massage), their mechanic (an honour and a privilege in the Italian teams, says Laurent Fignon, Tour winner in 1983 and 1984), and sometimes their doctor, whose job is not merely to attend to injuries (falls during races are not at all infrequent) but also to supervise the riders' diet and prescribe the many products riders need to accomplish such a gruelling feat. These include vitamins and minerals and, it is often alleged, stronger fare. Paul Kimmage, a successful Irish racer, has written about such practices in his book *A Rough Ride* (1990). As well as good-humoured games like 'hunt the syringe' in riders' back pockets, Kimmage also speaks movingly of the pressure he felt to conform with group practices in this illegal and dangerous area. The first ever English rider to wear the overall leader's yellow jersey, Tommy Simpson, died on a climb in the 1967 Tour from a combination of the exertion and drugs.

Inevitably, then, a group with such a variety of roles will have complex dynamics. To look just at the cyclists, it could seem that the key is to blend teamwork and a share of the limelight for each individual. Teams in recent times, however, have been sponsored by commercial firms such as Panasonic, Motorola and Renault who obviously want as high a profile as possible for their products. One result is that the cyclists fall into two categories, the leader(s) and the team riders. The leader is the star and it is the job of his team to do everything they can to help him win. These *domestiques* must shelter him from the wind, if he gets behind, pace him back into the *peloton* (the main pack, a minimum of about twenty riders who spend most of the stage together making the job that much easier for all its members), fetch food and water for him, give him their bikes if needed and even push him while he urinates. In return they get reflected glory and, as a consequence of their efforts, often most of the cash the star wins. All the riders are required to exhibit on their clothing the names of the many subsidiary sponsors who help with the cost of the venture, and are encouraged to wear team tracksuits at all non-racing times. In practice, rooming, planning, eating and, of course, racing together, mean that there is precious little time for partners or wives during the month of the Tour.

Clearly the task of the team manager/trainer is a particularly complex one. He has to handle the star, who sometimes demands more control than he should have, the jealousies and disappointments of the team riders, the esteem needs of absolutely vital contributors such as the mechanic, the solicitations from outsiders such as the media and hangers-on, the demands of the sponsors and so on. He needs authority but has to be a friend too, dealing with individuals from different social classes (unlike, say, the medical staff or indeed the first competitive cyclists, many racers come from working-class, often rural, backgrounds), frequently many different countries (since teams are no longer nationally representative), and different ages. The Peugeot team of 1982 actually had so many stars (Roche, Millar and Yates) that it did badly because they competed with each other. The new manager had to cut down the number of top riders to get the team back to winning ways.

Launched in 1903, the Tour's history is bristling with stories that add colour to the rather general description above. Racing had begun well before the Tour though, for manufacturers organised races to promote their cycling wares. They found that longer races were more effective for this and an early anecdote concerns the winner of the 1500-kilometre race in the *vélodrome d'hiver* in 1893, who devised a tube to urinate down while riding, thereby avoiding stops. To motivate racers now, the Tour offers prizes for practically everything: the longest breakaway, the most combative performance, the most elegant rider, the most amiable . . .

It was as prize money grew (well over a million pounds now in the Tour) that more working-class riders were attracted to the sport. One of the first champions actually rode a bike all day as a news courier and the competitiveness is aptly illustrated by the incident where a pretty admirer offered him a rose, which his manager snatched away just in time to avoid his rider being chloroformed by it. The Tour was launched as part of a circulation war between two sports papers and, in earlier races, competing commercial concerns and towns were not averse to scattering glass or nails on the road to halt the show in front of their patch. Even now, a rider might be permitted by his opponents to lead the field as he goes through his home village. But it was not unknown for riders to be deliberately obstructed, even beaten up, or for the riders themselves to take a train to get ahead. One photo of the 1927 Tour shows a group of riders having a break for a cigarette. When urine tests came in, competitors occasionally topped up their sample with someone else's offering. One tested cyclist, relieved to get a negative report was, however, surprised to find that he was pregnant!

Renowned for his aggression ('Being a racing cyclist makes you both aggressive and vindictive'), Bernard Hinault was, until 1995, one of only three riders to have won the Tour five times. His dealings with team-mate Greg LeMond were much criticised during his winning years, especially in the 1985 and 1986 Tours ('Americans seem to me to be lacking in humility!'). Less dramatic, but more interesting perhaps, is his reputation for being a highly professional cyclist who knew how to organise his team so that he would win with as little effort as possible. This is one area where the English *do* need tuition if they are to understand how careful planning can produce strategies which slow the race down, impede dangerous competitors, give up small prizes to secure the big one, and so on. It is a highly technical matter but a fascinating example of how the work group can control the job. Hinault took this attitude into the public arena when he led a riders' strike to stop the organisers making the riders take tiring train journeys between Tour stages in search of more demanding, dramatic and therefore lucrative routes. As it is, up to 40 per cent of the competitors fail to finish the race.

Despite his ruthless reputation, Hinault was very team-oriented, insisting on the sharing of plans, giving team riders their chances, seeing they received large parts of the prize money, arguing that rooming arrangements should be on a rota so that everyone got to know everyone else, changing places at the meal table – in other words insisting that the social and the task functions of the group were each attended to. 'You don't win races alone,' he said, 'you win because others help you and sacrifice their own chances.' When he changed to Bernard Tapie's team in 1983 he found there was a financial and public relations manager in addition to the usual mix. To be fair, too, Greg LeMond did win in 1986 and seemed to build on Hinault's example by being even more businesslike and determined. He was shot in a hunting incident in 1987, yet got back to fitness and won the Tour again in 1989 and 1990. The French often found his American approach to the race rather odd, especially the way he frequently had his family with him. But as he said himself, 'I have won for a team of which my family is part.' The 1990s star is not French either. Miguel Indurain, a Spaniard, rode in 1994 to become only the second rider in history to win the Tour four times in succession. Happily for the French, the first was a Norman, Jacques Anquetil.

For the comic writer Pierre Daninos, the Tour is distinguished by the fact that it is the police themselves, some twenty thousand of them, that actually paralyse the traffic. Cricket would hardly cause such a standstill. Twenty times more people watch football matches than cricket matches in Britain. And to some extent the popularity of a sport depends on media coverage. Television gave snooker a tremendous boost and the Tour could not do without such coverage since a spectator at the roadside can see no more than a few minutes of the race a day and needs papers to identify riders and television to understand the overall shape of the competition as it progresses. It was Channel 4 television that started to break down the ignorance of the British with regard to the Tour. Its daily coverage was so popular that it has had to go to repeats and moving the programme to prime time. In 1994 there was still no UK-sponsored team but the reputation of the Tour was considerably enhanced there when two of the stages of the Tour de France were raced in England, one from Dover to Brighton, and the other a circuit starting and ending in Portsmouth.

In 1994 the Tour attracted 149 000 visitors to Hampshire, generating an income of £8 million (for hotels, restaurants, pubs, cycling shops, £10-a-day car parks, etc.). Fifty-seven per cent of these visitors said they would definitely return to the area, making knock-on economic benefits look very promising. But for that prize the local authorities, as well as investing about half a million pounds, had to accomplish a huge organisational feat. They began three years before the event. Technical officers, police officials and newspaper people visited the Tour in action in France several times. A Joint Authorities Panel of Hampshire and Portsmouth was set up; negotiations entered into with other authorities through whose districts the route would pass; and a central project team was formed to coordinate the three big events of the 1994 summer: Portsmouth's 800-year celebrations, the D-Day anniversary and the Tour. The team comprised a project director and deputy, a coordinator, phone and desk receptionist, and commercial, advertising, hospitality, tourist, liaison, transport and associated events officers. A special booklet of instructions was produced for the thousand volunteer marshals who were organised into sectors with a supervisor for each section and a key marshal for every twenty or so volunteers. The project also galvanised a multitude of other groups such as the Southern Tourist Board, inter-county police committees and the Greater Portsmouth Hoteliers Association, whose particular job it was to provide hospitality for the visitors and who hit on the idea of representing, in their various hotels, food and drinks from various French regions. Businesses combined with local authorities to provide day-long festivities on village greens and in pubs and forecourts all along the race route.

The Tour entered the UK through the Channel Tunnel on 5 July and left on Brittany Ferries on 7 July after two days' racing, ready to start again in Cherbourg on the morning of 8 July. However, Bernard Hinault would not have needed to complain: the weary riders travelled from Portsmouth to Cherbourg by plane.

Activity brief

1 The Hawthorne experiments (see Mullins, pp. 58–61) suggested how groups can control their work tasks. How do racing cyclist teams illustrate such organisational behaviour?

2 On the basis of this account of the Tour, how far would it be true to say that a sporting group can provide its members with an outlet for high spirits, single-gender activities and even violent impulses that families, work and friends cannot? Does this idea help distinguish between the notion of team and group? How far do you think contemporary Western environments (television, feminism, private cars, etc.) might weaken the 'club mentality'?

3 Psychologists studying sport have paid a good deal of attention to the connection between group cohesion and effectiveness. They have suggested that they are causally connected in both directions and that the process changes over time (Lambert, 1968–9). Some experiments have even suggested that social tensions in a group can improve its effectiveness (Lenk, 1969). How far do you see the Tour as exemplifying any of these conclusions?

ACTIVITY: Build your own dinosaur!

Logistics

The group should be divided into sub-groups of between four and eight. You will require a large picture of a dinosaur, which you will then need to 'slice' vertically so that each group can be provided with their own 'slice' that they have to build.

An observer should be appointed to each group who will give feedback to the group at the end of the exercise.

Task

Using the materials provided (and only those provided) each sub-group is required to construct their assigned section of the whole dinosaur which is

- recognisable as such;
- creative in use of materials;
- with the maximum dimensions of 18 inches from head to toe and 18 inches from head to tail.

Materials provided

Plasticine	2 sheets of A4 plain paper
2 sheets of newspaper	Glue
String	Drinking straws
Felt-tip pens	Blueprint of dinosaur with only each particular sub-group's section indicated

Time allowed

The total time allowed for this exercise is 40 minutes. At the end of this period each group will take their part of the dinosaur to the co-ordinator and, while he or she is assembling the sections, sub-groups should listen to and discuss their observer's comments on their work.

Discussion points

Discussion can centre around the following areas:

- how small groups work together (or don't);
- the need for communication, co-operation and communication between groups in order to get a task completed successfully; and
- in a whole group session, comparisons between the observers' comments and the success or failure of the finished product (the whole dinosaur).

Activity provided by Beverley Wallace, Gowrings (Newbury) Ltd.

DEBATE

'Training in group dynamics, whilst interesting, has no practical value as a means of increasing group effectiveness.'

Starting points

For

- Group dynamics can identify and highlight more problems than it can solve and as a result can actually *detract* from performance.
- The group should exist to do, and, indeed, are paid to do, a job of work. They don't need cosseting and pampering – it's a waste of money.

Against

- A manager needs to know and understand how a group functions and how people relate to each other in order to be able to point them in the right direction.
- Knowledge of group dynamics can lead the group towards self-awareness which can result in empowering them to improve their own performance and effectiveness.

Further reading

Campbell, C. L. and Dunnette, M. D. (1968), 'Effectiveness of T-Group Experiences in Managerial Training and Development', *Psychological Bulletin,* 70 (2), 73–103.

Cooper, C. L. and Mangham, I. L. (eds) (1971), *T-Groups: A Survey of Research,* Wiley.

Luft, J. (1970), *Group Processes: An Introduction to Group Dynamics,* 2nd edn, National Press.

ASSIGNMENT 1

Using the Belbin Self-perception Inventory in Mullins (pp. 510–12) select a group of people to study. Your group could be from an organisation which you know, from an informal group of students or from a 'hobby' group (e.g. a sports club committee).

Explain to the group what you are planning to do (and why) and then administer the questionnaire. Ask individual members to score their own answers. Analyse the results and present the findings:

1 as an oral presentation with appropriate visual aids;

2 as a written report of not more than 1500 words to be submitted to both the group studied and your tutor.

Remember that, depending on both the group you choose and the results, you may raise more questions than you'll be able to answer. You may need to use a considerable degree of tact and patience, particularly with group members who disagree with their ranking, and you'll certainly need to be very fully conversant with the Belbin work in order to present it well and to be able to handle questions.

ASSIGNMENT 2

Working in a small group, elect an observer and then, starting with a brainstorming session (see Mullins, pp. 500–2), invent a board game based on the Tour de France.

Present your game to the wider group. Each group will be judged by other groups using the following criteria:

- creativity;
- presentation of the game;
- interest likely to be engendered; and
- simplicity and ease of playing the game.

Have your observer report on the group's functioning throughout the exercise, using theories such as 'groupthink', 'risky-shift', 'interaction analysis' and so on to help with the explanations.

APPLICATION 1

Making meetings function more effectively

FT

As organisations become more complex it is difficult to imagine a way of decreasing the need to get together, if only electronically. If the number of meetings cannot be cut, they can certainly be made more efficient. From questionnaires collected by London Business School we know that the way meetings are run by some managers causes dissatisfaction.

The most frequent complaints are that there are no clear objectives; meetings are of no specific length; they are cancelled; discussions ramble; there is no follow-up action; and too many people are present at the meeting.

The remedies are obvious: clarify objectives; prepare the agenda; fix the time period; and keep meetings small (six or fewer for a problem-solving, decision-making group).

But we also need to establish rules for the function of meetings – in particular, which meetings are decision-making units and which are not and, within meetings, which items require a decision and which do not. We should establish in advance whether an item on the agenda is open for discussion or is a decision the chief executive has made and simply wants to communicate.

Very few of the meetings I attend as a team member have any decision rules. We just plough laboriously through the agenda. The agenda might be divided into 'above' and 'below' the line items. This crude division tells the members that if it is below the line then the item is for information only. Items above the line are open for debate.

Some decisions should never be left to a group. If we are all ignorant and a specialist is available we may be best guided by the specialist. But ignorance is rarely a barrier to lengthy debate among executives. Other decisions benefit enormously from discussion and consensus. These are decisions where no one is an expert.

Some companies – the example that follows draws on a model used by Shell Exploration, the oil giant – have established decision categories or levels as a guide to what is up for debate and what is not.

- Level 1 decisions. The board decides. The communication style is 'tell'. The chief executive and his or her team is bound to implement this decision, which will appear in the board minutes.
- Level 2 decisions. The chief executive decides. Again, the communication style is tell. Executive decisions made by the chief executive are usually either strategic or resource allocation decisions. The chief executive exercises his or her power as the last word in the hierarchy. Inevitably, some decisions will affect others adversely.

  These decisions are often the most difficult and there is confusion in some organisations about their place. Some leaders go on team-building exercises and come back assuming that management is all about consensus. They reject unilateral decisions which have been negatively labelled as 'command and control'. They believe consensus is the right way to manage.

  But some decisions need a single decision maker, a face, a champion to make them. Effective leaders assert their authority to make decisions about resources or strategy when necessary. Managers who avoid these essential decisions come to be seen as indecisive. Such a reputation is bad news for would-be high achievers.
- Level 3 decisions. The chief executive consults the team and decides. Communication style is 'consult'. The chief executive asks his or her direct reports for input.
- Level 4 decisions. A joint decision of the chief executive and the team. Communication style is 'involve'. The chief executive asks for opinions, listens, and adopts the majority view.

- Level 5 decisions. The team decides. Communication style is 'consensus'. The chief executive may appoint another member of the team to lead discussion and come up with a team decision. The team may go away from the office to minimise status differences. A facilitator may be briefed to help the democratic processes and to see that hierarchical differences are kept to a minimum.

It is unrealistic to imagine that the number of cross-functional, cross-national, cross-product team meetings will be reduced. If anything, there will be more of them. So what should you do?

First, managers should be aware of the effect they have in meetings. Second, team leaders should not confuse executive decisions with other decision processes. Someone has to be in charge when it comes to resource issues if team members are divided. Third, as so much time is spent in meetings we need to make them more efficient. Classification of decision processes is one way to focus discussion and to make participants aware of their role.

Source: Professor John W. Hunt, *Financial Times*, 8 April 1998.

APPLICATION 2

Once upon a time a British company and a Japanese company decided to have a competitive boat race on the river Thames. Both teams practised long and hard to reach their peak performance. On the big day they were both as ready as they could be.

The Japanese won by a mile.

Afterwards the British team became very discouraged by their loss and morale plummeted. Senior management decided that the reason for the crushing defeat had to be found and a project team was set up to investigate the problem and recommend appropriate action.

Their conclusion: the Japanese team had eight people rowing and one person steering. The British team had one person rowing and eight people steering. Senior management hired a consultancy company to do a study on the team structure. Millions of pounds and several months later, the consultancy company concluded that too many people were steering and not enough were rowing.

To prevent another loss to the Japanese the following year, the team structure was changed to: four steering managers, three senior steering managers and one executive steering manager. A new performance system was set up for the person rowing the boat to give more incentive to work harder and become a key performer. 'We must get it right first time, every time' the British were heard to say.

The next year the Japanese won by *two* miles. The British company made the rower redundant for poor performance, sold off all the paddles, cancelled all capital investment for new equipment, halted development of a new boat, awarded high performance awards to the consultants, and distributed the money saved to senior executives . . . .

APPLICATION 3

Think back to your first day at college (and some of us have to think back further than others). It's 9.15, you're all in the lecture theatre and the course manager is about to do the 'welcome to the course and have a great time' bit. You listen with one ear and glance nervously around at the people who'll be your companions over the next three or four years. These are the people you'll work with, get drunk with, go out with and perhaps live with (although not necessarily in that order). Surprise, surprise! They're all wearing the same type of clothes: jeans which are just sufficiently worn out to be acceptable and a slightly faded sweatshirt (ideally either advertising a rock band's tour from about two years ago or, failing that, a brand of real ale). Then you notice a lone soul sitting in the corner in *brand new* jeans (with a crease up the centre) and a *brand new* chain store sweatshirt. They look totally out of it and you decide to give them a wide berth: definitely an oddity, that one. Still, the rest look OK.

What has happened here is that you've all been through the process of anticipatory socialisation: you want to be accepted by the group in general and so you start by wearing the sort of clothes which will immediately identify you with that group. Luckily for you, you got it right. Unluckily for the other one, they had the right idea but got it ever so slightly wrong.

(If you want a further example of anticipatory socialisation/group norms, remember back to the same period but a little later into your college life when the groups had began to form and courses and faculties began to differentiate themselves: the pharmacists always drank more than anyone else; the engineers always wore leather jackets; the computer boffins were altogether different (you know what we mean . . .).

APPLICATION 4

Kirk's Team Saves The World (Again . . .)

Captain's log: Stardate 8454.2

My senior officers and I have taken command of the new USS *Enterprise,* after six charges against us were dismissed by a Starfleet Federation Court Martial. The court was swayed in our favour because we had recently saved Earth from the depredations of an immense, intergalactic hump-backed whale, armed as we were with nothing more than a clapped-out Klingon bird of prey and Scotty's recipe for transparent aluminium.

This has prompted me to reflect on the qualities which enable my crew and me to function so successfully as a team and have found the writings of a twentieth-century management author, Dr. R. Meredith Belbin, most interesting in this context (as Spock would say). I therefore asked the ship's computer to undertake an analysis of our respective team roles using the Belbin model.

Science Officer Spock's sober logic, his capacity for accurate data-based analysis and his habit of making decisions only when he has fully evaluated all possible options mark him out as a *monitor-evaluator* in Belbin's typology. His somewhat clinical judgements mean, however, that he does not make an inspiring leader and his openly expressed criticism frequently causes him to clash with the ship's doctor.

Dr McCoy's outspoken and often argumentative cynicism makes him a prickly, but highly expert, individualist. He is quick to challenge and frequently expresses himself in a provocative, colourful, even hurtful manner. His courage, often born of outrage at stupidity or petty bureaucracy, is also typical of the *shaper*'s team role.

Communications Officer Uhura is a popular and friendly crew member; frequently confidante to Scott, Chekov and Sulu, and able to smooth over tensions and conflicts between senior officers. An accomplished singer and musician, she is always ready to entertain her colleagues during off-duty moments and this indicates her role as the sociable *team worker*.

Chief Engineer Scott is our *specialist*. Devoted to his dilythium-powered engines and knowing every inch of the *Enterprise* like the back of his hand, he is typically single-minded and dedicated, though sometimes too preoccupied with technicalities to bother with overall mission objectives.

Our extrovert **Helmsman, Mr Sulu**, is outward-looking, open to new ideas and experiences, though some of his enthusiasms are short lived. He shows many characteristics of the *resource investigator*.

Navigator Chekov is destined for Starship command. As a conscientious all-rounder, he is meticulous to the point of obsession, rarely leaving any task unfinished. He appears to be a *completer*.

As for myself, **James T. Kirk**, the computer indicates that my maturity and confidence, combined with my capacity to optimise the talents of others, make me a *co-ordinator*. However, it seems that I also exhibit the unorthodox and creative problem-solving tendencies of the *plant* which have led me into more than one clash with Starfleet Command.

We are receiving news of a hostage crisis on Nimbus III; can Belbin's Team Theory save the world once more? Ahead Warp Factor 5, Mr Sulu, and steady as she goes.

Provided by Gill Norris, University of Portsmouth.

AFTERTHOUGHTS

A student who went to the trials of his university basketball team was not very hopeful that he would get in because he wasn't particularly good at the game: he couldn't dribble the ball very well or do any of the 'fancy' things that basketball players do. He was taken on because he was the only one who could take the role of a team player.

A manager on a team-building course was heard to remark: 'This Belbin stuff is all very well but he obviously hasn't tried managing a gay pub as I have to. In addition to all the usual roles, all my staff are Drama Queens as well . . . .'

15 Organisation Structure and Design

CASE STUDY

Changing organisation structures and processes at Northern Taverns

This is a case study in organisational change. It is based upon what has been happening in one of northern England's largest public-house (or 'hostelry', as our preferred term) -owning companies. In order to preserve anonymity the name has been changed, along with certain details which are not crucial for our present purposes; the essence of what has occurred (and is likely to occur) has been retained.

The case study is organised as follows:

1 The organisation is briefly described.

2 The changing external contexts of Northern Taverns are outlined.

3 Certain key objectives set by the company are described.

4 You are provided with an activity brief and recommended reading.

5 A note on methodology provides guidance on how you might proceed to collect the necessary data.

Northern Taverns and Northern plc

The plc has its head office in the north of England, from where it runs a number of businesses in a divisionalised mode: taverns, leisure, soft drinks, wines and spirits, and hotels. It is one of the UK's larger operating companies in this sector, employing around 45 000 people. This case study is based upon what has been taking place in just one of these divisions – Taverns – although, of course, it is not possible to entirely divorce what has been going on there from what has been happening in the rest of the plc, for there are a number of links and interdependencies between the divisions, for example between Taverns and Hotels, Taverns and Soft Drinks, Taverns and Leisure. The plc agrees objectives and targets that the constituent divisions are expected to achieve over a given time period.

Northern Taverns runs the hostelries and restaurants business of Northern plc. It makes the largest contribution to the plc's profits (having generated over 50 per cent of total profits for a number of years), employs over 30 000 people, and has 2000 managed and 1000 leased hostelries located throughout the northern UK and the Midlands, which are organised into six regions, each region in turn being split into a number of areas; the structure is shown in Fig. 15.1.

A variety of specialist services are provided for the staff located at each of these levels, some of them having a presence at just one of the levels, others being duplicated across a number of levels; examples include Acquisitions (for new hostelries or restaurants), Marketing, Construction, Personnel and Training, IT and Finance.

Northern Taverns has recently introduced electronic point-of-sale systems into its outlets in order, primarily, to improve management control. This has involved substantial capital expenditure, and stock control has shown a marked improvement; however, as yet, the systems are being used less effectively for marketing and business development purposes.

A managing director heads up each of the regions and there exists a strong regional identity – an identity which has been nurtured by Northern Taverns over the years through devices such as distinct trading names reflecting each particular region. Territories and resources are jealously guarded. Risk aversion is the predominant ingredient of decision-making; accountability is thinly spread and this adds up to a conservative orientation. Take the processes involved in identifying and approving a new site for a hostelry. The following specialists take part: Acquisitions, Marketing, Operations, Catering, Personnel, and Finance; and authorisation proceeds from area to region to divisional board to Northern plc. The 'lowest common denominator' rules, and the result has often been, as a member of the company graphically put it, 'cosmic constipation', or 'nothing coming out'.

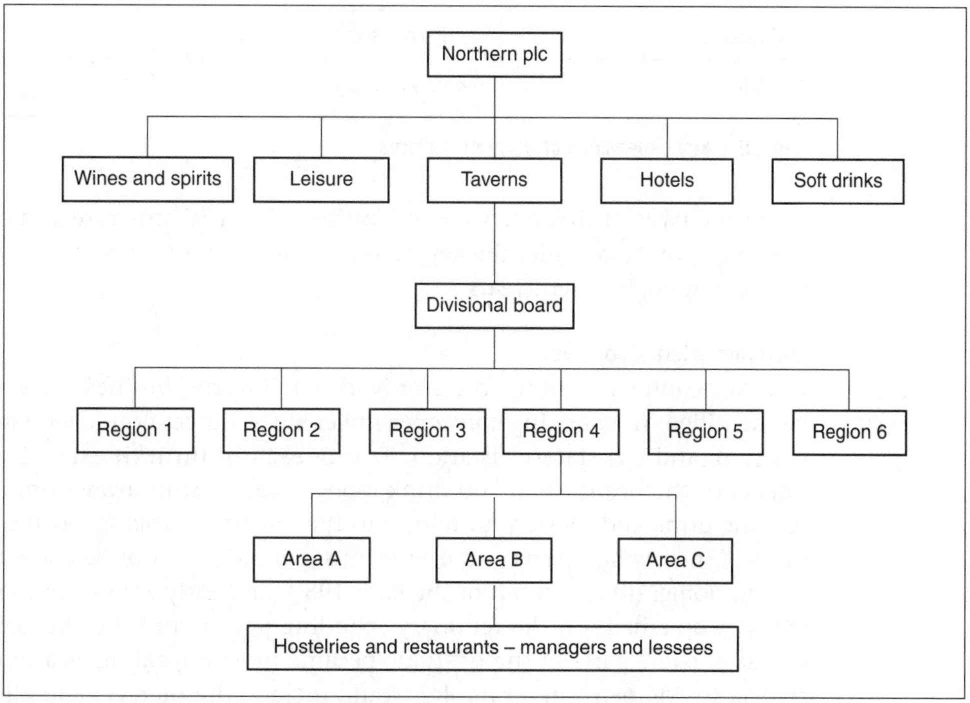

Fig. 15.1 Structure of Northern Taverns

The predominant orientation towards the hostelries and the staff who work in them in this retail sector (and Northern Taverns were no exception) can be summarised in the following three phrases:

1 'Hostelry managers are not to be trusted, therefore they must be controlled.'
2 'The hostelry is supply-driven – the "shop window" for a range of ales and lagers.'
3 'Individual outlet performance is the key consideration.'

The culture of the company may be conveniently captured along certain key dimensions as shown in Fig. 15.2.

Dimension	*The existing situation*	*Your proposed solution*
People	were *controlled*	
Structure	was *hierarchically based*	
Business expertise	was based upon *function*	
The manager	was the *supervisor*	
The board	act as *scorekeepers*	
Senior management's priority	was *control*	
Values	were *defensive*	
A VIP	was a *manager*	

Fig. 15.2 Key dimensions of Northern Taverns

On the basis of this overview of Northern Taverns' structure and culture, let us now move on to consider the key ways in which the contexts of its operations have been changing in recent years.

Changing external contexts

Four key contextual influences over Northern Taverns' business in recent years can be identified: (i) changing consumer preferences, (ii) economic recession, (iii) competition, and (iv) state/legislation. Taking each in turn: (i) examples include the impact of the health food and drink lobby, and the shift away from the 'on trade' (buying drink and food in hostelries) to the 'off trade': that is, people buying all or most of their wine, spirits and beer from supermarkets or off-licences for consumption at home; (ii) as a result of the later 1980s and early 1990s economic recession, many people had less discretionary spending power, and the cheaper prices to be found in some parts of the off trade became more appealing as a result; (iii) with respect to competition, examples would include the mergers and alliances which have been formed between brewing and retailing groups, the entry of foreign brewing companies into the UK market, and the regeneration of hostelries by smaller independent companies which have focused upon service, choice and variety of real ales, and a return to the basics of a 'good local'; (iv) finally, as a result of the 'Beer Orders' issued by the UK Government in the late 1980s, a ceiling was put on the number of hostelries which could be owned by a brewing group where those hostelries were tied in terms of supply to that particular group.

For Northern Taverns (as a division of Northern plc) this has meant that it was forced to sell off over 1000 hostelries during the period 1990–2 in order to comply with the 'Orders', and, although it is now below its ceiling, there is a strict limit on how many more hostelries it can open without simultaneously closing others.

Objectives

In 1996 Northern plc agreed the following objectives with Northern Taverns, to be achieved by 2001:

1 Outperform the 'on trade' competition by 10 per cent.
2 Increase net profit per £ taken from 8p to 16p.
3 Increase hostelry sales volume by an average of 10 per cent.
4 Open one new hostelry every month, and lease at least one hostelry every week.

Activity brief

1 Consider the options available to Northern Taverns for achieving the objectives set by the plc, focusing upon the people and organisational issues and possibilities. Outline these in report form, discussing the advantages and disadvantages of each. Make a recommendation as to your favoured option, justifying this choice.

2 Critically outline and discuss the concepts, models and perspectives which can be drawn upon from the behavioural social sciences in order to make sense of the social structures and processes which characterise this organisation.

3 Show how a use of the above (2) could be of help to those managers and other actors who have been given the responsibility for achieving the necessary social and organisational changes.

4 Return to Fig. 15.2, take each of the dimensions in the first column and produce a new third column which indicates in summary terms what you think the company should move towards from the present situation as described in column 2 (for example, you might want to recommend that the people dimension moves from *control* to *empowerment*). Write a sentence or two on each of them, explaining why you have made this choice.

Further reading

Annual reports of regional and national brewery and public-house-owning companies.

Buchanan, D. and Boddy, D. (1992), *The Expertise of the Change Agent*, Prentice Hall.

Carnall, C. (1990), *Managing Change in Organisations*, Prentice Hall.

Dawson, P. (1994), *Organizational Change: A Processual Approach*, Paul Chapman.

Huczynski, A. and Buchanan, D. (1991), *Organizational Behaviour: An Introductory Text*, 2nd edn, Prentice Hall (esp. Chapters 15, 16, 18, 19 and 20).

Kanter, R. M. (1983), *The Change Masters*, Allen & Unwin.

Kanter, R. M. (1989), *When Giants Learn to Dance*, Simon & Schuster.

Pettigrew, A. and Whipp. R. (1991), *Managing Change for Competitive Success*, Blackwell.

A note on methodology

We recommend that students read a sample of the annual reports of the national and regional brewery and pub companies; examples include: (i) under the national banner: Whitbread, Scottish & Newcastle, Bass; (ii) under the regional banner: Greene King, Wolverhampton & Dudley, Eldridge Pope, Marstons, Thompson.

It is perfectly possible to answer all the above questions on the basis of knowledge of the behavioural social science literature, and, indeed, it is *essential* that students draw upon and use this understanding in responding to the questions. In other words, it *can* be treated as a library/secondary material-based exercise. However, as strong advocates of fieldwork or 'getting involved in the action', we recommend that, if time and opportunity allow, you visit some hostelries and talk to/interview the bar staff and managers (indeed, if you are an undergraduate student, it is quite possible that you do part-time bar work yourself, thus facilitating the process). You can pick up information simply by sitting in the hostelry or standing at the bar, that is, through a form of participant observation. The better answers are likely to be based upon a sound reading around the area *and* fieldwork, where the information and ideas coming out of the former are fed into the latter, and vice versa, in an iterative mode.

So, when you next go down to your local hostelry for a pint or two of real ale, you'll be able to inform your friends and tutor that you have been taking the research for your coursework seriously, and that you got so absorbed in the work that you ended up staying all evening . . . Cheers!

Case study provided by David Preece, Gordon Steven and Valerie Steven: People, Innovation and New Technology Research Group. The People, Innovation and New Technology Research Group consists of members from three UK universities (Portsmouth, Coventry and Nottingham) and one of the UK's major brewing and pub retailing companies. It was founded by the authors of the present case and is based at the University of Portsmouth.

ACTIVITY

For this activity you can work either individually or in small groups.

Using the pictorial example given in Mullins (p. 547), refer to an organisation with which you are familiar (this can be either a traditional 'work' organisation or a voluntary organisation) and draw the formal organisation chart. Identify key people in the organisation and interview them informally. From your discussions with them draw the 'alternative' organisation chart.

In a presentation to the rest of the class, attempt to answer the following questions:

- Is there a difference between the two? Why or why not?
- What are the significant variables impacting on the 'alternative' chart?
- Which of the two should the organisation retain? Why? What difficulties do you foresee?

DEBATE 1

'All organisations of a certain size must have a bureaucratic orientation.'

Starting points

For

- Bureaucracy, in the Weberian sense of the word, ensures rationality; co-ordination and standardisation are products stemming from this which are a vital survival mechanism for any large-scale organisation.
- Bureaucracy allows us a high degree of predictability about human behaviour in a large and complex organisation.

Against

- Whilst it might have been a suitable organisational model for the first sixty years of this century, it is now becoming outdated, particularly so given the need for diversity in an unstable and changing environment.
- Managerial behaviour has changed to the extent that we have a greater understanding of human needs. This replaces the bureaucratic concept of coercive power and mechanistic, depersonalised values.

Further reading

Blau, P. M. and Meyer, M. W. (1987), *Bureaucracy in Modern Society*, Random House.

Mieward, R. D. 'The Greatly Exaggerated Death of Bureaucracy', *California Management Review*, 13 (2), 65–9.

Perrow, C. (1986), *Complex Organizations: A Critical Essay*, Random House.

DEBATE 2

'The structure of an organisation is unimportant. What matters is whether individuals do their job or not.'

Starting points

For

- Work is done by people, not by concepts like 'groups' or 'organisations'. As Mullins puts it: 'Strictly, organisations have no goals; only people do' (p. 118).
- Individuals work hard because they are motivated (they need the money or find the work compelling), not because they know they are in a 'tall' or 'flat' structure, in a wide span of control, or on a scalar chain.

Against

- An individual can be as motivated as possible, but if another individual is pursuing different goals, pulling in another direction, there will have to be some organising done to avoid inertia. Look how frustrating a bureaucrat's rules can be to a would-be innovator; lateral communication channels on a scalar chain can avoid problems of that type.

- 'Organisation' may be an abstract term, but so are 'love', 'home' and 'justice'. People have very strong attachments to such concepts, and very vivid images of them – and not just organisational charts either.

Further reading

Argyris, C. and Schön, D. (1980), 'What is an Organisation that It May Learn?', in M. Locket and R. Spear (eds), *Organisations as Systems*, Open University Press.

Goss, D. (1994), 'Investing in People: Human Resource Development and Organisational Change', in D. Adam-Smith and A. Peacock (eds), *Cases in Organisational Behaviour*, Pitman.

Morgan, G. (1986), *Images of Organisation*, Sage Publications.

Morgan, G. (1989), *Creative Organisation Theory*, Sage Publications.

ASSIGNMENT

Task

With reference to the Bains Report (see Mullins, pp. 130, 169 and 524), write a 1500-word essay assessing the merits and demerits of changes in the structure of local government.

Tips

- Your local authority offices and libraries should hold leaflets presenting the case for one or other of these choices. There was renewed discussion of the issues in the press when the chairman of the Commission, Sir John Banham, resigned in March 1995, feeling his committee's recommendations were being ignored.
- Diagrams can often save a lot of words when expressing notions about organisational structure.
- Remember that many councils had already contracted out or privatised many of the services traditionally provided by them including refuse collection, school meals, and communal transport, a trend which, surely, has a bearing on this question of structure.

APPLICATION

Is matrix management a recipe for chaos? FT

Matrix structures have been with us for centuries, though many ignorant consultants think they are new. Any family is a matrix in the sense that there are potentially two bosses, the mother and father. Government departments have been operating dual authority structures – with civil servants reporting to their permanent head and to a minister of state – for more than 100 years.

Some designers of organisations regard matrices as flawed and unstable because of the ambiguity that arises from two reporting lines. Others argue that their looser structural form has advantages: it brings the service provided much closer to the customer or client; it focuses on performance, with peer pressure, rather than formal systems and procedures controlling behaviour; and the matrix liberates teams and individuals to make decisions, be creative and behave in an independent, adult way.

Take the example of the operating theatre. The way it works evolved because traditional hospital design is organised around professional affiliations, rather than patient care. If we look at the organisational chart of a hospital there will be functions called Medical, Nursing, Accounts, Consultants, and so on. To get treatment, the patient usually goes from one professional group to the next. It is not surprising that the hospital trolley has become such a famous form of transport.

But in the operating theatre, multiple services for the client must be delivered simultaneously. The trolley is stationary and a matrix team operates on your body. The matrix will include a team leader, usually the surgeon, and specialists from the various vertical blocks who bring their skills to the patient. Each professional reports to the head of his or her function (axis 1) and to the team leader (axis 2). The structure is designed to react to time pressure and an uncertain environment. The surgeon and the team are not sure precisely what is going to happen, therefore their jobs are described rather vaguely so they can improvise. You call this a recipe for chaos, I would call it a flexible structure which relies on the experts in the team contributing their skills if and when needed. No traditional structure could work as effectively.

Turning to companies, international organisations sometimes run into trouble using matrices when they are trying to reconcile local and global objectives. Consumer products companies such as Heineken, Ford and Unilever have marketing and human resource functions both centrally and locally. This means the marketing manager in, say, Singapore, has to report to two bosses – their geographic boss and the central marketing boss.

Globally, it is unlikely you will get the market conditions which make a matrix structure effective in New York, for example, in all other parts of the world.

But, overall, if you ask whether the matrix structure is the best design we can produce for uncertain times, the straight answer is yes. The traditional military or feudal model of one person one boss may be admirably effective for simple tasks, a stable environment or vertical integration of expertise. But it is not very effective when it comes to handling highly complex tasks performed by numerous experts in unpredictable markets. Nor is it very effective, except when the company is small, in relating to the customer or client.

So if you are trying to get a matrix to work, what are the main points you need to keep in mind?

First, matrices work best where the market is demanding. In a stable, non-threatening marketplace, staff working in matrices begin to play political games; interpersonal skills, rather than expertise or merit, begin to determine who gets resources.

Second, people working in matrices need to understand that they will have a much less stable set of relationships because the market the matrix is serving is less stable. Trying to write manuals to cover every eventuality is a nonsense. You either accept that this is an ambiguous structure, or you get out of it.

Third, in some cultures where a feudal model of managerial control persists, it is unwise to introduce matrices. Alternatives are smaller units, more segmentation into divisional or local units, with overlays of matrices which affect only small parts of the workforce.

Fourth, while I strongly suggest you do not produce massive manuals and attempt to turn the matrix into a bureaucracy, there need to be clear ground rules about what each axis can or cannot do. It should be possible to document this knowledge on two pages.

There are no correct forms for matrices. They are dependent on people and what works for one company may not work for another. Thirty years ago it was a common belief that the hierarchical structures of organisations were designed to be independent of the talents of the people involved. Indeed, I can recall receiving a very low grade when I was doing my MBA for designing an organisation around the main players. My professor explained that structures were pure forms and it was people who mucked them up. Nowadays, any design consultant knows that while the design logic of working from strategy to objectives, targets, jobs and lateral thinking processes is enticingly seductive, the reality is that the design must suit the people involved, not the reverse.

Source: Professor John W. Hunt, *Financial Times*, 12 January 1998.

16 Patterns of Structure and Work Organisation

CASE STUDY

Midshires Housing Association: Coping with success?

Background

Housing associations are non-profit-making bodies, run by voluntary committees, providing housing, including hostels and associated amenities. They may be bodies registered with the Registrar of Friendly Societies, trusts registered with the Charity Commissioners or companies which are also registered as charities. However, in order to receive public funds for the provision of housing they must register with the Housing Corporation, which acts as the regulatory agent for central government.

The origins of the movement date back to the twelfth-century almshouses but it was during the nineteenth century that the movement developed. However, the spur to creating the movement as it now is came in the late 1960s and early 1970s – the time of *Cathy Come Home* and the reawakening of public awareness of the housing problems facing many people.

The 1974 Housing Act enabled the movement to receive considerable public funds with which to build new homes for rent at a level that those in housing need could afford. New associations were formed at this time either as a consequence of pressing local needs that local authorities were perceived not to be meeting, or as a reaction against the policies of redevelopment of areas through demolition rather than refurbishment. In 1974 the movement provided some 200 000 homes and by the late 1980s this had risen to over 600 000 involving some 26 000 voluntary committee members and a similar number of staff.

The change of government in 1979 heralded changes for housing associations. Whilst the 'right to buy' policy did not apply to charitable housing associations, the 1980 Housing Act provided the opportunity for new associations to be set up, specialising in initiatives that enabled people on low incomes to buy their own homes on what is described as a 'shared ownership basis': that is, to buy part and rent the remaining part of the equity until such time as the remainder could be afforded.

The 1980s were also a time when the responsibility for providing homes began to shift away from local authorities to housing associations and the idea of wholesale transfer of local authority housing to new or existing associations took hold. Now, in the mid 1990s, housing associations are perceived as the main providers of new social housing.

However, at the same time, public expenditure came under greater scrutiny and the Housing Act of 1988 introduced an important change in the way that the development work of housing associations was funded. From a position of having the total costs of a scheme met by grants from the Housing Corporation, now only a proportion of those costs are met, the remainder have to be found by borrowing from funding institutions such as banks and building societies. Any overspend has to be met from the association's own resources. Additionally, they have to set their own rents rather than relying on 'fair rents' being set independently. 'Risk management' is the phrase bandied around at management committee meetings now.

As the focus has shifted from local authorities to housing associations, so questions have been raised about who the voluntary members are that sit on the management committees. These are unpaid people who have the ultimate responsibility for the work of the association; they are not appointed by local authorities or, indeed, the government, but rely on being voted into office from the voluntary membership of the organisation. More often than not there is no necessity for an election since these people often stand unopposed. The issue of governance has come to the fore: phrases such as 'Are the days of the amateur now over?' are often heard.

The tensions within the movement are increasing, partly as a consequence of the increased focus being placed on them from external sources, but also from within, given the diverse nature of the organisations themselves. The movement includes associations which are very small (so small, in fact, that the committee does the work and no staff are employed) to national organisations who are responsible for thousands of properties, operating on a regional level with staff resources to match. These larger organisations are the ones that have thrived in the current climate.

The pressures for change and the dilemma facing many people in the movement are such that for those involved in still locally based associations, working within a couple of local authority areas, the words of Michael Simmons ring true: 'It is all a far cry from small knots of people crowding into tiny, improvised committee rooms agonising over how to provide decent accommodation for people in need. These same small knots of people, in many instances, are still meeting, trying to hold things together. But in many instances they are wringing their hands and wondering why they bother' (*Guardian*, June 1994).

Midshires Housing Association

In the late 1960s and early 1970s the city of Midtown was pursuing a policy whereby large areas of terraced homes were demolished rather than being refurbished and let. This, coupled with increasing problems of homelessness, created an environment where local people came together to find ways to help meet these needs in a manner more sympathetic than that expressed by the local authority. In 1973 Midshires Housing Association was formed from a local Shelter group. It had no staff and no office premises, and was run on a voluntary basis by the founding members. In 1975 the first house was completed ready for occupation and by the end of 1976 there were two members of staff. Once the group were able to demonstrate their ability to deliver their promises they were able to work with Midtown City Council whose support enabled them to receive significant funding from the Housing Corporation. On the back of the Housing Act 1980, a new association was formed to provide homes for sale on a shared ownership and low-cost basis. Soon, the association, whilst maintaining its roots and focus of activity within the local area, acquired a reputation for innovation and willingness to provide a broad range of housing serving different needs. This innovative approach even extended to the creation of an organisation that provided employment opportunities under the government-funded Community Programme. The table of stock shown in Fig. 16.1 illustrates the growth experienced by the association.

Year	*Rent*	*Special needs*	*Shared ownership**	*Other*
1976	1	–	–	–
1977	8	–	–	–
1978	66	4	–	–
1979	194	6	–	–
1980	286	55	–	–
1981	355	55	–	–
1982	383	91	–	–
1983	422	91	5	5
1984	538	106	103	22
1985	605	121	146	29
1986	657	121	162	36
1987	696	157	176	37
1988	775	160	259	39
1989	820	198	296	40
1990	876	198	341	40
1991	994	231	396	95
1992	1142	272	466	96
1993	1338	273	465	123
1994	1410	273	470	133
1995	1439	284	485	140
1996	1458	290	460	140
1997	1601	298	470	152

*Once a property has been bought outright, it falls from the table.

Fig. 16.1 Midshires Housing Association: stock in management

Therefore, within twenty years the Association grew from having no housing stock to managing over 2000 units – still a small to medium-sized association in national terms but nevertheless one with a sound reputation, both locally as well as with the Housing Corporation.

However, there was a recognition within Midshires that, if the problems associated with homelessness were to be combated, simply providing housing was not enough. To enable new activities to be pursued, a trust was formed in 1985 from which grew a network of day centres for those in bed and breakfast accommodation and the task of fund-raising from non-government sources began.

Staff numbers have grown from a zero base in 1973 to two in 1976, eleven in 1979, seventy in 1989 and some 130 in 1998. The first offices were situated in a church which gave part of its premises to community use, but since then space demands have meant two moves, in 1982 and in 1987 to its present offices.

Once staff were employed the involvement of the voluntary members in day-to-day work gradually changed. From one committee of some seven people at the beginning, the organisation soon spawned subcommittees and other committees so that the number of voluntary members grew to fourteen, with fifteen co-opted members, in 1982 and by 1989 to twenty-five members, twenty-three co-optees and eight committees. By 1994 there were twenty-eight members and twenty-three co-optees for nine committees. In 1998 arrangements for a group structure were put in place that incorporated three small local associations, adding to the number of members involved with the organisation.

By 1998 the last of the founder members had left the main management committee. Although there still remained a number of members with experience going back to the early 1980s, it was the chief executive who became the main focus for the link with the past. He had joined Midshires in a voluntary capacity in 1977 but by 1979 was an employee and, in 1981, its chief executive. With the original band of founder members, who pushed to find new ways of helping those in need, he has been the driving force behind the investigation of new initiatives.

The chair's statement in the annual report of 1997 set the tone for the late 1990s: 'There are two things that worry me greatly. One is that Midshires Housing Association faces the problem common to almost every organisation that grows – it is in danger of becoming too bureaucratic, losing touch with its roots and thus pulling its punches with the Establishment, to the possible detriment of those it most needs to help. The other is more serious in that while all those working in public sector housing report a growing need, resources from central government are reduced.'

Activity brief

1 Assuming the role of an outside consultant, consider Midshires Housing Association, describing those internal management issues which would need to have been addressed as the organisation grew, indicating what steps you would have expected to have been taken to resolve them. Looking to the future, assuming a constant growth projection, how should the interests of the voluntary committee members and the full-time staff be addressed in order to achieve an agreed way forward? In

particular, how should the management style of the chief executive have changed up to now and how should it change in the future?

2 We have already seen that Midshires is becoming more bureaucratic in its structure and is actively seeking policies of innovation and competitive advantage. Given that salaries, although competitive in the voluntary field, are probably lower than in industry, how would you gain and maintain commitment and motivation levels of employees?

Further reading

Handy, C. B. (1988), *Understanding Voluntary Organisations*, 4th edn, Penguin.

Case study provided by Chris Jenkins.

ACTIVITY

Make a diagrammatic representation of *one* of the following organisations:

- a power station;
- a dairy farm;
- a subsidised theatre;
- an army; or
- a car factory.

Aim to illustrate:

1 The variety of inputs (staff, capital, energy, etc.).

2 The ways goals and feedback influence those inputs (e.g. union policy affecting recruitment practices or EU directives determining stock size).

3 The ways outputs might be made to fulfil social responsibilities in some measure (e.g. actors running morning workshops in day centres for the disabled, or water, warmed from being used as a coolant, being piped to a local shellfish farm).

If you decide to use the input/output systems model (see Mullins, pp. 99–100 and 124), try adding a new box through which both goals and feedback pass to be processed together before being passed on to influence inputs. The box could be called 'strategic planning' (see Mullins, p. 129). Thus the difficulties overly institutionalised soldiers can experience when seeking employment in 'civvy street' could influence the kind of training programmes the army might purchase or design, or the assessment tests used for selecting recruits to the force.

DEBATE

'The current trend towards flatter organisational structures leads to a decline in staff motivation and in the desire to succeed.'

Starting points

For

- Motivation is engendered by the prospect of promotion and the challenge of a new role.
- Multiple-tiered structures offer a clearly defined promotion route linked to pay and status.

Against

- Promotion is not the only method of rewarding effective performance. Job rotation and job enrichment are alternative ways to develop professional and personal skills.
- Flat structures encourage delegation of responsibility and can motivate a greater proportion of staff than those rewarded by promotion in a bureaucratic structure.

Further reading

Hall, L. and Torrington, D. (1998), *The Human Resource Function,* FT Pitman Publishing.

Senior, B. (1997), *Organisational Change,* FT Pitman Publishing.

Thornhill, A. *et al.* (1999), *Managing Change – A Human Resource Approach,* FT Pitman Publishing.

Debate provided by Joyce Dargie, The Fremantle Trust.

ASSIGNMENT

An article appeared in *Management Issues,* a journal aimed at both academics and managers, with the following synopsis:

'It is predicted that by the turn of the century at least half of the British workforce could be working at least part of the week from home. This idea of "teleworking" will have far-reaching implications for organisation design.'

In *not more* than 2000 words, complete the article as if you were submitting it for publication. You should bear in mind the following:

1. Your target audience will be both academics who know the theories of organisation design in detail and practitioners who probably won't have the same understanding but will have a basic knowledge (in other words, you don't need to draw lots of diagrams depicting a functional structure, a matrix structure, etc.). The non-academics who read your article will be practising managers and you will therefore need to relate your theoretical arguments to the workplace.
2. As with all academic journals, your article will be sent to at least two people with a knowledge of the area in order to obtain their views prior to it being accepted for publication. Your arguments, therefore, must be clear, logical and lead the reader to an obvious conclusion.

3 Your work must be referenced (for an example of referencing using footnotes, see the final pages of any chapter in Mullins). There is nothing wrong in quoting other authors' views or opinions, but at least give them the credit for having stated the point before you did!

APPLICATION 1

Gillian, one of our part-time management students, is a freelance management trainer. As part of an assignment for us, she produced the following story.

Phillippa MacIntyre Associates is a management consultancy whose main area of activity is in interpersonal skills training. Before becoming self-employed, Phillippa was training manager for a leading chain of high-street fashion stores who not only had their own shops but also operated a shop-in-shop concept in large department stores.

The recent economic recession caused the company to think long and hard about its overhead costs and, as is usual, training was the first thing to come under the corporate axe. However, the company was rather more proactive than its rivals and rather than axing training altogether, they offered generous redundancy packages to their training staff and then bought back their services on a consultancy basis. It was a solution which suited both parties: overhead costs were reduced and Phillippa and her colleagues had the opportunity to become self-employed but at less risk than would normally be the case. Thus Phillippa MacIntyre Associates (PMA) was born. PMA consisted of just Phillippa and an administration assistant – the other associates, some ten in total, whilst working primarily for PMA, were self-employed and free to pursue their own sales leads as they wished, a point which Phillippa continually stressed.

PMA went from strength to strength, largely due to Phillippa's dynamic personality. She believed wholeheartedly in her company and her drive and enthusiasm brought in a steady stream of work which kept most of her associates busy, working solely for her. As the economy began to pick up, Phillippa was offered a huge contract from a rival fashion chain which amounted to 1000 days of consultancy. Clearly the existing ten associates were not going to be able to cope with this massive influx of work and so she advertised for other freelance trainers to join PMA on a subcontract basis so that the total complement would number fifty. The response to the advertisement was considerable and Phillippa spent a long time interviewing candidates to ensure not only that they were competent to do the job but also that they had the right attitude and personality to be able to fit into her culture. Successful candidates were invited to an induction day to ensure that they not only were *au fait* with the training programme but were also inculcated into the PMA culture. Our student, one of the freelance trainers, did not go away empty-handed . . . on the contrary she left the meeting with three lever-arch 'bibles' containing background information and paperwork including all the returns she would need to make to PMA after each training visit (six in total plus two invoices).

When we asked her how she was getting on, she replied, 'Well, I thought it was going to be the perfect subcontract: some guaranteed days work and no ties to

PMA. Unfortunately that isn't proving to be the case; Phillippa gets really upset if you can't make meetings because you have other work not generated by her and the operations manual keeps changing – I've got enough paper to make a rain forest. I'm thinking of giving it up.'

Chandler suggests that structure should follow strategy. If the structure becomes outdated, people are added on with little thought resulting in a loss of control. Can you see where PMA didn't take an open systems approach and didn't consider the inputs, outputs and the effect of the environment?

Also, taking the contingency factors into consideration, the increasing size would indicate that she needs to be more mechanistic in her approach and although she is trying to do this in terms of paperwork, she is operating an essentially organic organisation.

APPLICATION 2

For this one we'll need to go back to Midshires University (see the case study in Chapter 12). The Law Department is in the faculty of Humanities but actually only has one pure law degree. The rest of the teaching is 'serviced out' to other departments. This is by no means a rare occurrence in colleges and it happens when other degree courses have a specialised unit of some sort and no expertise in their own department to teach it, and the demand is such that it would be uneconomic to employ a lecturer specifically to teach it.

Thus law lecturers may find themselves with the timetabled courses set out in Fig. 16.2. The timetable for this particular lecturer means that they don't actually teach in their own department nor, since Midshires has a campus which is spread over quite a wide geographical area, even on their own site. Whilst they are ultimately responsible to their own head of department, they also have a reporting responsibility to the course manager in whose department the particular course is located.

Course	*Department*
BSc Engineering	Mechanical Engineering
BA Architecture	School of Architecture
MA Human Resource Management	Business School
Employment Law Short Course	Management Centre
BA Hotel and Catering Management	Business School

Fig. 16.2

Prior to incorporation, this arrangement worked well, probably because it was informal in nature and relied on personal contacts and unofficial reciprocal trading. However, after incorporation, the culture of the 'new' university changed subtly and an 'official' matrix structure was brought in. We can see from the case in Chapter 12 that there was greater pressure to 'perform and deliver' both teaching and research. Demands on lecturers now became formalised and much of the earlier goodwill began to dissipate.

A fly on the wall in the staff coffee room overheard the following comments:

- *'I didn't mind going to Boards of Studies and Boards of Examiners before, but I object to being notified formally of my requirement to do so – especially having to complete the tear-off slip with the reasons* ***why*** *I can't attend: it's like being back in school.'*
- *'I don't teach one single course in this faculty and yet my head of department is supposed to be doing my appraisal under this new scheme they've brought in. How can he when he doesn't really know what I'm doing?'*
- *'I'm supposed to be schools liaison officer – how can I find the time to do it when I'm never on site and I'm supposed to be on the committee for a new exam in the Engineering Department?'*

Here we can see that prior to incorporation, the 'unofficial' matrix structure worked because the culture of the organisation and the attitudes and behaviour of the members made it work. However, once the matrix was made 'official' throughout the university, the structure became too complex and the attendant problems associated with this form became all too apparent (see Mullins, p. 543).

APPLICATION 3

We hear much these days about 'delayering', 'downsizing', 'business re-engineering' and the like. We are exhorted to be 'leaner and fitter' and to 'think globally and act locally' (the latter slogan appearing everywhere from the lips of the management gurus to local authority bottle banks). It seems that senior management are taking an organisational machete to hack out layers of management, seemingly, sometimes, without much thought to the consequences (we suggest they read Mullins, pp. 543–4, for a synopsis of the consequences of a badly designed structure).

We are bombarded with articles and case studies about companies who have 'flattened their pyramid' and even, on occasion, turned it upside down. Ricardo Semler, however, has gone one further and 'rounded it out' (Semler, 1993). Claiming that the traditional pyramid is dysfunctional not only for efficiency and effectiveness but also for personal growth and development, he has replaced it with a series of concentric circles, the smallest forming the core of senior, strategic managers (renamed 'counsellors'). The next circle out from the core encloses seven to ten business unit leaders (now renamed 'partners'), and the final circle would comprise everyone else in the organisation who would be renamed 'associates'. 'Floating' outside the circles are six to twelve triangles, each composed of one person (a 'co-ordinator'), who would, in the old system, be the first level of management but who, in the circular system, co-ordinate such activities as marketing, sales and production.

Semler claims that although this new design took a while to be accepted it is now working successfully. Movement around the organisation is as easy and as quick as individuals want (or don't want) and decision-making has both speeded up and improved through a weekly team briefing and a further meeting of the counsellors and a representative from each unit. In Semler's words: 'Just three circles, four job categories, and two meetings. That's it.'

But is it? Semler is accepted as an entrepreneurial leader, a maverick (indeed, that is the title of his book). This, together with his charismatic personality and lateral-thinking approach, has clearly worked for Semco. Would it work for, say, a local authority Trading Standards Department or a university? Has the time come to call a halt to these 'me too' approaches to organisation design and, instead, consider incremental changes over a much longer period of time when their long-term effects on structure, performance and people can be assessed?

APPLICATION 4

Co-operative's wheels of fortune

FT

Imagine a company where corporate strategy is decided not by the general manager but by 20 employee shareholders at the annual meeting. And the general manager, whose post did not exist two years ago, has to be re-elected by shareholders every 12 months.

Yet what could otherwise be a recipe for muddle, stagnation and financial loss may explain why Edinburgh Bicycle, a workers' co-operative, has become one of Britain's biggest independent bicycle retailers. Its turnover has nearly trebled since 1990 in a sluggish UK bicycle market and last year grew 20 per cent to £2.8m. It consistently makes modest profits. Edinburgh Bicycle runs a large shop in Morningside, Edinburgh. It designs its own bikes, including models for the city's hilly and cobbled streets, and has them manufactured under contract. About 20 per cent of its business comes from outside the Edinburgh and Glasgow area, thanks to an annual 132-page catalogue and its own web site. Customers are offered evening classes in bicycle maintenance.

In principle the people in command at Edinburgh Bicycle are the 20 members of the co-operative, which can include any employee who has worked there for two years, though several have been there since the business was founded in the late 1970s by a group of graduate cycling enthusiasts.

The co-operative members appoint the general manager and a six-person executive team to run the business and agree the rolling five-year plan. 'You could call ours an inverted management structure,' says Lindsay McDermid, promotions manager.

But the procedure is not as formal in practice as it looks on paper. To devise the five-year plan the company's six departments draw up their own plans, and give Mike Sweatman, the general manager, the task of incorporating them into a single scheme. But he is unlikely to have to reconcile big differences over strategy because the members will have sorted these out in informal discussions.

The co-operative also meets once a quarter to discuss how things are going. It may sometimes hold a team from a department to account if its performance, shown in the weekly sales figures, is unsatisfactory. 'We probably spend more time talking in meetings than people in other companies but we believe the co-operative structure is a source of strength,' Mr McDermid says. One advantage, he says, is that 'people who work here feel fully involved in the business, and that makes them committed to doing their best for the customers'.

A further strength, he says, is security of employment for staff, whose numbers range between 30 and 50 depending on the time of year. 'The idea of the co-operative is to be here for the people who work here, not to produce dividends for someone else or for the boss,' he says.

'In a co-operative a small number of people can't destroy the livelihood of the many by taking their money out of the business, as can happen in a conventional company or partnership,' he adds. 'In Edinburgh Bicycle the maximum amount of money a member can take out is the nominal £1 investment needed to belong to the co-operative.'

Most co-operatives in the UK, he says, tend to break up after their membership reaches about 12 because members want to continue deciding detailed issues in a business now much larger than when the co-operative was formed. Edinburgh Bicycle has survived as a co-operative, he thinks, because members are expected to trust the different teams to take detailed decisions although they can have access to all the information they want.

'You have to be a particular sort of person to work here,' Mr McDermid acknowledges. 'If you're stubborn or self-centred or have grandiose ideas, you probably won't fit in.' More than in other businesses the general manager has to have the full consent of staff for everything he does. The company has a relatively flat pay structure, with the highest paid employee receiving only 3.8 times the pay of the lowest paid. 'We're not out to become super-rich,' says Mr McDermid. In addition to salaries all employees may occasionally receive a bonus related to profits which could be a few thousand pounds.

The expansion in the company's sales in the 1990s has been against stagnation in the UK market, according to figures from the Bicycle Association which represents retailers. But might Edinburgh Bicycle have done even better if it had been structured like a normal company and did not have the limits entailed in being a co-operative?

With share capital of only £20 it does not have the comfort of a large equity base. Instead it relies for finance on an overdraft and bank loans, as well as on retained profits which now amount to more than £300 000. Its annual pre-tax profit of around £60 000 is small compared with turnover.

'It would obviously be nice if we had unlimited capital,' Mr McDermid says, 'but we get by. It makes you concentrate on what is realistic. We've never said to ourselves: if only we could have been a conventional company.'

Source: James Buxton, *Financial Times*, 24 February 1998.

APPLICATION 5

Questions of commitment

FT

The majority of employees in most countries work in hierarchically controlled, functional organisations. In the UK, for example, out of a workforce of 28m, employees account for 21m and just 4 per cent is self-employed. The free-forming units of liberated individuals we keep hearing about are still rare.

But this is not to say each corporation is made up of an homogeneous mass. There have been usually at least two main groups of contributors: 'them and us', or 'line and staff', 'white and blue collar', 'head office and local office'. They were and are different, and are managed differently. The huge growth of the service and knowledge industries has been largely responsible for highlighting these differences. Although most workers in these industries are still employees, their relationship with the company and with each other has undergone great change, and a number of contributor groups can now be identified.

Charles Handy, the management writer, was one of the first to notice this a decade ago when he pointed to the shamrock or clover leaf design of many firms. Each of the three main leaves represents a different type of contributor to the organisation's objectives.

First, there is a core of full-time, highly-paid professionals, technicians and executives who generate the intellectual capital, the organisational knowledge, which differentiates a firm from its competitors. Second, there is a contractual fringe of individuals who provide material and service inputs to the core. Third, there is a flexible group of part-time or temporary workers called on to handle peak workloads.

According to the model, instead of one workforce there are three, each with a different kind of commitment to the firm, a different contractual arrangement, a different set of expectations – and each must be managed differently. Mr Handy predicted an increasing number of part-time workers, an explosive rise in the importance of knowledge workers and the opportunity for a minority to end their dependence on the firm by developing alternative activities.

This model has been extended by Peter Saul, an Australian strategy consultant, to include customers/clients and what he calls 'social regulators'.

He argues that the customers are increasingly 'paid' for the work they do. For example, those who pay their bills early may gain a discount, and loyal airline passengers earn air miles.

He defines the role of social regulators as monitoring the enterprise as to how it meets the community's needs. The importance of regulators has come to the fore since privatisation became popular during the 1980s.

In any single organisation, only some of these five types of contributors may be employees in the traditional sense. Others, such as the flexible workforce, may contribute to the objectives of several organisations in the same industry.

Mr Saul notes two dimensions that differentiate the contributions of different groups. First, the length of the relationship between the contributor and the firm: is the relationship a long or short-term one? Second, the nature of their primary contribution: are they there to maintain a service or output for the firm, or to ensure its competitiveness? Those who make short-term contributions have different expectations from those there for the longer term. Further, those whose primary function is to maintain output and service will have very different expectations from those whose primary function is to maximise competitiveness.

Contributors to the strategic core are usually involved in long-term relationships to maximise competitive advantage. Roles can be negotiated and refined over time. Some protection from the hassle of the immediate market allows these contributors to build mutual trust and develop teamwork. Suitable performance measures are established to help people learn from their experience. Subtle judgements can be made about these contributors' motivations, potential and loyalty.

In contrast, short-term relationships apply to those in the flexible workforce, customers/clients and those providing contractual services of a trouble-shooting nature. These contributors are seen as visitors to the organisation and not particularly interested in the vision or long-term goals of the company. Because they are not emotionally involved they have some objectivity but are dispensable. They can be dropped brutally without ceremony in a way members of the strategic core rarely treat each other. Another group, also short term but concerned with competitiveness, includes management consultants and advisers. While they are employed they articulate the approved vision and values, but when the assignment ends they move on. The importance of both Mr Handy's original analysis and Mr Saul's development of it is the clarity it gives to the question of different commitments of contributors to the same organisation. At best the firm is a loosely coupled set of relationships.

This raises the question about the value of attempting to establish shared visions and values among different contributors. It highlights the fallacy of many human resources policies and practices based on some average employee.

Much of the advice to chief executives on how to lead more effectively is based on the assumption that the only people who matter are in the strategic core. Who ever mentions motivating the contributions of the flexible workforce or the contractual partners or the growing army of consultants?

Source: Professor John W. Hunt, *Financial Times*, 20 May 1998.

AFTERTHOUGHTS

'I tell you, sir, the only safeguard of order and discipline in the modern world is a standardised worker with interchangeable parts. That would solve the entire problem of management.'
Jean Giraudoux, The Madwoman of Chaillot

A doctor's first duty is to his or her patients unless you work for Homewood NHS Trust where the first duty is loyalty to the employing organisation . . . .

17 Technology and Organisations

CASE STUDY

Using an intranet: What does it mean to employees?

This brief case study is derived from a research project which is looking at the social and organisational issues arising out of and connected with the adoption and implementation of intranet technology. Two organisations are being studied; this study is based upon the data gathered from one of them – a computer supplier company based on the south coast of England, employing around 1500 staff across the US and Europe, with the great majority working at this head office and main manufacturing plant. Over forty individual interviews have been conducted to date, half of them when the intranet was in the early process of introduction (in June and July, 1997), and the other half some six months later. A wide range of people from the company were interviewed, from vertical and horizontal slices of the organisation. The extracts below are taken from the second round of interviews.

The interview transcriptions and analysis have been drawn upon in order to generate below two sets of the more polarised views of staff about the company intranet: those people who feel that 'little has changed' and those who are of the view that things have changed noticeably as a result of the intranet implementation. Of course, there were also many people who took a perspective somewhere in between, that is, talking about some amount of change, whilst at the same time arguing that things haven't changed that much; other people had views which might best be referred to as ambivalent or 'mixed'. These views are not reproduced here – for purposes of the case study, the intention is merely to illustrate how it is possible to find a wide divergence of views about 'exactly' the same technology, to which everyone interviewed had, in principle at least, equal access.

The notation used for the transcripts is as follows:

INT = Interviewer
IS = IS/IT specialist
LM = Line manager
NM = the company IT software which the intranet replaced
PD = Personnel Director
SEC = Secretary
SM = Senior manager
TS = Technical specialist

'Little has changed'

LM: 'But I haven't accessed a single departmental home page or a single personal home page for any useful business reason since the intranet has been in effect.'

TS: 'I think maybe this is part of ah sort of use, not even use of culture but intranet culture which we are just putting up with ahm I don't know why we have got ah an organised way of producing departmental and personal pages on the intranet, there seems to be a fad that had grown up on the intranet and we have paid homage to and lip service to and put in place on our intranet rather than recognising it for the complete waste of time and effort I believe it is.'

SEC1: 'Yeah, I don't think it was that, I don't think it was that a big a change, I thought it was wonderful, marvellous, hooray let's move into the twentieth century at least. But I don't know if things have really changed that much for most of the people out there because they still use it in exactly the same way as they used NM.'

SEC2: 'They still have too much mail, coming to them personally, still too much actually gets sent out individually as opposed to being posted on the web page, but maybe that's because they haven't quite grasped the idea of the groups and the user pages and things. We're only now doing this course, Intranet Best Practices, where they go, where they explain a bit more about posting things on group pages or user pages or whatever. I don't think people really have been fully aware of what the intranet can do unless they are particularly keen on PCs and enjoy playing with things, but a lot of them I think just use it to send messages and look in their diary, they don't really know what it should be used for.'

IS: 'I think that initially there was a huge bubble of work to get it in and then there was the kind of, well now we have got it let's do what we did before, but using intranet rather than NM, and so the initial access was almost look this thing that you did before you know with NM, you can now do with intranet like this, that's what people were driving for, people were saying how do I do exactly the same thing that I did on NM but on the intranet? Not really saying, how can I best do my job using intranet as a tool.'

SM: 'I don't find really that there's been any substantial change ahm as I say from that point of view. I think that people don't like change, if the people have been around for a long time using a diary management system through NM and got used to the quirks and things, if somebody is going to put in a totally new system, they will think oh this isn't going to work as well, but I don't have any problems ahm now the majority of the time the secretary sets up the diary and does all the diary work but I am just as competent at doing that myself.'

'Things have changed'

LM: 'The system is streets ahead of what we used to have, and the way you can structure it, the sort of linkages, so you have got one set of data in one place and you can click on an icon and get through to the core piece of information from pretty much wherever you happen to be in the network, it is streets ahead.'

PD: 'I think having things like our own home pages, and it just feels like our system and not the system that many of us were used to for many many years, it makes people think slightly differently, and I think whenever you have a change event, and you will know this, it allows you to have, you can use it as a way of putting in other changes like, if you want to know, you can put announcements on the home page, you have to keep yourself up to date, you have to look at the home pages, its not going to be delivered to you, once you make a change it allows other changes to happen, so I think yes the technology is very powerful.'

TS: 'Well, yeah, we have a virtual organisation anyway when you think about it, my department is across two continents, and we communicate fairly effectively, I think. We wouldn't have been able to communicate effectively if we didn't have IT. The fact that I can send and they can send me video pictures if they wanted, sound files or competitors' software very easily says a lot I think of the way we do our business.'

LM: 'And the difference with this is obviously if you are issuing that new plan you can just append a spreadsheet to the note and send it as a piece of electronic mail, ahm, which is great. So, yes, I think some of the communication has stopped, some of the communication is easier to deal with and some has changed medium. So people, I believe, are using the telephone where they used to send notes, which is absolutely excellent, and people are sending faxes where they used to send notes.'

INT: 'Does it make it easier to find out what it is going on elsewhere?'
LM: 'Yes, it has, because one of the things you have got is the functional home pages, the QMS content and the departmental home pages makes it easier to understand who does what, and what their processes and procedures are. I mean, that is much more readily available and much more easy to understand than it ever was before . . . . Now, if you click on another area, like business unit or support area, you will probably find some quite sophisticated flow charts and relating procedures and organisation charts, which are very easy to look at and understand, and probably because of this they are more up to date than they used to be. So that, in that respect, it is easier to find out what other people are up to, and I don't know how much it is used, but there is some useful information pages set up.'

Activity brief

Why is there such a wide range of views about the company intranet from staff who work in the same organisation, and who have access to the same technology? How can this be explained? Draw upon your knowledge of organisational behaviour in general, and your reading of Chapter 17 of Mullins in particular.

 The author wishes to acknowledge the contribution of Ken Clarke, University of Portsmouth Business School, to the design, conduct and analysis of the intranet research project through which the data reported here were gathered.

ACTIVITY

ABC & Sons is a third generation family business, producing components for manufacturers of luxury consumer goods. It has established a reputation for quality and service and exports a quarter of its output overseas.

Family members have generally entered the business as new graduates and, starting on the shop floor, have spent several years working in every department of the company. They have later broadened their knowledge by attending courses on new developments and technology, and on various aspects of management. As a result, the company has kept up to date in its production and administrative techniques and is making use of sophisticated levels of information technology in several areas. However, it has paid little attention to the development of its other managers beyond essential updating in, for example, health and safety regulations.

Until recently, ABC & Sons had a relatively stable workforce of 500 employees, was seen as a good employer, and was viewed with pride by its many long-serving employees who encouraged their own children to work there. The skilled workers have traditionally been men and the assembly, packing and clerical workers have been women, many from ethnic minorities.

More recently, however, there have been some significant changes. The introduction of the new technology has necessitated the recruitment of new technical managers and some graduate management trainees. Some of the older craft skills have become redundant, while new technical skills are now needed in many areas. Moreover, although the new technology has given the company a competitive edge, the market world-wide for its customers' products has dwindled and, indeed, some of its major customers and key suppliers are in difficulties. While so far avoiding redundancy, the company has responded to natural wastage by taking on most newcomers on part-time contracts and has increased the proportion of women and young people employed.

The senior management of ABC & Sons is beginning to recognise that the company is facing more than recession and that the industrial sector as a whole is in decline: the company needs to plan its future strategically. It is also becoming aware that the changes introduced over the last few years have radically altered the nature of the company. Senior managers have recently been dismayed by incidents that suggest a growing cynicism among the longer serving employees and desire for early retirement, and among the young a lack of commitment and a disappointingly narrow range of skills. To deal with all these issues, a new post of human resource manager has been created, reporting to the managing director's daughter who is the board member responsible for staff and administration. The existing personnel and welfare officer will now assist the new manager.

You are the newly appointed human resource manager.

1 Have recent changes to technology really improved the company's ability to compete?

2 What human resource development issues confront you in this situation? List your priorities for dealing with them.

You may work either on your own or in a group.

Source: Adapted from Beardwell, I. and Holden, L. (1997), *Human Resource Management: A Contemporary Perspective*, 2nd edition, FT Pitman Publishing.

DEBATE

'To make the best use of technology we must use it to support and develop our business, not adapt the business to the technology – technology should be our servant – not our master.'

Starting points

For

- Technology can provide expensive solutions to irrelevant problems.
- Technology can drive change at an accelerating pace which actually diverts our attention away from real customer needs.
- The 'best' solutions from a technical viewpoint may not be the ones our customers most need or want.

Against

- Technology throws up whole new ways of doing business which we need to adapt to.
- If we don't keep up with technological change we may fall behind our competitors.
- If we don't keep up with technological change we may lose key employees who like to work at the leading edge of technology.

Further reading

Hamel G. and Prahalad, C. K. (1994), *Competing for the Future*, HBS.

Jones, T. *et al*. (1990), *The Machine that Changed the World*, Rawson Associates.

ASSIGNMENT

Consider the introduction of a new technology you have experienced or witnessed in an organisation. Typical examples might include:

- a network of computer terminals providing electronic mail and notice boards;
- company bicycles for travelling round a large industrial plant (e.g. an oil refinery);
- electronic databases replacing card filing systems in a library or hospital;
- student study packs (audio- and videotapes, manuals, etc.) for open or distance learning;
- mobile phones or pagers for employees in a construction firm or university;
- drop-in computer-based training stations in the workplace;
- video- or conference-phones to reduce travelling to meetings in an aviation engineering firm;
- telesales (i.e. selling by telephone and/or television);

- laptop computers issued to sales staff, maintenance workers or consultant accountants;
- home-based electronic offices to enable commuting staff to 'telework' part of the week.

Focusing on one such change write a 1500-word essay that assesses the extent to which working practices will be, or have been, altered by it, and evaluate its impact on efficiency and job satisfaction (see Mullins, pp. 107–8).

Key issues that might impinge upon your evaluation could include: access, control, reliability, safety, cost, training, pace of change, consultation, privacy, health, and law.

APPLICATION 1

Companies seek IT directors with sharper business focus FT

Breakdown of communication between IT directors and company boards means that many of the hopes for IT as the key to new ways of working and partnerships with suppliers and customers are being eclipsed by a desire to use it simply to cut costs.

This is one finding of recent research commissioned by Korn/Ferry International, executive search specialist, with the *Financial Times*, which shows that IT directors are being kept outside the boardroom rather than at the heart of business strategy.

The survey of IT directors and chief information officers finds considerable differences in IT representation at board level across the US, the UK, Germany and France. This ranges from just 13 per cent in France to 36 per cent in the UK and Germany and almost half in the US.

Nonetheless, when asked whether IT directors will regularly make it to chief executive in the next five years, less than 30 per cent of those in the US believe this will happen, compared with 46 per cent in France and a third in the UK.

'The IT function is seen as enabling business plans to happen, but not as a contributor to those plans in the first place,' says Mina Gouran, managing partner of Korn/Ferry International's European advanced technology practice. 'Company boards consist of people who have immediate impact, so IT should be there, alongside finance, manufacturing and marketing, because IT knows the potential.'

The fact that only a minority of IT directors are on the board 'is perhaps a reflection of the type of people leading IT,' she adds.

This last comment underlines the finding that IT directors see their main obstacles to the top as being their lack of business experience and a perception among other executives that they are too technical. This applies especially in the US and the UK.

IT directors themselves believe they need business experience outside IT – not just to get on the board but simply to do their own jobs well. Around 80 per cent across all four countries agree here. Indeed, 80 per cent in the US and two-thirds of those in France and Germany believe an MBA or other academic grounding in business skills is important to success in IT management. In the UK, 54 per cent support this notion.

In addition, more than 90 per cent across all the countries believe the ability to communicate key messages to top management is necessary for success as head of IT – this is even more than the vote for in-depth knowledge of IT as a key success factor. The US respondents, in particular, are almost unanimous here.

Other recent research has also highlighted communication as vital for full business exploitation of IT – and revealed the IT function's shortcomings. A particularly telling analysis by CSC Research Services of its 10 annual international surveys of IT directors' top concerns goes as far as to suggest that directors are getting bored with hearing about the wonders of information technology.

'Aligning IT and company goals has been in the top three issues for the last 10 years – and number one for the last two years,' says managing director John Cooper. 'This is worrying, as it implies that there's been little progress. It is probably also unique to IT: do marketing and production people feel unaligned with the business?

'IT people have complained for 30 years that their business colleagues do not understand them – and they are now concerned about continually pushing the importance of IT, because they think directors are bored with it and still cannot get to grips with what it can do for the business.'

This lack of understanding means business executives fall back on viewing IT as a cost, rather than an investment, says Mr Cooper. This is confirmed by the CSC Research Services finding that cutting IT costs has been in the top four issues for five years.

'Unless business people come to understand that IT is an enabler, they will continue to see it as a cost,' he says.

The Korn/Ferry International and *Financial Times* research supports this idea that many business directors have a simplistic view of information technology. In particular, it highlights the continued view among many business executives that IT's role is only to cut costs.

Almost half the US IT directors and more than 40 per cent of those in the UK say this is their most successful argument when seeking more investment. The prospect of improving customer service is some way behind and other issues, such as improving communication, are a long way back.

The future does look a little brighter: IT directors certainly see their role changing. Around two-thirds say their role is already changing, the main reasons being business and IT uncertainty, plus to increase business focus.

Asked how their role will have changed by 2003, 'more business focus' receives the biggest vote in the US and the UK.

This change is in line with board directors' expectations, says Ms Gouran at Korn/Ferry International: 'In our IT executive searches, business employers specify varying characteristics – but all of them want business awareness. This has become far more pronounced in recent years, because of rapid business change.'

Philip Schneidemeyer, vice-president of Korn/Ferry International's advanced technology practice in the US, sees IT directors' own ambitions playing a role here: he has job candidates increasingly asking if their peers are reaching chief executive level (his simple answer is, 'No'). Meanwhile, he sees some companies extending the IT directors' role into business: for example to cover logistics as well as IT. Indeed, he believes companies seeking the best IT directors will have to show commitment to IT as part of business strategy.

But at the same time IT directors should examine their own abilities, Mr Schneidemeyer says – especially if they want to get to the top: 'What distinguishes the best IT directors are leadership and the ability to communicate – which is just the same as in other executive jobs.'

Source: John Kavanagh, *Financial Times*, 1 July 1998.

APPLICATION 2

Working the system by remote control

FT

The concept of providing employees with access to a corporate network 'anytime, anywhere, anyhow' is a strategic goal for many IT departments, but one few have achieved.

Three years ago British Telecommunications set up a project team to build a system which would enable more than 10 000 of its mobile and teleworking employees to access its core IT system. Since then the British Telecom Remote Access (BTRA) scheme has grown into perhaps the biggest remote access project ever undertaken in the UK.

The system, built around multi-protocol wide area network (Wan) access switches from Ascend Communications, the US-based networking equipment supplier, enables remote access users to connect to BT's internal intranet and central site applications. It uses standard analogue or digital ISDN lines and GSM services, giving the same level of security and ease of access as if their machines were attached to a local area network (Lan).

Engineers, sales representatives, management and support staff can now remotely access systems ranging from contact databases and mainframe fault diagnosis applications. to word-processing and e-mail.

Fifty Ascend MAX 4000 switches in four regional centres are used to support BT's remote access users. Additional switches are being installed to provide more than 20 000 staff with remote access by the end of the year.

'With local access numbers in eight countries worldwide, BTRA enables our remote and mobile employees to connect to BT's corporate data networks from anywhere on the globe, 365 days a year,' says Ian Yeadon, BTRA project manager.

BT staff simply use their PC modems, ISDN cards or GSM data cards to dial one of the four regional centres and are transparently connected to BT's data networks, as if they were directly connected to a Lan. Users include sales, marketing and customer support engineers as well as all BT Shops. One factor affecting the choice of network switches was the need to support a wide range of data networking protocols, including IPX, which is used to connect to BT's internal mail systems, as well as allowing for access to centralised resources held geographically on Novell servers.

'Security was another key consideration for the BTRA project,' says Phil Holcroft, Ascend's UK country manager, 'especially when you consider this network is the only internal remote access network approved to meet BT's rigid security requirements.'

Mr Yeadon says BT is already working on the next phase of the project. 'This will include new additional services being made available to our users including improved international access,' he says. As part of the expansion BT has recently ordered Ascend's new high density MAX TNT hardware to support the fast-growing number of BT employees using the remote access network.

BT's customers are expected to benefit in a number of ways. For example, if a system fails during the night, an engineer can log on from home and remotely manage and fix the problem rather than making a journey to his office. In addition, sales staff can remotely access up-to-date pricing and order entry systems for BT's products and services, speeding up customer quotations and orders.

Source: Paul Taylor, *Financial Times*, 29 July 1998.

APPLICATION 3

TFW Images

TFW Images was formed in 1989 by two ex-employees of IBM who became the Managing Director and Creative Director of the company. They were very soon joined by a Sales Director with experience from a range of companies, mainly manufacturing. The main business of TFW Images is communications in its widest sense. Examples of its activities are: designing corporate brochures which might include annual reports as well as advertising material, designing and organising conferences and all the material that goes with them, and creating company logos and other symbols of corporate identity.

TFW Images' main client was, and still is, IBM. In fact, the rise of the company coincided with the large-scale changes which IBM went through as it refocused its efforts away from the mainframe computer market towards that of the personal computer market. As technology began to replace people, TFW Images was able to take advantage of the willingness of companies like IBM to outsource some of their design requirements.

From a high point of employing, directly, 17 people (two of whom were in Paris), TFW Images now has seven direct employees. Of the original three directors, one remains, the Creative Director, although he does not currently carry a particular title.

In a volatile market – there are other competitors and the fortunes of IBM are less certain nowadays – one reason for the company's success is its ability to maintain a flexible structure which can be tailored to the demands of the market. Essentially, TFW Images is an organisation which 'brokers' services from other organisations to bring its products to the market. Thus, rather than employing printers, photographers, illustrators, market researchers and additional writers and designers directly, it closely associates with other companies and independent consultants who offer these services. The use of sophisticated computer systems facilitates the transfer of the part-finished products from one part of the network to another, wherever it might be in the world.

Most recently, TFW Images has joined in partnership with Omni-Graphics, a well-established design company operating mainly in the publishing and arts spheres of activity. Examples of Omni-Graphics' activities are: the design of calendars, brochures for and layout of art galleries, and the design of news magazines.

Given the equality of skills and size of the two organisations, the benefits of the partnership will come from their complementary activities (TFW Images is business oriented while Omni-Graphics is arts oriented) and the financial advantages which will flow from this. The management of the two partner organisations will remain separate and both will keep their own names. Thus, to any client, nothing will have changed. Yet, conceptually and financially, a new overarching organisation has been 'virtually' created.

Source: Senior, B. (1997), *Organisational Change*, FT Pitman Publishing.

18 Job Satisfaction and Work Performance

CASE STUDY

A nasty shock for Eric Evans

ABC Ltd: A study in (lack of) job satisfaction

ABC Ltd is a private sector organisation which manufactures air-conditioning systems and sell them worldwide. Its head office is located in the north of England, although there are outposts of ABC in Spain, Norway, Australia and Japan.

ABC has always been run as if it were a small organisation even though its founder sold it to a big electronics concern some five years ago and it has grown from an original staff of twenty at the outset to employ 500 people at head office and something of the order of 3000 across all locations. It has never had a personnel department, therefore there are very few policies and procedures governing the organisation. Decisions regarding employees (for example, hiring and firing) are usually taken on an *ad hoc* basis by the relevant manager(s), with the particular circumstances of the case being taken into account. Furthermore management have always refused to recognise trade unions, believing that relations within the organisation are good enough for employees to be able to air grievances without the need for formal representation.

Indeed employee relations have never been seen to present a problem for ABC; the only area that management sees as cause for concern is the shop floor, where the systems are actually manufactured. The unskilled and repetitive nature of the work in this department is recognised to make unrest more likely and indeed several attempts to unionise this staff group have been launched in the past. Other sections, by contrast, are considered not to be in any need of special monitoring – the service maintenance department, for example. The staff in service maintenance are highly skilled engineers who are employed to maintain and repair the systems that ABC sells. They are available between 6.00 a.m. and midnight should any of ABC's customers require them. Everyone in this division has personal pagers and takes turns being 'on call' which, in the main, means attending to out-of-hours calls as the pager records them and telephoning the relevant client to give them advice. If the problem cannot be solved over the phone and it is urgent (for example, the air-conditioning system in a hospital has broken down), the engineer will have to go to the client. Because of the breadth of ABC's market, the job also involves a good deal of overseas travel. The service maintenance department is considered to be one of ABC's selling points, as the cover provided by the team enables the company to promise all their customers a five-year warranty. Recently it has also been necessary to provide cover for the overseas branches of ABC – there has been a secondment to the Norwegian office for the last six months and Japan have also requested that a UK engineer go out there to work until they can recruit to their several vacancies. There are twenty engineers in the service maintenance department, as well as the manager and his secretary. All but one are male.

It was only when Eric Evans (the service maintenance manager) realised that he had recruited no less than five engineers in the previous two years, three of whom had left after a very short time and whom he was still trying to replace, that he began to perceive that all was not necessarily well among his team. When he thought back to those who had left he realised that all of them had gone to jobs elsewhere in the local area. In other words, his staff were leaving because they were dissatisfied with the company, not because they were moving away, or retiring, or any of the other reasons why people leave employment.

'Well, it can't be the money,' he thought. 'Those guys get a good whack out of this place plus a company car. Other places don't pay so well or offer cars. It must be something else. I'll have to have a chat with them, see what's going on.' At this point, Eric was interrupted in his reverie by his secretary reminding him of his 10 a.m. meeting with the company directors. He made a note to himself to look into the matter before gathering up his files and leaving the office.

In fact Eric didn't need reminding of the problem he had been considering that morning. He returned from the meeting in the early afternoon to be told that a local customer had called, furious because they had had to wait three hours for an engineer to repair their system. The client's offices had grown so hot in the meantime that they had had to let their staff go home and by the time the system was fixed it wasn't worth calling everyone back in. So they had ended up losing a day's work and were blaming it on ABC.

'But I don't understand!' he protested to Carl Peters, who had the unfortunate task of breaking the news to him. 'We've got enough people in, haven't we? Why were they kept waiting?'

'Well, we've got four people sick, Eric, and there's about five others abroad. We need five people to stay here and cover the phones, so that only leaves three to go out to calls. And it's been manic these last couple of days 'cos the weather's so hot. Martin had to drive from here to Glasgow and then on to Manchester yesterday to answer urgent calls. The call from Barnes Brothers just got shoved to the back of the queue. It's not our . . . .'

Eric broke into Carl's explanation: 'Four people sick! Have they called in? I haven't been told about this, otherwise I would have tried to arrange cover.'

'I dunno if they called in or not, Eric, but I know we've been down on staff constantly recently. There's always someone off, and it's usually two or three.'

'Right, OK, Carl, I'll ring the customer and eat humble pie. But I want a meeting with the lads tomorrow, 9 a.m. sharp, and we're going to get to the bottom of this. Can you let them know for me?'

At 9 a.m. the following morning, the service maintenance staff began to gather in Eric's office. Eric opened the meeting by telling them that he was concerned about morale in the department and would appreciate any comments they had regarding their own job satisfaction. At first they were reluctant to say anything but Paul Feather, one of the longest-serving members of staff, eventually got the ball rolling: 'Well, what I hate is never knowing what we're up to, Eric. I'm getting sick of being called out to places, then having to work really late 'cos the client's left it till the last minute to call. The times I've driven back from London at 2.00 in the morning – and I've got a sick wife, as you well know.'

'Yeah, and we never know how far ahead we can plan our social lives and stuff,' broke in Carl. 'The only way to ensure not being called away is to book holiday time. I remember when I was due to go and see my parents and you wanted me to fly off somewhere – I'd had the trip arranged for months and suddenly find out the day before that I'm supposed to be going to Switzerland. Then when I wouldn't go, you got really mad with me.'

'Speaking of being called out, I got a page the other night at 3.30 a.m. I didn't turn my pager off 'cos I was on again at 6.00 and one of the customers thought he'd chance his arm. So I got woken up in the middle of the night. It's not on – they know when they can get hold of us, and to leave a message if it's an emergency. This wasn't even urgent – he was just working late and got a bit warm. It could have easily waited till the morning,' added Paul.

'Plus the salespeople always make rash promises to the customer – they say they can get the system installed in such and such a time. They never consult us – they just come back and dump the order sheet on us.' This came from George Browne, who went on: 'And what's more, the job's actually quite dull, you know. I know it's good money and everything, and we get a car, but we always go to the same companies, here and abroad. Also there's very little opportunity to train on any system that you don't already know. So you end up doing the same work, the same installations and the same repairs, week in, week out. The only training that seems to go on here is for people who come in from outside! Another thing – if we were trained in other systems we could fill in for people more easily.'

At this point Robert Fields was heard to mutter, 'Yeah and the car thing . . . that director who bought the flash new company car for herself, fifty grand or whatever it was, when we just got told we had ten grand to spend on our cars, take it or leave it. She doesn't have to do thirty thousand miles a year for the company, it's just for posing.' Everyone murmured in agreement.

'I'm with George on the stuff about the training – I've not been here long and I'm bored of the same round of places. There's something else too,' said Sarah Jones. 'It's true about the money being all right but if you look at other departments, they're getting more money than we are, even if you take the car into account. Look at pre-sales – they're all on at least five grand more than we are. The only way to get a rise around here is to threaten to leave, like Carl did that time.'

'Now that's not fair,' Eric burst out. 'What about appraisals? You get an automatic increment after your appraisal, if it's been OK.'

'I can't remember the last appraisal I had – and anyway, when I did have it you'd forgotten to fill out the form, so it wasn't much of a discussion. You just sat there and told me I was doing OK and not to worry, you'd do the form soon. Anyway, those increments are only in line with inflation, so we'd kind of expect them anyway – they're not really because you're working hard or whatever. We haven't had a proper performance-related rise in three years,' Sarah replied.

'I never even got my increment after my last appraisal – you sent me a letter saying I hadn't been awarded one, but you never said why! You said at my appraisal that my work was good and you were pleased with me, so I was expecting one,' chipped in Colin Sanderson, who hadn't spoken up until then.

'And you said that I had to improve, and then I got an increment anyway – which I thought was kind of daft. Then you sent me to America to do that really big job, booked me away for a week and totally ignored me when I said I'd never get it done in that time. You had to send John Carter out to help me,' Carl commented.

There was a brief silence as Eric took all this information in, and the group wondered if they'd gone too far. When he didn't say anything for some minutes, George leapt in to fill the gap: 'Can I just say something else? It's too bloody hot in here most days in the summer 'cos of the great big glass windows – they let all the heat in and then when you open them, papers go everywhere. For an air-conditioning company, we've got rubbish ventilation up here. I had to go home early last week because it was so warm – you just can't concentrate.'

Finally Eric spoke: 'OK, OK, I get the gist. There's quite a lot here needs dealing with, it seems. Can we just summarise what the grievances are and I'll make a point of trying to deal with them as soon as I can.' Eric was starting to feel somewhat beleaguered. He had had no idea that things had got this bad. He made a resolve to act as fast as he could – it seemed that he would have no staff left at all if he did not.

Activity brief

1 There are some obvious indicators of lack of job satisfaction in the text. What are they? What other factors should managers look for which may demonstrate that morale is low?

2 At the meeting the staff are encouraged to air their grievances. Summarise the points they raise.

3 Looking at the summary from the previous question, how do Mumford's five contractual areas (see Mullins, p. 631) help to explain current problems?

4 How could ABC use job design to help them reduce the causes and effects of stress? (See Mullins, pp. 670–4.)

5 What actions would you recommend Eric to take to improve employee commitment at ABC? (See Mullins, pp. 651–3.)

Case study provided by Joanna Brewis, University of Portsmouth.

ACTIVITY 1

1 Most of us belong to a number of organisations (college, firm, church, etc.) and a number of groups (family, hockey team, drama society, etc.). Make a list of yours and alongside it try to sum up in a short phrase or sentence why each one is important to you. Do this part of the exercise before reading on.

2 One of the difficulties in theorising about attitudes is their close connection with values and interests. Going through your list now, which of the three are you stressing each time?

3 Considering next the factors that affect your level of satisfaction at work in particular, which of the following do you want from it?

autonomy
authority
variety
status
money
stimulus
challenge
to be creative
excitement
to be useful
social interaction

Do your answers change if you ask the question of any unpaid or voluntary work you have or intend to do? Do they change again if you think in terms of a temporary post only?

ACTIVITY 2: Quality of Working Life (QWL)

'As a philosophy, QWL views people as "assets" capable of contributing skills, knowledge, experience and commitment, rather than as "costs" that are merely extensions of the production process. It argues that encouraging involvement and providing the environment in which it can flourish, produces tangible rewards for both individuals and organisations.'

(ACAS advisory booklet No. 16, p. 7)

In a small group discuss the sorts of ethical dilemmas which might confront a manager adhering to a QWL philosophy.

Source: Adapted from Beardwell, I. and Holden, L. (1997), *Human Resource Management: A Contemporary Perspective*, 2nd edition, FT Pitman Publishing.

DEBATE

'Offering counselling for people who are stressed out because of organisational pressure is an insult to their intelligence.'

Starting points

For

- Organisations which offer counselling are simply trying to avoid their real responsibility – to stop putting so much pressure on people that they need help from counsellors.
- Offering counselling makes 'guilty' managers feel virtuous.
- Counselling identifies 'needy' people – the ones who take up the offer.

Against

- Stress is cumulative and seldom derives simply and only from our work situations.
- Counselling can provide a simple and healthy solution for some people.
- Counselling can form one, very useful part of a complex overall strategy for managing pressure effectively.

Further reading

Cartwright, S. and Cooper, C. (1994), *No Hassle! Taking the Stress out of Work*, Century.

Cooper, C. *et al.* (1988), Living with Stress, Penguin.

ASSIGNMENT 1

Reducing the causes of stress

Consider what could be done within an organisation which you know well, to reduce levels of stress.

1 How can management make changes at an organisational level which help all of its employees to recognise the symptoms and causes of stress and ultimately to cope, or change the organisation?

2 What can individuals do to help themselves and their colleagues to deal with stress?

Write a two-part report on (a) reducing the causes of stress and (b) coping with the symptoms of stress at the organisational/individual levels.

ASSIGNMENT 2

The successful executive

This is the story of Lynette Thompson, who runs a very successful business. She started out as a self-employed European Community legislation consultant. For the first three years, Lynette balanced the tasks of designing and running consultancy programmes for a select group of clients.

As time progressed, Lynette's workload became increasingly difficult to cope with. She travelled extensively in the UK and Europe providing consultancy programmes for her client companies. At the same time, she was her own bookkeeper, administrative assistant and researcher.

Gradually, Lynette's workload increased to such an extent that she found herself working seven days a week. She felt she could cope as her office was in her home. However, Lynette's constant fear was that she would become ill, and not be able to work. She also had a home, a husband, a teenager and two dogs to think about and make time for.

Lynette did not feel her earnings justified the hire of a secretarial assistant or a researcher, so she continued to work an increasing number of hours; she also increased her travelling. She felt compelled to take on more challenging consultancy programmes in order to make a name for herself, and to grow and develop professionally.

Lynette believed in networking as a way to increase business. She joined two successful international business organisations. Soon, she found herself on a subcommittee, with more responsibilities. She agreed to run a monthly advisory programme without a fee. This was a good networking strategy, but it increased the pressures on her already overloaded life.

Adding further pressure, in the third year of running her own business Lynette began to publish a monthly newsletter for her clients. This provided a useful complement to her consultancy activities, and kept her clients abreast of new developments in the labyrinth of European legislation.

In year four, Lynette began to feel the physical repercussions of her activities. More fatigued than usual, one day she found herself almost unable to get out of bed. This frightened her, particularly as she prided herself on eating well, staying healthy and keeping fit.

She adhered to a daily routine of fitness. Even so, Lynette often rose at 4.30 a.m. to fly to a European destination, and worked with her clients until late each evening. She did try to make an hour for herself every evening prior to dinner, and kept up a regular routine of personal and professional reading.

What had gone wrong? Lynette began a round of visits to her doctor and to the local hospital for tests. The tests showed that she was extremely fit – great blood pressure, no cholesterol problems, good heart, and so forth. Yet she was beginning to feel more and more ill. She began to have regular headaches, lose her naturally clear complexion, suffer weight loss, and find her energy level severely depleted.

Despite these signals, Lynette felt she had no choice but to persevere with her strenuous programme. One day, she found she could not go on. Her system collapsed. Out of sheer desperation, Lynette went to an acupuncturist and a naturopathic doctor. This doctor discovered the problem. He diagnosed an infection of the liver and the malfunction of her adrenal glands – the accelerator pedal of the body. This came as a great shock to Lynette, who couldn't understand how this could have happened to her. She had no choice but to cancel most of her consultancy engagements for the next two-month period, and began a strict dietary regime, taking recommended minerals, vitamins and medicines to eliminate the liver and adrenal problems.

Gradually, over a period of six months, Lynette began to recover her mental and physical well-being. However, her illness caused her to look seriously at her working life. She realised that some radical changes were necessary. But where to begin?

1 What could Lynette have done differently to deal with her pressures, and cope with the immense stress she was under?

2 What would you recommend she do, once she reached the point of having to submit to her illness and cancel some of her work?

3 What role do you think gender played in the case of Lynette? Could that have been one of the issues which drove her on?

Further reading

Brewer, K. C. (1991), *The Stress Management Handbook*, National Press Publications.

Froggatt, H. and Stamp, P. (1991), *Managing Pressure at Work*, BBC Books.

Hamilton, R. (1993), *Mentoring*, The Industrial Society.

Motivation cassettes based on the book by P. Makin and P. Lindley (1994), *Positive Stress Management*, Kogan Page.

Mullins, L. J. (1999), *Management and Organisational Behaviour*, 5th edn, FT Pitman Publishing, 474–6, 637–40.

Scott, D. (1993), *Stress That Motivates*, Kogan Page.

Shea, G. F. (1992), *Mentoring*, Kogan Page.

Contributed by Sunny Stout, Sun Training.

APPLICATION 1

A salary can't buy happiness

FT

The American researcher Fred Herzberg was the first to propose that employees' salaries were a major cause of dissatisfaction but not necessarily a cause of satisfaction. Writing in the 1950s he introduced the concept that what makes people happy about their work and what makes them unhappy are in fact different things.

What makes them happy or satisfied, he proposed, were characteristics of the job that met what he called their motivator needs, such as a desire for achievement, recognition, interesting work, power of self and/or others and promotion.

What makes them unhappy arises from what he called hygiene needs related to the context in which the work was done.

These 'dissatisfiers' are company administration, the boss, salaries, peers and the physical working conditions.

This theory became part of the management training package for millions of managers around the world. It had all the appeal of any good theory: it was practical, simple, memorable and consistent with the gut feel of many managers. Unfortunately, over the next 40 years no other researcher was able to replicate Herzberg's findings with such clarity.

Today most researchers would agree that what excites people and what irritates them about their jobs are often different factors, but these may reflect personality differences as much as they reflect either the work or the job context.

However, it is on salary, particularly, that Herzberg's neatness lets us down. Salary is not just a contextual factor. It also establishes our place in the scheme of things. It affects our sense of equity, impinges on our sense of personal worth, our self-esteem. Salary crosses the barrier from hygiene to motivator need and casts serious doubt on the theory.

No one would argue today that salary is not a motivator. There are people for whom money is an important motivator. They are attracted to jobs which pay a fee every time the person performs and are found in the professions, commission-based sales jobs and in personal services.

But for the majority of reasonably paid employees salary is not a prime motivator on a day-to-day basis. Few people get up each morning and say 'I am off to get my money today'. For most of us other factors – challenging work, variety, control over our work, recognition, power, autonomy – are the prime motivators day to day. (This does not exclude the power of money in large lumps. Everyone has a price and, given enough money, you can motivate your employees for short terms with large lumps.)

Financial rewards are one of the most complex areas of managing. It is well nigh impossible to get it right. We preach equity and fairness, yet most reward systems are blatantly unfair. We preach transparency and openness, yet there are anomalies which persist.

Our reaction to these anomalies is a periodic shuffle in our basis of assessment. On each occasion we tend to think that this time we will get it right but the very nature of incentives to work are so idiosyncratic that, whatever your system, it will bug some people a lot of the time.

Over the last 40 years there have been at least four management movements which have attempted to fix the anomalies. Two of these – management by objectives in the 1970s and 1980s, and performance related pay from the 1990s – became universal cults.

Bureaucratic information-based reward systems are now a booming business. Yet their underlying assumption is false. They are based on a belief that organisations can be administered scientifically – that inequities and emotions can be squeezed out to provide a rational scheme.

But organisations are about people who have emotions: love, hate, pleasure, pain, satisfaction and dissatisfaction are essential ingredients of life at work. And if we are successful in producing a totally rational reward system then we would be in danger of squeezing out the creativity and innovation that companies need to survive.

So what might you do with your reward system? A middle path between an obsessive belief in a rational scheme and the idiosyncratic effects of labour market forces would be sensible. If your people are unhappy, you should concede that salary systems are imperfect – that they are rarely fair and that transparency is not guaranteed to improve them.

Resist the temptation to buy a bureaucratic, information-based system that will eliminate some of the very behaviour your company needs to survive. Do establish performance criteria because measured performance does outstrip unmeasured performance. But remain flexible.

Do not concentrate on salary as a major reward. Most of your people come to work to satisfy other motives. Use other rewards such as recognition, having fun, interesting work, and new challenges to excite your people. Finally, from time to time make such adjustments to your salary scales as market intelligence and common sense would dictate. After 40 years of trying, we should admit there is no better strategy.

Source: Professor John W. Hunt, *Financial Times*, 11 March 1998.

APPLICATION 2

Performance pay takes off . . . but mainly spurs on high achievers

FT

The use of performance-related pay (PRP) in large companies is on the increase, although most companies that use it believe its greatest impact is in motivating their top people, rather than poor or average performers. A survey published by the Institute of Personnel and Development looked at 1158 responses from public and private sector organisations. The findings appear to contradict those who say PRP is in decline, says the IPD. 'Contrary to popular belief that organisations are becoming disillusioned with performance pay and with IPRP (individual performance-related pay) schemes in particular, the results strongly suggest that the use of all forms of performance pay is growing.'

IPRP is still largely confined to managers, but there are signs that it is growing among other employees, with a quarter of the employers using such arrangements outside management.

A closer look at the figures, however, reveals that while the most common approach is to adopt IPRP, other forms of performance pay – such as team-based pay and skill- or competency-based pay – are growing more rapidly, albeit from a smaller base.

The survey asked questions to gauge the impact of IPRP. More than half of employers questioned believed the schemes rewarded people in a way that the employees thought was fair, although some 14 per cent of the respondents reported that employees thought the schemes were less fair than what had gone before. Some 13 per cent of employers said that IPRP had led to a deterioration of teamworking.

A fifth of those questioned said they believed that IPRP had improved the work of top performers. 'These high performers may be precisely the type of employees that many organisations wish to nurture and develop,' says the study. Only 4 per cent thought it had had a great impact on average or poor performers. A larger number thought it had resulted in a small improvement in these groups.

The average value of performance pay awards was 10 per cent of base pay, while the median was 4 per cent. This suggests that, while a minority were receiving big pay awards, the majority of employees were receiving much smaller bonuses.

Ten employers out of those surveyed awarded at least 100 per cent of base pay, while three-quarters thought their awards too small to motivate people. Overall, 74 per cent said IPRP encouraged employees to focus on company objectives.

Source: Richard Donkin, *Financial Times*, 5 February 1998.

APPLICATION 3

His master's voice

FT

The UK workplace is widely believed to have changed beyond recognition over the past 10 years as a result of technological innovation and the need to compete in the global economy.

This is said to have transformed relations in the workplace by giving employees more control over their work and increasing their participation in company decision-making. As a result, we are supposed to have seen an end to the more traditional and allegedly oppressive methods based on scientific management and the production assembly line.

The trouble with much of this familiar picture is that it is based more on anecdote than on empirical evidence. A massive study of the UK employment relationship challenges this comforting view with an impressive analysis of what is actually happening in the workplace. It suggests that behind the much acclaimed modernisation of employment relationships lies a much more familiar pattern of workplace behaviour shaped by the attempted reassertion of managerial power.

The co-authors, led by Duncan Gallie at Nuffield College, Oxford, produce some startling findings about UK employees. They point to what they see as an impressive improvement in workplace skill levels. As many as 63 per cent of all employees surveyed said the skills required in their particular job had increased over a five-year period while only 9 per cent said they had suffered from deskilling.

As many as 65 per cent of employees reported an increase in their responsibility at work, mainly as a result of those improved skills. The authors point to the 'spectacular' spread of new technologies so the proportion of employees using automated or computerised equipment rose from 39 per cent to 56 per cent.

They conclude that the second half of the 1980s and the first half of the 1990s 'saw a marked decentralisation of decision-making within organisations' with a resulting loss of middle-level management. There was also evidence that 'work has grown intrinsically more satisfying and less degrading'. But the survey also found upskilling had brought 'ambivalent' consequences for the quality of working life because of intensified work pressures.

Moreover, the greater 'task discretion' required from employees has not brought a greater willingness by employers to trust their employees more and give them more autonomy and participation. It seems there has been no significant shift in power from managers to employees.

On the contrary, the authors claim that the UK has seen the intensification by management of 'extensive and expanding control systems', helped by the spread of advanced technologies. 'Almost everyone is supervised and four in ten supervise others to some degree,' they argue. While managers and professional staff enjoy increased personal discretion at work, 'more manual workers are experiencing tighter supervision than before', with 30 per cent having their pay linked to work-pacing and target-setting and with appraisal and merit pay covering 40 per cent of them.

This conclusion is strengthened by the study's other findings on the limited degree of employee participation and representation. Only 32 per cent of employees said they had 'any significant degree of say over changes in work organisation' with half saying they could exercise no influence at all. The study claims 'the capacity of employees to affect their employment conditions appears to have diminished since the mid-1980s, although they may have become better informed about organisational activities'.

The lack of an employee voice in the UK workplace is stark. Only 22 per cent of workers said they had a consultative works council or similar structure in their establishment and a majority believed such a body enjoyed little or no influence.

The study found consultation committees were strongest where trade unions were recognised. As in Japan and the US, so in the UK a correlation exists between high worker participation levels and innovative workplaces.

But Mr Gallie and his colleagues suggest that in a period of rapid technological change and competitive pressure, 'UK employers have very widely failed to carry through the institutional reforms in their organisations that would have enhanced co-operation in employment relationships and led to a higher level of social integration of their employees'.

The lack of a worker voice may help to explain the alarmingly low levels of commitment among workers to the company that employs them. The study found only 8 per cent said their own values and those of their organisation were 'very similar', while a mere 14 per cent said they were 'proud' of their organisation and only 30 per cent felt any loyalty towards it. This contrasts with 28 per cent saying they 'felt sufficiently attached to their organisation to say they would turn down another job if it offered higher pay'.

The study provides evidence of the increase in employment insecurity, especially for young male manual workers, which has grown markedly since the 1970s. But gender differences are less obvious when it comes to the experience of being without work. The authors point out once a man or a woman becomes unemployed it tends to lead to further spells of unemployment as his or her job prospects become more problematic.

But on the other hand, there is no evidence the work ethic is dying out. Going to work in a society dominated by fragile family values provides an increasing number of people with 'a basis for personal autonomy', says the study. Workers work not merely to earn money. They are more concerned with employment security, job interest and the quality of their personal relations with management.

The main conclusion, however, is rather bleak. The quality of employment may have improved for those in higher and intermediate skilled employment, but the brunt of change has hit the non-skilled manual worker hard. 'The UK employment structure still remains fundamentally divided by class', argues the report. It warns that this could lead to a resurgence of workplace conflict. Apparently there are few signs that a new model of the employment relationship is becoming more widespread in the UK.

Source: *Financial Times*, 1 July 1998.

19 Human Resource Management

CASE STUDY

ACT Ltd

ACT Ltd is a thriving electronics manufacturing and distribution company. Set up ten years ago, the company produces components for the PC assembly market. Growth has been rapid, with a lot of new business won on a reputation for product innovation and high quality. The company currently employs 150 people at a greenfield site in the south of England. It is now planning a further expansion of its facility to take advantage of the new markets which are opening up in Europe and beyond.

Although the company is a success, the managing director is feeling uneasy about the way the company is managing its human resources. There are two areas that give him cause for concern. The first involves the way non-technical training is organised.

Training organisation

The company has always invested heavily in training its workforce. Indeed, the managing director is convinced that ACT's reputation is mainly attributable to its highly trained workforce. In the past, training was confined to technical areas. However, with the expansion of the company, it has been necessary to develop the training organisation to provide additional skills in areas such as administration, finance, marketing, team-building and communication.

There is no Personnel Department. Training has always been left to the line managers to organise. With technical training, this was never a problem. It was always well organised, consisting of mainly on-the-job training and day release courses provided by the local college. However, now that training is extending into non-technical areas, the managing director is having increasing doubts about the effectiveness of the training organisation within his company. A recent incident serves to highlight this.

Walking through the production department a few weeks ago, the managing director spotted a memo and a list on the notice board. It was written by the department manager and alongside the memo was a 'glossy' brochure from an external training consultancy advertising a wide range of administration and supervisory courses. The memo invited staff to study the brochure, select a course they felt would benefit them and add their name to the list.

The managing director studied the list. Many of the courses that people were applying for appeared to be peripheral to the needs of their job. Then he realised that if everybody who was applying actually went on the courses, a serious hole would appear in the company's training budget! He removed the memo and brochure and made a mental note to have a word with the manager concerned.

As he walked back to his office, he reflected upon the incident. There was no doubt in his mind that something would have to be done to ensure that training was organised in a more structured and professional way. The company had to ensure that it obtained a return on its training investment.

The managing director's second concern is with the capabilities of his management team.

The calibre of the management team

The management team consists of three board directors, four departmental managers, and four supervisory staff (see Fig. 19.1).

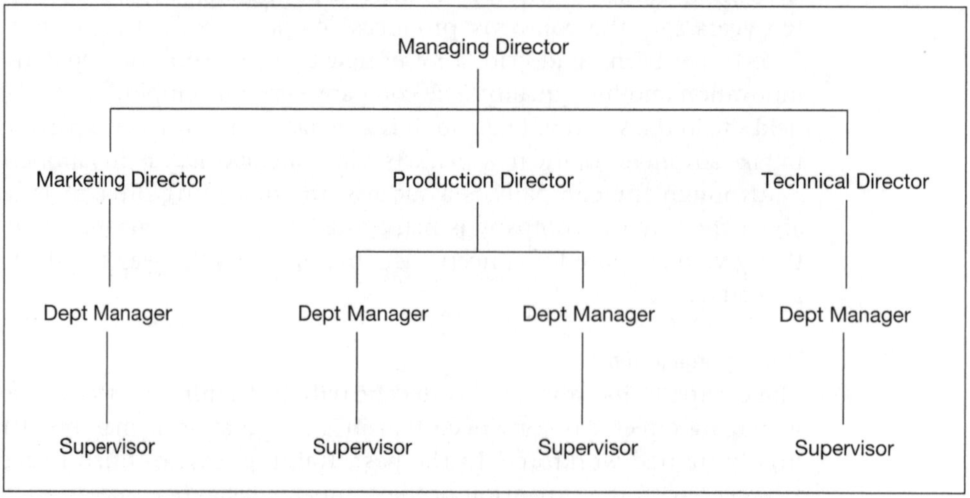

Fig. 19.1 ACT Ltd organisation chart

With the company's rapid expansion, emphasis has always been on product design, quality, achieving high levels of output and maximising sales. What has now become obvious is that in the rush to achieve business growth, the development of core management skills has been neglected. Without these skills, the managing director fears there will be a real threat to the future survival and success of the company. A number of examples highlight the managing director's concern.

In the boardroom, none of the directors seems capable of discussing and dealing with strategic issues. The other day the managing director wanted to discuss the exploration of new markets in Europe and the sourcing of components from the Far East to reduce production costs. But the meeting was taken up with a discussion about the technical details of the latest semiconductor design!

The departmental managers are all good engineers and are respected by the workforce for their technical capabilities. All of them have grown with the company and promotion has largely rested on the possession of sound technical skills.

But the department managers seem unwilling to delegate and 'step back' from the day-to-day running of the company. The other day, the managing director heard one of the supervisors complaining about the level of interference she was experiencing from her department manager. 'He won't keep his nose out. He takes all the decisions so I just let him get on with it.' He has also noticed that some of the supervisors are too 'laid back' with the workforce while others seem to be managing through a culture of fear and intimidation.

The managing director has tried to communicate his concerns at management team meetings but his managers keep avoiding the issue. When he presses them, they become defensive and withdrawn. The managing director is approaching retirement age and wants to resolve these issues before he retires.

Activity brief

Imagine you are a firm of management consultants that has been approached by the managing director for advice and guidance. You have been asked to review and make recommendations that will improve the way training is organised and develop managers to achieve organisational goals.

Source: Adapted from Beardwell, I. and Holden, L. (1997), *Human Resource Management: A Contemporary Perspective*, 2nd edition, FT Pitman Publishing.

ACTIVITY

HUMAN RESOURCES MANAGER – EUROPE

The position will support a sales, marketing and support organisation in several European countries and will be based in the Thames Valley area.

Key responsibilities include salary and benefit surveys; recommendations; administration; recruiting and staffing; employee relations; performance improvement planning; training needs analyses and employee communications. The candidate will be responsible for ensuring consistent human resource policies and procedures and translating corporate programmes to meet local needs.

To fill this challenging position we are looking for a high profile candidate with the following qualifications:

- University degree preferably in psychology or business or related, with postgraduate courses in human resources.
- Ten years' experience in progressive personnel functions with positions in US-based companies; experience in field generalist roles.
- High-tech background.
- Expertise in compensation, benefits, recruiting, staffing, employee relations, training and organisation development.
- Fluency in English, French and German. Spanish and Italian an asset.

The company offers excellent social benefits and pleasant working conditions in an international environment.

If you fulfil these requirements do not hesitate to send your résumé to Bob Smith who will treat your file confidentially.

PERSONNEL OFFICER

UK Head Office and a number of Sales Divisions are moving to new headquarters in Thames Valley in September this year. In anticipation of this move we need a Personnel Officer to join us now.

Located at our new Head Office you will be responsible initially for recruiting local staff. During the period between appointment and September it will be necessary to spend some time in existing company locations. After the move the position will involve providing support to several Divisions. Reporting to the Personnel Manager, the areas of responsibility will include: recruitment; advice on procedures and conditions of employment; personnel administration and training.

Applicants should be graduates with a minimum of three years' experience in a general Personnel Department. Preference will be given to someone studying for, or having completed, a recognised course in Personel Management.

Excellent salary is provided, together with good Company benefits including pension scheme, BUPA, and free life assurance.

1 The two advertisements reproduced here are separated by 15 years and have been selected from commonly available advertising sources for personnel posts. One post was advertised in 1983 and one in 1998. Analyse the respective employment philosophies behind the two adverts and decide which advert appeared first. What are the significant factors that you would point to in comparing and contrasting these adverts?

2 If you have organisational experience (either in your current or previous occupation, or as a result of work placement in your course) draw up an advertisement for your job in that organisation to reflect that organisation's current needs and employment philosophy. Would your advert differ from one that might have been drawn up in the 1980s? Indicate the major differences that might be made.

3 If you *do not* yet have organisational experience, select a job known to you, of a relative or a friend, and draw up an advert for it based on the issues that are discussed in Chapter 20 of Mullins. What issues would you emphasise in setting out the requirements for employees?

Source: Adapted from Beardwell, I. and Holden, L. (1997), *Human Resource Management: A Contemporary Perspective*, 2nd edition, FT Pitman Publishing.

DEBATE

'Having a separate HR department leads poor line managers to abdicate responsibility for their people.'

Starting points

For

- Poor managers may prefer to get rid of difficult and messy 'people problems' so that they can concentrate on what they see as important technical and financial issues.
- By trying to be helpful HR staff can set up a feeling of dependency on their service to sort out personnel problems, rather than managers accepting their own role and responsibility to staff.

Against

- HR staff do not take on day-to-day responsibility for all staff but they can answer specialist queries.
- HR can support and develop the competence of line managers by offering behind-the-scenes advice on staff issues.
- HR have other important and separate areas of staff activities which support line managers in the strategic use of staff as a resource.

Further reading

Graham, H. T. and Bennett, R. (1998), *Human Resource Management*, FT Pitman Publishing.

Hall, L. and Torrington, D. (1998), *The Human Resource Function*, FT Pitman Publishing.

ASSIGNMENT

Write a briefing paper of no more than 800 words to be presented to the board of your own, or an imaginary organisation in which you present a cost/benefit analysis of implementing a large-scale organisational improvement programme such as Investors in People.

Costs should be reviewed in terms of all the resources which may be used and not simply monetary estimates of such a policy.

Benefits should also include analysis of the potential personal and business growth and development for those involved.

Consider carefully what sort of data you might collect for such an analysis – although in this case you can use estimated figures for your presentation where necessary.

APPLICATION

Does the human resource department have a future? FT

If the late spaghetti western producer Sergio Leone had a made a feature film about personnel management – and the likelihood of that was about as remote as the planet Pluto – he would probably have billed it *The Job With No Name*. Its sheer fuzziness and lack of hard performance measures are a constant source of frustration in management circles, as well as provoking suspicions among employees and scepticism among academics. The Trades Union Congress, for instance, recently wrestled with the meaning of human resource management – as personnel is sometimes called – describing it as a 'slippery concept' and questioning the motive behind some HRM practices.

The formation earlier this year of the Institute of Personnel and Development – the professional body combining the old Institute of Personnel Management and the Institute of Training and Development – came at a time when some companies were dispensing with their personnel departments completely, choosing to assign the responsibility to line managers. Indeed at this week's annual conference of the IPD in Harrogate, which finishes today, Sir Brian Pitman, the chief executive of Lloyds Bank, told delegates that removing the central personnel department at Lloyds was one of the most effective changes the bank had made.

He said: 'Line managers now understand the pains of some of the decisions that personnel has to take.'

However, in spite of this, there seems a sense among delegates that their time has finally come.

Mike Bett, the IPD president, summed it up by pointing to a growing recognition that the survival and success of organisations will increasingly depend on their ability to build highly skilled workforces and to release the full potential of employees. 'There should be a professional personnel and development specialist on all top management teams: in the boardroom and on the executive committees,' he suggested, adding that personnel should be involved in developing front-line boardroom strategy.

Bett's confidence in a rosy future, however, is not universally shared. Earlier in the year a team headed by David Metcalf at the London School of Economics described personnel specialists as 'big hat, no cattle' with lots of pretensions and few results. Its research suggested that the presence of a personnel manager was associated with poorer employee relations.

Drawing from the same body of research as that used by the LSE team – the third Workplace Industrial Relations Survey – but taking a different definition of personnel, David Guest, of Birkbeck College in London, and Kim Hoque, a researcher at the LSE, presented a more positive picture. Their study concluded that HRM was producing superior performances in the workplace. The contribution of personnel specialists, said Guest and Hoque, had been difficult to identify because they often worked by exercising influence in partnership with line managers. This sometimes created ambiguity about personnel responsibilities so that when things went wrong it proved expedient to blame the personnel specialist.

Personnel's influence on strategy is equally a subject of debate and contradictory research. Guest and Hoque quote earlier research which suggests that personnel departments often have insufficient responsibility to influence human resource strategy. They noted another study, however, by Cranfield School of Management and Price Waterhouse International, which found that 43 per cent of personnel directors claim to be involved in the formulation of corporate strategy from the outset.

The IPD's response to personnel's uncertain role has been to place a strong emphasis on sifting good practice from bad in an effort to position itself, in Bett's words, as 'the pre-eminent professional body influencing and improving the quality, thinking and practice of people management and development'.

One the other hand the IPD is promising to extend training and support for often hard-pressed personnel professionals, on the other it is wedging open the door, making itself accessible as a consultancy service and provider of books, reports, seminars and conferences.

Conscious of the jargon, Geoff Armstrong, the IPD's director general, has also committed the institute to encouraging greater clarity of the personnel role. 'By removing jargon and barriers to understanding, we must spread the message that the development and management of people is much more than a series of fashionable programmes,' he said shortly after the formation of the institute. He believes personnel is 'a systematically learnable discipline, with a wide range of explicit competencies which need to be applied appropriately by everyone who has responsibility for other people'.

The IPD has warned against what Armstrong calls the promotion by gurus of 'the wonders of human resource management' at the expense of collectivism, industrial relations and some personnel procedures. 'Performance management, single status and individually tailored payment packages are presented as the new snake oil which can achieve miracles anywhere', he says. 'Such dogma is misleading and dangerous.

'Useful tools have been packaged up under the banner of human resource management and sold as panaceas, to be applied at any time and place. Without proper regard for the organisation's established culture and particular needs, most such flavours of the month prove deeply disappointing.'

The role of the personnel officer or manager, argues Armstrong, is to apply new practices where they are helpful and where they can be adapted to the specific needs of organisations. 'We have seen recently the immense problems which arise when performance-related pay, decentralised bargaining and commercial imperatives are imposed as though they, in isolation, can provide all the answers in our schools and hospitals,' he said.

He is distancing the IPD from the concept that HRM should be used as an exploitative tool of management. What lessons can be drawn from human resource management? Will it be a distinct learnable discipline at the cutting edge of organisational and employee development in the 21st century or will it fade away, remembered only as a brave attempt to bag up an elusive set of ideas? The challenge for personnel is to maintain its separate identity in the shifting emphasis within rapidly changing organisations. Leading that shift could ensure that it has a bright future.

Source: Richard Donkin, *Financial Times*, 28 October 1994.

20 Staffing the Organisation

CASE STUDY

Graduate training at Midcounty Hospital

Chris Evans joined Midcounty Hospital as a management trainee after completing a four-year Business Studies degree at Midshires University. When he was interviewed for the position, he was told by the interviewing panel that the hospital was still coming to terms with its successful application for Trust status and things were going to be a bit chaotic for a time. They then asked him how he would cope. Chris responded by telling the panel that he saw this as a development opportunity and went on to explain in detail how he intended to put into practice many of the skills he had learnt at university and during his industrial placement year.

Chris's response impressed the panel and he was offered a place on the graduate management training programme. The programme is administered by the Personnel Department. Trainees on the programme are rotated at six-monthly intervals through the main administration departments where they gain knowledge and experience of the complex systems and processes required to run the business side of the hospital. At the end of the training programme, trainees are assessed by their supervising managers, and those who are successful are appointed to permanent positions as junior managers within the hospital.

Chris began his training in the Finance Department, working as a deputy for Jeff Thomas, the Director of Finance. Jeff is a recent appointment to the hospital. He was headhunted from a major firm of City accountants three months ago. Although an experienced accountant, Jeff has had little management experience, apart from supervising a small office of secretaries and filing clerks in his old company. In fact he never really liked that side of the job and was lucky to have an experienced supervisor who dealt with 'the people problems'.

At the beginning things went well. After a brief welcome Jeff introduced Chris to Sarah, the supervisor in the Finance Office and told her to 'show Chris how things operate in the office'. Sarah was a bit taken aback. Jeff had not discussed this with her and she wasn't really prepared for Chris's arrival. However, as the department was putting together its first budget, an extra pair of hands was very welcome. After a bit of rearranging, she was able to spend a couple of hours with Chris explaining how the office worked and then gave him a job checking invoices. Chris set about the task with enthusiasm and two days later reported to Sarah that the job was complete. When Sarah checked the work, she found Chris had done a first-class job and he had discovered a number of errors for correction. Pleased with his initial performance, Sarah gave Chris another job working on the office computer inputting data onto the sales ledger file.

A couple of weeks later, Sarah noticed that Chris was becoming withdrawn and spending frequent periods looking out of the window. His work was becoming careless and when he completed a task he would not come and report to her. Instead, he would wander away from the office to see another trainee working on the other side of the hospital.

Sarah decided to speak to Jeff because Chris's behaviour was disrupting the work in the office. Although always busy, Jeff promised to speak to Chris and, after frequent reminders and eventually protests from Sarah, he called Chris into his office. Jeff explained what Sarah had told him and asked him what the problem was. Chris began by explaining that the work he was doing was routine and boring and not really making full use of his skills. At this point, Jeff interrupted him and pointed out rather frostily 'that in the financial world, everybody has to cope with routine, boring work'.

Chris left the office dejected and worried. He knew that he had to obtain a favourable report from Jeff and he hadn't got off to a very good start. When he arrived back at his desk Sarah presented him with a six-inch-thick computer print-out for checking.

Activity brief

1 What do you see as the main issues or problem areas?

2 What actions would you suggest might be taken to overcome the current difficulties?

3 How can problems be avoided in the future through changes to:

(a) the current recruiting process;
(b) the current induction process?

Source: Adapted from Beardwell, I. and Holden, L. (1997), *Human Resource Management: A Contemporary Perspective*, 2nd edition, FT Pitman Publishing.

ACTIVITY

Imagine that you are a regional personnel manager responsible for food retail stores in a growing regional economy. You have 36 stores in your area, ranging in size from small local grocery-style stores in which there are typically only about seven people employed, to large city centre superstores usually employing a store manager, two assistant managers, twelve line supervisors, 24 full-time employees working as check-out specialists, 45 full-time warehouse and stores staff, and 35 shop floor assistants.

Over the last six months you have noticed a steadily increasing demand for your products within the region as a whole. Your chain is not renowned for paying particularly high wages relative to other employers in the area.

Your managing director is looking to extend the opening hours of the city centre stores from 8 a.m. to 6 p.m. Monday to Saturday, as they are currently operating, to 6 a.m. to 10 p.m. Monday to Saturday.

1 Carefully draw up an initial HR plan for the organisation, indicating when and where staff are currently employed within the organisation, how long they are likely to stay in that position, and the future projections for staffing requirements. You can assume that within your region there are seven city centres in which you have two stores each. The remaining 22 stores are located in small to medium-sized peripheral towns.

2 Imagine now that you have been given the responsibility for designing an alternative method of planning and utilising human resources in line with the new opening hours. In your efforts to construct a new HR plan and utilisation process you recognise that there are a number of aspiring career-minded individuals within the organisation. How are you going to reconcile the organisation's desire to maintain high productivity and low cost together with individual employee requirements for progression and change?

3 How might the existence of a trade union affect the design and final outcome of the HR planning process?

Source: Adapted from Beardwell, I. and Holden, L. (1997), *Human Resource Management: A Contemporary Perspective*, 2nd edition, FT Pitman Publishing.

DEBATE

'An organisation's need to discover as much information as possible about prospective candidates so that sound selection decisions can be made outweighs an individual's right to privacy.'

Starting points

For

- Many jobs give people potential access to large resources – organisations must at least check how honest potential employees are.
- Interview situations offer temptations to lie or embellish the truth to enhance the candidate's chances of being recruited. If someone is honest at interview, they may be expected to be honest later.

Against

- The organisation is setting up the relationship in a culture of mistrust from the start.
- Privacy may be seen as a fundamental right which cannot be interfered with for the employer's benefit.
- Confidential information may be misfiled or misused and taken out of context.

Further reading

Graham, H. T. and Bennett, R. (1998), *Human Resource Management,* FT Pitman Publishing.

Walton, J. (1999), *Strategic Human Resource Development*, FT Pitman Publishing.

ASSIGNMENT

ShopCo is a nationwide high street retailer which recruits 100 graduates each year into trainee management positions. A recent decision has been taken to adopt a competency-based approach to recruitment of this group and the following 11 competencies have been identified as key indicators:

- analytical ability
- achievement motivation
- business awareness
- competitiveness
- effective decision-making
- drive and enthusiasm
- leadership
- oral communication
- written communication
- planning and organising
- interpersonal sensitivity.

1 Design an assessment centre which will provide at least two pieces of evidence for each competency outlined, detailing the exercises, timing and potential costs involved.

2 Outline the training requirements for assessors.

Source: Adapted from Beardwell, I. and Holden, L. (1997), *Human Resource Management: A Contemporary Perspective*, 2nd edition, FT Pitman Publishing.

APPLICATION

Multinational recruitment and selection

'During the start-up phase McDonald's drew upon the expertise of their employees from around the world. Initially there were 45 Western managers from various countries. This number was gradually reduced, so that by March 1991 only seven remained. All these managers were replaced by Soviets . . . .

[For crew members] Moscow McDonald's placed a single advertisement in Moscow newspapers soliciting applications. By the fall of 1989, when they started to hire workers they had received approximately 27 000 applications. This created a base for selecting the most energetic, motivated, intelligent and outgoing young men and women . . . following its practice widely used in its US restaurants, McDonald's decided to hire Moscow teenagers as crew members . . . people with no prior work experience. The idea was that it would be easier to instil McDonald's work habits and standards in people who knew no other way to work than to disabuse people of unacceptable work habits they had acquired in previous job' (Vikhanski and Puffer, 1993: 104).

'All the Directors at Nissan UK are British, except the finance director and deputy managing director. None of the managers are Japanese. Only a handful of Japanese are to be seen in the factory, mostly specialist engineers on temporary assignment to help iron out problems in the early stages of production of the new car' (Popham, 1992).

- Discuss the extent to which these examples correspond to the patterns of recruitment and selection associated with multinational corporations, i.e. ethnocentric, polycentric, regiocentric and geocentric.

References

Vikhanski, O. and Puffer, S. (1993), 'Management education and employee training at Moscow McDonald's', *European Management Journal*, 11 (1), 102–6.

Popham, P. (1992), 'Turning Japanese', *The Independent Magazine*, 12 September, 25–9.

Source: Adapted from Beardwell, I. and Holden, L. (1997), *Human Resource Management: A Contemporary Perspective*, 2nd edition, FT Pitman Publishing.

21 Management Control and Power

CASE STUDY

Brownloaf MacTaggart: Control and power in a management consultancy

Background

Brownloaf MacTaggart (BM) is the engineering consulting division of Watkins International, a large international firm of chartered accountants and management consultants.

Watkins was established as a chartered accountancy practice in 1893. Following decades of moderate growth it entered the management consultancy market in 1955 primarily as a 'spin-off' from audit and taxation work. In the following years this diversification proved to be profitable. What had started as a very small side-line activity has developed into a multidivisional management consultancy business employing in the UK alone some 700 people. Worldwide Watkins employs around 70 000 people through a network of firms and associate firms. The international firm has at least one office in most countries, and in the early 1990s has established new offices, particularly in Eastern Europe.

Watkins has endeavoured to grow primarily by acquisition and internal growth, but acquisition has been by far the most successful strategy, particularly in the 1980s when a software development company and BM were acquired. The firm now has five consultancy divisions in the UK covering information technology and software engineering; public sector management; financial services and treasury; leisure and retailing; and general engineering.

Brownloaf MacTaggart and Co. had started business in 1962 as a two-man partnership. Alex MacTaggart had been a successful production engineer, who had assiduously built up a long list of good contacts while working for blue-chip engineering companies. Duncan Brownloaf had been a successful engineering company salesman selling diverse products such as hydraulic pit props and mining pump equipment. The two men combined their undoubted strengths by taking small premises in Walsall, in the West Midlands. The business flourished and in 1977, now employing 20 people, two additional employees were admitted into partnership Heinrich Grubber, a German national, and William Smallpiece, a native of Shropshire.

Having admitted the two new partners, both founder partners were beginning to think of retirement. Duncan Brownloaf's health was failing and perhaps it was time for a change. In 1980 the company moved into bigger offices in the heart of Birmingham. One month after the move both Alex MacTaggart and Duncan Brownloaf were gone. It was suggested, although never proven, that both men suffered a 'palace coup' led by Heinrich Grubber.

The BM name was continued, after all the goodwill generated was considerable, and Heinrich Grubber and William Smallpiece set about planning for the future. For some time both partners worried about future strategy. Should they stay as a small stand-alone company or actively seek merger or acquisition? In 1988 the future direction was effectively settled. Watkins International had been looking to acquire an existing engineering consulting company. Merger negotiations were started with BM. These negotiations proved to be unusually protracted. Besides issues of partner capital, there were a number of issues surrounding managerial autonomy. Surprisingly, merger was nearly aborted by the insistence of the BM partners that young Eric Reliant be admitted into partnership. The partnership qualities of Eric were not immediately obvious to the senior partners of Watkins. A redemptive new age traveller, he tended to be seen as a disorganised blue sky thinker (or 'head in the clouds' visionary). Underneath, however, he was an artful schemer who had carefully flattered and fawned around the BM partners. What he lacked in technical engineering skills he more than made up for in low-life cunning.

With agreement reached on the admission to partnership of Eric Reliant, the way to merger was clear. Following the merger life appeared to continue much as before. BM continued to occupy the same premises, and to all intents and purposes operated as the same company. The BM name was retained for the sound commercial reasons of client goodwill and recognition, but now operated as the Brownloaf MacTaggart Division of Watkins International.

For eighteen months it was business as usual. The head office of Watkins was two miles away – in many respects out of sight and out of mind. Surprisingly Watkins did not rein in its new division. Procedures stayed more or less the same although the house style of reports to clients now had to conform to strict and elaborate Watkins requirements. The name of the overall firm had changed but the three partners continued to behave as if BM was an independent company. Heinrich Grubber was particularly proud of now being a partner in an international firm with all the apparent prestige and jet travel this implied.

The situation

Watkins International began to introduce firm-wide standardised practices early in 1990. First the time sheet recording system linked to client billing was changed from a manual system to a computerised system; later, standardised routines and forms were introduced for a number of administrative procedures, including holiday requests, staff appraisal, expenses and assignment control. All curricula vitae were placed into a computerised database linked to a proposal (or bidding for work) administration system. Updating of each curriculum vitae takes place after each consultancy assignment by the project manager completing the relevant form and sending it to the marketing department. Surprisingly, despite the relative sophistication of this system, matching the personnel with the requisite experience to project requirements is rather hit and miss, and depends more on an informal reward and punishment system (consultants who conform to the company culture are rewarded with interesting and prestigious assignments, which may help career advancement, while consultants who do not conform, for whatever reason, can be impeded by a succession of mediocre or difficult projects). BM employees began to recall nostalgically the 'old days' of BM before merger. Little did they know that more was yet to come.

In May 1991 Watkins secured three floors of a prestigious office block located adjacent to their head office in Birmingham. This office block consists of ten floors, four of which are occupied by a commercial bank and architectural practice. All Watkins' management consultancy divisions were located, in August and September 1991, on to one floor of the new office. Some 700 people (including all management consultancy support staff such as accounts, personnel and office management) are housed in a huge open plan office (although partners have individual, if small, offices). Individual consultants are assigned to a desk; each desk accommodates at least two consultants. If both consultants are working in the office, working space becomes a simple matter of early desk possession. All consultants are required to log on to a computerised staff locations system, which records contact telephone numbers and physical location for every hour of the working day. The same system acts as a message recording point when consultants are working outside the office.

The change from a relatively small office away from the main management consultancy to the big company environment came as quite a shock to several BM staff. For many staff there was a realisation, perhaps for the first time, that they were working in a large, rather impersonal, increasingly automated and tightly regulated environment. Above all they were expected to sink or swim in a fiercely competitive environment. There was also a realisation among staff, and indeed the BM partners, that although they may be well known in the engineering industry, within the Watkins empire they were minute in terms of size of turnover, number of projects, number of employees and profitability.

In 1992, in order to improve its competitive advantage in a stagnant management consultancy market (by being seen to conform to the highest service quality delivery standards) Watkins introduced a new quality management system, in an effort to secure BS 5750 Part 1 certification (the British Standards quality award). This new system required a complete rethink of the way consultancy assignments are managed, and introduced an essentially mechanistic approach to quality management based on an accountant's view of correct filing, record keeping and random assignment audits. Elaborate quality procedures became progressively refined during 1992 and became encapsulated in a beautifully printed Watkins Quality Manual. This manual was revised five times in as many months, and not surprisingly, many consultants became confused as the quality system appeared to be used by partners as part of a reward and punishment system; it is all too easy to miss completion of a form or a section of a form, neglect to obtain a partner's signature on a form or miss a quality plan review. The threat of periodic quality audits hangs over every consultant and, instead of using the quality management system as a means of improving services to clients, many consultants have become increasingly antagonistic towards it. The whole quality management system has become a bureaucratic nightmare instead of the aid to successful service quality and client satisfaction it should be.

Recruitment policy within Watkins is generally rudimentary but calculated. There is no shortage of well-qualified applicants. In normal economic conditions the Watkins management consultancy thrives on a constant inflow and outflow of bright young staff, although in the past three years recession has generally slowed down this movement such that Watkins has made around five per cent of its management consultants redundant since the end of 1992. The typical management consultant is aged around 30, with a few years' professional accounting or industrial experience. He (for the typical consultant tends to be male, although exceptionally gifted women are being recruited in greater numbers) generally has a first degree from a well-known university plus an MBA from one of the top three British business schools. Occasionally an accounting qualification has also been obtained. He or she is also highly motivated with an almost obsessional ambition to climb the career ladder. Because of this obsession with success, the typical consultant is prepared to work all hours of the day and night, and working at weekends in the office is thought to be particularly important, provided, of course, a partner is made aware of this fact.

Entrants to the BM Division are somewhat different to the typical Watkins consultant. A typical BM consultant is aged around 29 to 33; has a first degree in engineering, usually from one of three universities, plus membership of a professional engineering institution, such as the Institution of Mechanical Engineers. Possession of a higher degree is rare. As a consequence, the average BM consultant and partner are less well qualified than other Watkins consultants and partners. A climate of almost anti-intellectualism has therefore flourished in the BM Division, particularly since the merger with the Watkins empire, along the crude lines of 'we're only the oily engineers – ignorant but proud of it'.

As with the Watkins company as a whole there is never a shortage of young hopefuls eager to join the ranks of BM and as such, the BM partners have over the years developed a callous and cavalier attitude to personnel management. Such attitude by the partnership would have been unthinkable during the time of Alex MacTaggart and Duncan Brownloaf. The Watkins management consultancy personnel function is small and subordinate to the wishes of the partners.

Motivation of staff is rarely considered and their well-being is secondary to the business of improving profitability. Heinrich Grubber, in particular, takes a cool and calculating approach to staff management. He tends to select bright new consultants and then invariably burn them out with sustained hard work until the next young person comes along to take their place. It takes around eighteen months to two years of relentless hard work in the BM Division for the true nature of the situation to dawn on the more perceptive consultant – basically promotion to the next grade is rarer than a Norwegian parrot and, while one or two consultants have recently been promoted from consultant to senior consultant, only one person in the past fifteen years has been promoted from senior consultant to managing consultant.

The allocation of consultancy assignments within the BM Division is based primarily on either 'the warm body' principle (who is available) or as part of a none too subtle punishment and reward system. Generally there is a perceived hierarchy of jobs, ranging from an international assignment in some exotic location, working for Heinrich Grubber and the well-respected associate Nigel Redcoat (rated as a top job) to the managing of a small engineering business under receivership, working for Eric Reliant and the loathed and feared associate, Rupert Wormwood, famous for his unprincipled ways and ill-disguised alcoholic binges (most certainly a low-rated job). A succession of either top-rated jobs for prestigious clients or small insignificant jobs managed by poor job managers can make or break a Watkins career in around four months.

Advancement in the steadily deteriorating atmosphere of the BM Division is always likely to be a rather haphazard process. Surprisingly, technical engineering skills *per se* are not the key to career success in this organisation. Advancement, if it comes at all, may occur by a combination of conformity to, compliance with, and dependence on the sub-culture of the BM Division, within the wider culture of the Watkins company. Conformity, compliance and dependency can be demonstrated in a number of ways – being seen to work all hours in the office; flattery of the partners resulting in appalling sycophancy; exercising personal responsibility by undertaking small marketing and selling exercises designed to bring in new assignments; completing already time-pressured projects before schedule and under budget (which generally can only be achieved by under-recording time expended on a project), and the honing of good old-fashioned Machiavellian techniques of back stabbing.

It is against the background of difficult trading conditions in an environment that is uncertain, together with the absorption of a relatively small firm into an international management company with all its standardised procedures, and where mistrust, intimidation and fear are common emotions, that this case is developed.

Activity brief

1 Identify the different ways in which managerial control and power are being exercised in both Watkins International as a whole and the BM Division in particular.

2 Having identified the different aspects of managerial control, examine how appropriate these are in managing the different types of employees in Watkins International.

3 Explore the nature of the apparent dichotomy and tensions created in allowing highly qualified creative and essentially autonomous consultants room to reach creative solutions to client problems (often under considerable time pressures within an uncertain environment) and the employing organisation's need for order, stability and reliability.

4 Considering the Watkins International approach to quality assurance, which appears to be primarily bureaucratic and perhaps at variance with the image management consultants would wish to present to clients, is this likely to affect the way consultants consider and make recommendations for the implementation of total quality management systems in client organisations?

Further reading

Huczynski, A. and Buchanan, D. (1991), *Organisational Behaviour*, 2nd edn, Prentice Hall, Chapter 22 'Management Control' and Chapter 19 'Leadership and Management Style'.

Kakabadse, A., Ludlow, R. and Vinnicombe, S. (1998), *Working in Organizations*, Penguin, Chapter 8 'Power: A Base for Action'.

Morgan, G. (1986), *Images of Organization*, Sage, Chapter 6 'Interests, Conflict and Power'.

Mullins, L. J. (1999), *Management and Organisational Behaviour*, 5th edn, FT Pitman Publishing, Chapter 21 'Management Control and Power' and Chapter 22 'Organisation Development'.

Sveiby, K. E. and Lloyd, T. (1987), *Managing Knowhow. Add value by Valuing Creativity*, Bloomsbury.

Thomas, K. W. (1976), 'Conflict and Conflict Management', in M. D. Dunnette (ed.), *Handbook of Industrial and Organizational Psychology*, Rand McNally, 889–935.

Source: Adapted from case study by Gary Akehurst. In Adam-Smith, D. and Peacock, A. (eds) (1994), *Cases in Organisational Behaviour*, Pitman.

ACTIVITY

Whitewater Engineering Ltd

A large engineering firm specialising in the manufacture of marine engines and casings has developed to separate business units operating as individual profit centres. At plant 1, a new HRM director has been appointed with the mandate to review the existing employment relationship. The firm has the following characteristics:

- a multi-union site with the AEEU representing the majority of the employees who are skilled workers, although the TGWU and MSU are also present on site;
- the site has a reputation for 'good' industrial relations with a professional personnel department in place – there is a well-established system of collective bargaining which encompasses both integrative and distributive issues;
- in recent years the company as a whole has experienced falling profitability and a declining market share. The response to date has been to negotiate voluntary redundancies through the corporate structure and to establish local profit centres, but it is now felt that further measures must be taken. The workforce is aware that the company is experiencing recessionary pressures and will need to consider alternative strategies to ensure long-term survival.

As HRM director, your mandate is to outline a series of initiatives aimed at the labour process which you believe will improve the efficient operation of your site. In your report you must recognise the implications for the collective bargaining process of your plans, identify possible areas of conflict and suggest ways to bypass potential problems.

Source: Beardwell, I. and Holden, L. (1997), *Human Resource Management: A Contemporary Perspective*, 2nd edition, FT Pitman Publishing.

DEBATE

'The task of assessing students' work at post-secondary school level should be transferred from the staff to the students themselves.'

Starting points

For

- Stress, which can have 'an adverse effect on the level of individual performance' (Mullins, p. 475), may be relieved if workers are given 'greater discretion in how their work is performed' (Mullins, p. 636).
- Such delegation of power would help change students' attitudes towards teachers and knowledge for the better. 'Beware the boss who walks on water' (Townsend, 1985, p. 141).

Against

- According to McGregor's Theory X, the average person is lazy, has an inherent dislike of work, avoids responsibility, and prefers to be directed (Mullins, p. 209), so students will resist self-assessment.
- Transferring the task of quality control to the worker, or indeed the customer, is simply a cost-cutting exercise by managers looking for an easy life.

Further reading

Fox, S., Caspy, S. and Reisler, A. (1994), 'Variables Affecting Leniency, Halo and the Validity of Self-appraisal', *Journal of Occupational and Organisation Psychology*, March, 67, 44–56.

Glen, F. (1975), *The Social Psychology of Organisations*, Methuen, Chapter 2.

ASSIGNMENT

Given the flexible structuring and rapid rates of change in many modern organisations, control has become a very complex issue.

Write a brief management report (not more than 800 words), in which you look at the benefits/drawbacks/interesting points which will be associated with an attempt to simplify control systems in a medium-sized multinational operation.

You can add any detail you wish to profile your 'imaginary' company, but keep it brief and to the point in line with the question.

APPLICATION 1

A case of political competence?

A new finance director joined a large manufacturing company and brought with him an experienced credit control manager with whom he had worked closely at his previous organisation. The close relationship continued in the new organisation and together they put together a detailed proposal for sweeping changes in the finance function which were designed to improve its overall efficiency.

After a number of months, it became apparent that the finance director was having problems persuading his senior management colleagues to accept the fundamental changes contained in the proposal and it was rumoured that his position in the organisation was under threat.

The credit control manager heard the rumours and decided to distance herself from the proposal by letting it be known that she disagreed with many of the changes. She also took steps to reduce the number of informal meetings held with the finance director and to communicate through formal memos.

- Do you think this manager was being politically astute?

A case of political incompetence?

An experienced middle manager was seconded to manage a major project. The project team was effectively managed and a feasibility study carried out on time and within budget. The manager circulated copies of the team's report to the board of directors and arranged a presentation. During the presentation it became obvious that the feasibility study was being seen as a threat by certain directors who criticised it heavily and successfully blocked its recommendations. Amid much recrimination and argument, it was decided to shelve the report and disband the project team.

- Where do you think this manager went wrong politically?

Source: Beardwell, I. and Holden, L. (1997), *Human Resource Management: A Contemporary Perspective*, 2nd edition, FT Pitman Publishing.

APPLICATION 2

Success at office politics comes from years of practice

FT

It is a stark fact that all organisations – whether businesses, government departments or voluntary organisations – are political systems.

Politics is a necessary part of the process. All organisations have limited resources. Everyone wants more of those limited resources and there are two ways to achieve that. First, to convince those with more power over the allocation of resources to give you a greater share and, second, to become more powerful and grab more resources.

Either way you will become involved in the politics of dividing up the cake. Some people are distressed because there must be winners and losers in the allocation game: your gain could be my loss. And, invariably, the winners seem to be the political players because they put more time and energy into selling their case.

What irritates the less competent political players is when resources are divided in a way they consider to be blatantly unfair. For reasons that are not always clear to an outsider, certain functions have bigger budgets, better facilities, smarter cars and larger salaries. While people may argue that these differences reflect labour market forces, it is also true that they reflect decisions based on political clout.

If you are tempted to believe that politics could be eliminated through a rigorous rule-bound procedure, that is quite independent of the people involved, then let me tell you this is naive. If the second half of the 20th century has taught us anything at all about managing organisations, then it must be that massive control systems, designed in the name of rational decision-making, can result in crippling structures which become ends in themselves.

For people motivated by power, the real allure of the top jobs is to make things happen, to change events, to create the new, to break with the past. Not surprisingly, most of those who make it to the top are experts at playing politics. For them, it is intoxicating stuff and just to experience power they will devote seven days a week and 24 hours a day if necessary to the political processes involved.

London Business School has a data bank of what motivates managers across the world and there are interesting differences between cultures when it comes to accepting that power is essential to get things done. But, regardless of culture, the most effective chief executives enjoy the exercise of power and have served very similar apprenticeships.

Most of these men and women come from families where they were the eldest; where they learnt their managerial skills from a dominant parent (of either gender); where they practised their use of power first on their siblings and second on their peers at school, university or on the playing fields. For them, the exercise of power in order to make things happen is not a transient interest. They have been watching and imitating role models, reading about heroes and thinking about political tactics for a long time before they secure positions of real power.

These chief executives far outclass that relatively new breed of CEOs born in the 1950s and 1960s who clambered up hierarchies through professional expertise rather than any real interest in the exercise of power. These chief executives, whose interest in managing people is often minimal, seek the space to do what they consider to be their real job of making deals or evolving strategies or conducting research or designing new structures and systems.

It is ironic that at a time when we are desperate for leadership an increasing number of these introverted, autonomous specialists, who have a minimal interest in power, are being appointed to chief executive positions. They need management gurus such as Tom Peters to tell them to 'walk about' and 'walk the talk'; managers motivated by power, meanwhile, who get their greatest buzz out of managing and processing relationships to make things happen, do not need gurus to tell them what they already know.

Comments such as 'I do not have the stomach for the sort of political games some of my colleagues play' are most often first expressed by people in their 30s as they begin to realise that their career is not a dress rehearsal; that peers with better political skills may pass them by. It is a period of recognising that each of us is on his or her own, that managing others is about respect, not friendship. It is a time when the importance of politics and patronage in medium to large organisations becomes undeniable.

If the politics distress you then you should ask whether you are right for a large organisation or whether you would be better in a smaller company or selling your skills as a sole trader. You might be better suited to working as a consultant if you want autonomy, to mix with a small number of other professionals to solve other people's problems, and to see a direct relationship between what you do and what you earn. You will enjoy a different form of power based on your expertise but you will also lose some of what you have. You will no longer run things; you will live, vicariously, on the successes of others who are the real movers and shakers.

The alternative is to accept the world for the way it is: accept that you are in a political system and learn by observing others. Concentrate on your best political skills and develop those. Strong managers use their political skills with great subtlety to achieve specific ends. When political games become ends in themselves they become destructive. Discourage non-directed political games within your team. As a manager you are an exemplar. If you want to encourage openness and trust in others then remember you are their role model.

Source: Professor John W. Hunt, *Financial Times*, 23 February 1998.

22 Organisation Development (Culture, Conflict and Change)

CASE STUDY

Rover Group: Building a learning organisation

Background

The announcement in April 1995 that Rover Group had made record profits and that its domestic and export sales were continuing to forge ahead merely confirmed what many observers believed – that Rover has turned itself into one of Europe's leading car companies, and is approaching a position where it can challenge the best in the world. It was this potential for world-class performance which lay behind BMW's purchase of Rover in February 1994. As the BMW Chairman, Bernd Pischetsrieder, commented on BBC TV's *Money Programme* at the time, 'The objective is that BMW and Rover together will be the largest specialist manufacturer worldwide.' The purchase of the company by a German firm renowned for its commitment to quality, flair and financial soundness was a major vote of confidence in Rover, and set the seal on what has been one of the most remarkable turnarounds in British corporate life.

The genesis of learning business

Yet when Michael Edwardes first became Managing Director in 1978, the company had become a byword for industrial militancy – a common joke at the time was 'only Bobby Charlton strikes faster than British Leyland'. One of Edwardes' first priorities was to tackle the industrial relations strife at the company and establish, or re-establish, 'management's right to manage'. Obviously, he did much else, including establishing the link with Honda, but it was his fierce determination to restore managerial authority and end union militancy which characterised his reign.

In 1982, Edwardes left and was replaced by Harold Musgrove. By this time, employee relations were on a less volatile footing. It was under Musgrove that management, strongly influenced by Rover's alliance with Honda, came to recognise that the rapid development of new models and attendant changes in processes and techniques required a substantial retraining of the workforce, and an end to the 'them and us' culture which still dominated the organisation. It was not until 1986, however, with the appointment of Graham Day as Chairman, followed shortly after by the appointment of a new managing director, that 'people' moved to the top of the agenda.

Under Edwardes and Musgrove, Rover's priorities had been profits, products, procedures and people, in that order. Day became convinced that Rover's only hope of long-term survival was to stand the company's objectives on their head. Profit, he argued, would be the result of people concentrating on producing superior products by way of distinctive processes. People came first, profits came later. It is difficult to overestimate how much of a challenge this was to the established view held by managers in Rover. They had spent three or four very painful years in the late 1970s and early 1980s establishing their right to manage, and fully subscribed to the traditional management macho ethos of the British motor industry. Suddenly they were being told that employee initiative was the key to success, that there must be a partnership between managers and workers.

Nevertheless, through a succession of meetings and brainstorming sessions, senior managers began to craft a new personnel approach for the company. The effort began with a new quality initiative in Rover which stressed that 'quality is about people' and a new mission for Rover 'to achieve extraordinary customer satisfaction'. The personnel function also adopted a new mission statement:

> *The purpose of personnel within Rover is to achieve success through people and the purpose of the personnel team is to gain success for the business through the success of its people.*

From this time, as the following quotations demonstrate, senior managers began to speak a new language: 'We want to change the emphasis from training – people having something done to them, to learning – people doing something for themselves'; 'we want to unlock the potential of everyone to make a contribution to the future'; 'we want to bridge the gap between management and workforce'; 'we want to achieve success through people'; 'it's our people's contribution which will give us our competitive edge'. Furthermore, the emphasis moved from managers managing to managers leading: 'We see excellent leadership as the key to unlock those [employees'] contributions so we focus heavily on encouraging our line managers' leadership skills.'

Since 1986, a whole raft of measures and policies designed to open up the opportunities for and to promote learning have been developed. Rover now estimates that, at any one time, over half of all employees are engaged in some form of learning. In order to facilitate this process and create a corporate learning environment, the company has attempted to remove barriers which separate one employee from another. It has flattened its management structure and removed the bewildering plethora of job titles and job descriptions that used to exist. It has committed itself to end the divide between blue-collar and white-collar jobs, and the insecurity that had often been a feature of the former. This commitment was demonstrated in 1992 with the launch of the company's far-reaching 'Rover Tomorrow – The New Deal'. This included:

- *a company undertaking not to make compulsory redundancies, in return for a commitment from employees to continuous improvement and flexibility;*
- *the harmonisation of terms and conditions between white-collar and blue-collar staff;*
- *the coining of a new term – 'associates' – to describe all Rover employees, regardless of what job they did or where they worked;*

- *the expectation that white-collar staff should be prepared to be redeployed onto assembly-line work;*
- *a requirement that all new graduate recruits had to spend their first three months with Rover working on the production lines;*
- *the expectation that all Rover employees, even directors, should wear the same grey overalls.*

In order to accelerate that pace of change at Rover, in 1990 Rover Learning Business was created to bring together and give focus to the company's various learning initiatives.

Rover Learning Business

The idea of creating a separate business within a business to promote organisational learning appears at first strange, especially given the enormous effort Rover put into creating a learning culture between 1986 and 1990. However, senior managers came to believe that the push for continuous improvement through the provision of opportunities for continuous learning could lead to a mass of fragmented and unco-ordinated initiatives, unless a group was established with the sole purpose of directing, co-ordinating and developing the company's learning initiatives. This view was strengthened by the evidence from employee attitude surveys, which the company had conducted for a number of years. These had consistently shown that (a) employees did not feel the best use was being made of their talents, and that they were prepared for faster and more radical change than the company had so far experienced; and (b) employees felt they were not well enough informed about opportunities for involvement, development and progression within Rover. Consequently, there was a strong view among both managers and workforce that the pace of change could and should be accelerated and, despite past efforts, that a more coherent, co-ordinated and publicised approach to learning was required. Rover Learning Business (or RLB, as it is generally referred to in Rover) was launched on 14 May 1990. It was given a budget of around £30 million, and a remit to help Rover Group achieve a number of specific objectives:

- *to distinguish Rover Group as the best in Europe for attracting, retaining and developing people;*
- *to emphasise the view that people are its greatest asset;*
- *to gain recognition by its own employees that the company's commitment to every individual had increased;*
- *to unlock and recognise employee talents and to make better use of these talents;*
- *to improve the competitive edge of the company.*

In addressing the first RLB Open Conference in 1993, Sir Graham Day, Rover Group's Chairman, summed up the philosophy that underpins the work of RLB:

> *Neither the corporate learning process nor the individual one is optional. If the company seeks to survive and prosper, it must learn. If the individual, at a minimum, seeks to remain employed, let alone progress, learning is essential.*

The Change Management Process

RLB has put a great deal of effort into assisting staff in Rover to plan and implement change. Out of this, they have developed an approach to change which is both rigorous and effective. The approach is based on teamwork, and stresses the need to seek information on best practice and benchmarking, and to involve those most closely affected. The process is driven by business needs, and takes the change team step-by-step through the various stages necessary to plan and implement change. RLB point out that it is also a learning tool. Once a project has been completed, the team evaluate what worked and did not work, and what lessons they can learn for the future.

On a recent visit by the author to Land Rover, staff explained how they had used the process successfully to plan and implement the introduction of a new production line for the Discovery. They had assembled a team and had gone off-site for four days. They were accompanied by a fellow manager who was familiar with the RLB Change Management Process and who acted as a facilitator. At the end of the four days, they not only had a plan for introducing the new Discovery line, including a timetable and resource implications, but had also developed a presentation to explain to managers and.other associates what they intended to do. One of the team members commented that it was the smoothest and quickest change project he had ever been involved in. In addition, the team had managed to introduce the new line at no cost to the company and with no additional resources or loss of production.

On the same visit to Land Rover, staff at all levels were enthusiastic and complimentary about the changes which had taken place at Rover, and especially the opportunities for learning.

The outcome

Rover's strategy is to stimulate changes on a broad front, aimed ultimately at achieving a competitive advantage through the efforts of all managers and employees. The view it takes is that in an industry of fast followers, those who learn fastest will be the winners. So Rover does not necessarily need to invent new methods and new processes itself; however, it must be capable of identifying them and utilising them more quickly and better than its competitors. For Rover, the emphasis is not on technology (though that is important to the company), production methods (though the Honda link has put Rover at the forefront in these), or design (though its cars are extremely well thought-out and designed), all of which can be copied relatively quickly. The emphasis is on developing people as the key to achieving a competitive edge, and on creating a learning organisation which can draw on ideas from a wide range of industries and sources and adapt them to Rover's needs.

The result of this has been to transform relationships and working practices in Rover Group. The 'them and us' philosophy which permeated the company has been replaced, though probably not in everyone's mind, with a much more team- and company-oriented approach. Perhaps the most dramatic example is that not only was the company prepared to ask white-collar staff to take shop-floor jobs, but some actually have

In cases such as this, where companies receive a great deal of media attention, it is important to try to separate the hype from the reality. What can be seen objectively is that Rover has changed out of all recognition since it was rescued by the UK government in 1975. Though the foundations for this were laid in the

Edwardes era (especially the link with Honda), the step change in performance appears to have come in the last ten years, with the development of a new attitude towards staff, and the move to creating a learning organisation.

Source: Adapted from case study by Bernard Burnes, based on research carried out with Penny West of Edge Hill College. In Burnes, B. (1996), *Managing Change*, 2nd edition, Pitman.

Activity brief

1 How well do you think Rover has responded to the changing needs of its business environment?

2 What drove the company's move to change management–worker relations?

3 How influential do you feel the attitudes of Rover's leaders have been at successive stages in the company's development? To what extent did the organisational culture mirror or detract from the vision of its successive leaders? How has the organisational climate changed at Rover?

4 How important is the concept of organisational learning to modern business development?

ACTIVITY

The following is an extract from *Doing the Business in Europe: A Guide to Chinese Exporters* written by Hay-lo and S. F. Profesee, published by Shi-Ster Press in the year 2003.

BEHAVIOURAL CHARACTERISTICS

Always remember that the European nations exhibit quite distinct patterns of behaviour among their citizens. *These can be both positive and negative!* The following provides a summary of some of the key points about the people you will meet.

Germans

For

Always punctual and hospitable. Disciplined. Flair for production. Don't allow women in the boardroom. Don't joke at work. The only nation unaffected by BSE (mad cow disease).

Against

Little imagination or humour. Regimental. No flair for marketing. Don't allow women in the boardroom. Consider they are the best business nation in the world. Worriers (e.g. about BSE (mad cow disease)).

English

For

Fair-minded and courteous. Entrepreneurial. Low staffing costs. Not given to emotional outbursts. Unique sense of humour. Sang-froid (e.g. over BSE (mad cow disease)).

Against

Xenophobic. Rude public service workers. Repressed soccer hooligans. High strike rate. No dress sense. Consider they are the best business nation in the world. Largely wiped out by BSE (mad cow disease).

Draw up a similar list of plus and minus characteristics for any two of the following nationalities:

French	Italian	Swedish
Japanese	American	Greek

Compare your list with those of other people in your group and then discuss the following questions:

- What logic do we follow when we culturally stereotype people in this way?
- What are the dangers from both a psychological and business point of view of stereotyping others?
- Why should individuals be regarded as unique?

Activity provided by Dr Ray French, University of Portsmouth.

DEBATE 1

'The socialisation of new members into an organisation's culture is no more or less than the manipulation of the individual and is therefore unethical and should be condemned.'

Starting points

For

- The inculcation into a culture serves only the organisation's goals and to produce compliant employees to continue the culture. Any satisfaction gained by the employee is a spurious one gained from conforming to the organisation's wishes.
- Not only is it unethical but in the long term it could prove detrimental to the organisation. Overly compliant employees are less likely to be creative and innovative.

Against

- In order to survive, an organisation needs members who are all pulling in the same direction – otherwise divisiveness will lead, ultimately, to the downfall of the organisation.
- Studies have shown that there are clear links between culture and satisfaction (Hellriegel and Slocum, 1974); socialisation is therefore an important and necessary mechanism.

Further reading

Feldman, D. C. (1981), 'The Multiple Socialization of Organization Members', *Academy of Management Review,* April.

Hellriegel, D. and Slocum, J. W. Jr. (1974), 'Organizational Climate: Measures, Research, and Contingencies', *Academy of Management Journal,* June, 225–80.

Van Maanen, J. and Schein, E. H. (1977), 'Career Development', in J. R. Hackman and J. L. Suttle (eds), *Improving Life at Work,* Goodyear.

DEBATE 2

'Culture is such a deep-seated phenomenon that it is impossible to change successfully.'

Starting points

For

- Culture develops over years and is therefore deep-rooted with strongly held core values. Rituals, stories and management style serve to sustain this culture in a way which is too difficult to change.
- The culture of an organisation is self-perpetuating through its selection and socialisation procedures; these alone probably guarantee that culture cannot be changed.

Against

- Culture *can* be changed, although it is an extended process involving changing both attitudes and behaviour.
- Culture *is* a deep-seated phenomenon but it can be changed by changing the determinants of culture – the rituals, selection process, and so on – which will therefore change the core values.

Further reading

Anthony, P. (1993), *Managing Culture,* Open University Press.

Gagliardi, P. (1977), 'The Creation and Change of Organizational Cultures: A Conceptual Framework', *Organization Studies,* 7 (2), 117–34.

Kilman, R. H., Saxton, M. J. and Serpa, R. (1985), *Gaining Control of the Corporate Culture,* Jossey-Bass.

ASSIGNMENT 1

Take two contrasting types of organisation and using the Handy influences on the development of culture (Mullins, pp. 805–6) as your model, compare and contrast your two organisations.

Your two different organisations could be:

- private and public sector;
- for profit and not for profit;
- service sector and manufacturing sector;
- production and academic.

In not more than 1500 words critically analyse your findings, suggesting reasons for any differences.

How would you describe the current culture of the two organisations? Do you consider this to be a suitable culture for the environment of the organisations?

ASSIGNMENT 2

1 List the characteristics of the 'ideal' organisational culture or suggest which of either the Handy or Deal and Kennedy typologies (see Mullins, pp. 803–5) you would try to foster if you were appointed as a senior manager in three of the following organisations:

- a wheel clamping contractor
- a research laboratory
- a battleship
- a private hospital
- a second-hand car business
- a high-fashion clothing store
- a fast-food chain
- an advertising agency.

2 How would you go about fostering that culture if the prevailing culture were different?

Assignment provided by Ron Rosen, University of Portsmouth.

APPLICATION 1

One of our summer school students was an overseas student who joined our programme having completed his compulsory military service. Over coffee at the start of the programme he told us about it.

'First you have your hair cut, even though it might already be short enough, and then you get issued with your kit which you have to put on immediately. You catch sight of yourself in the mirror and you *know* you're in the Army – all your individuality has gone and you look just like everybody else. You get given a bunk with army-issue bedding and a cupboard which looks like all the rest – you can't even fill it up as you want, there's an order for how you put your gear in it. You sit on your hard bed and look around at all the others – the people you'll be spending at least the next six months with, whether you like it or not. Their expression mirrors yours: "We knew we'd have to do it sometime, we just have to get through it with as little hassle as possible."

'The next few weeks merge into a blur of following often apparently illogical orders. Your life becomes dominated by Senior NCOs shouting at you, bells and klaxons ruling your every move from when you get up to the time you have to go to bed. You have to change uniforms at the drop of a hat for no reason and go through mindless drills and marching at all hours of the day and night. If you dare to question anything you end up peeling potatoes, cleaning out baking tins or painting the stones around the parade ground. You even get used to the terrible food. Throughout it all, you have to wear your uniform and stay on the base, you get a pass-out only when you've finished basic training.

'Eventually that day arrives and you get your next set of orders. Even then you probably won't get what you asked for. I'm a computer programmer so for my first posting I was put in the kitchen. As you march out of training camp for the last time you notice the next batch arriving. You look them over and catch yourself saying, "look at that lot – he'll have to get his hair cut, that one will have to stand up straighter, *he's* going to get a rude awakening . . . what a shower!" You pull yourself up short and suddenly you realise you *are* the Army – it's crept up on you . . . .'

Can you see where the role of socialisation fits in here? Using a variation of the socialisation model suggested by Feldman (1981) we can see the *encounter stage,* in which the new employee sees what the organisation is *really* like and faces up to the fact that expectations and reality might differ. The second stage is *metamorphosis* where the new employee adjusts to their workgroup's values and norms. These two stages result in outcomes of productivity, commitment and turnover, although presumably in the case of military service the latter is not acceptable.

(For those of you old enough to remember UK National Service, this may bring back some memories. For those of you too young to remember, perhaps you should be grateful.)

APPLICATION 2

Gerry is currently employed by Solent Marine as a ship's laminator. Solent Marine is a boat-building company which specialises in the construction and refitting of yachts and although Gerry is principally employed on GRP laminating of hulls, decks, and so forth, his job description also requires him to turn his hand to whatever needs doing (this bit of the job description is often called 'the slave clause' and usually begins with 'any other reasonable duties which may, from time to time . . .').

On this particular day, Gerry was painting something on the deck. He did the classic thing: stepped back to admire his handiwork and promptly fell through the forward hatch and into the cabin space below: a descent of about fourteen feet. On climbing back up he realised that he'd bruised his back muscles where they'd caught the edge of the hatch and was in considerable pain. He reported sick to his chargehand who said, 'You'd better drive yourself to hospital, then, and get it checked!' As Gerry limped off the chargehand shouted after him, 'Can you drop Mr Durrant at his house on the way to hospital?' Gerry said afterwards, 'Not only did I have to drive myself twenty miles to hospital when I was in so much pain that I couldn't put the clutch in, but I also had to drive up this pot-holed lane to give a customer a lift home. To cap it all I've got a trapped nerve and a cracked rib and I've found out that the company doesn't even pay sick pay. . . .'

What does this tell you about the particular culture and likely levels of commitment engendered by this company? Would *you* work for them?

Note: When one of the authors told Gerry that his example would be included in this book but he was not to worry because the example would be presented as fictitious, his reply was: 'The whole **** company ought to be fictitious if you ask me!'

APPLICATION 3

Over forty years ago Whyte (1956) described 'organization man' as a person who not only worked for the organisation but also belonged to it. This was echoed two years later by Lawrence (1958) two years later who wrote: 'ideally we would want one sentiment to be dominant in all employees from top to bottom, namely a complete loyalty to organisational purposes.'

Thirty years later this theme was still being hailed by leading management writers such as Peters and Waterman (1982) and Kanter (1983) who suggested that strong cultures which supported organisational objectives were vital prerequisites for success.

We have, then, an assumption that strong culture and high levels of commitment need to go hand in hand to ensure organisational success: we need a company peopled by 'organisation men'. However, what happens to creativity and innovation when this happens? It is interesting to note that some of the organisations identified by Peters and Waterman as 'excellent' have had serious declines in their financial performance (for example, Caterpillar Tractor and Schlumberger) – is this in spite of or because of their culture and levels of commitment?

What, then, is the answer? Do organisations deliberately employ people who are not 'organisation men' in order to foster a climate of creativity and innovation? If so, what is likely to be the commitment levels of these people and, therefore, the subsequent effect on organisational performance?

APPLICATION 4

The last few years have seen a dramatic increase in organisations investing in customer care programmes. Larger companies have spent considerable sums of money not only in training their employees but also in telling the world at large about it – remember 'We're getting there' (British Rail) and 'Ask for Tom' (Texas Homecare)? For the most part, these programmes were introduced in order to give the organisation a competitive edge in the marketplace: 'We may not be cheaper than Company X but we care for you, the customer.'

However, after a while, the bandwagon became so popular that an in-house customer care programme became a necessity, a way of 'keeping up', rather than trying to gain or sustain competitive advantage. One of the authors was inundated with consultancy requests to 'change the attitudes of my shop floor with a half-day customer care course', followed by 'No, the rest of us have got the right approach, it's just the shop floor/front facing staff who've got the attitude problem'. What is actually needed here is a long-term programme of culture change rather than an ineffective quick-fix solution (as one employee said, 'Why should I care about the customer when the company doesn't care about me . . . ?'). All too often these programmes, including a recognition of the need to change the culture itself, are seen as quick-fix solutions and then the organisation wonders why it hasn't worked – except that it's all the fault of the staff, isn't it?

Customer care is now being replaced with 'empowerment' as the ultimate panacea for the organisation's ills. Will we be updating this feature in a few years time by replacing the references to 'customer care' with references to 'empowerment' and adding in the latest fad at the end of the piece?

APPLICATION 5

'A change is as good as a rest', they say, so you go abroad for a good holiday (even if you don't like the food), because foreigners are such a change. But *working* with them is another matter: there the difference can be stressful rather than restful.

Books and articles advising managers about cultural differences abound, especially since the Single Market pushed Europeans even closer together, causing a spate of mergers and takeovers.

The *Independent on Sunday* (3 July 1994) tells of the frustration of Japanese consultant Chihiro Nakao, for instance. He is used to gauging the commitment of managers by how much shoe leather they wear out 'walking the factory', but at Porsche he found that the Germans had their shoes resoled. To write *Riding the Waves of Culture* (Economist Books, 1993) Frans Trompenaars compiled a database of thirty companies in fifty countries, and recommends that managers stop seeing cultural problems as other people's stubbornness. The *Guardian* (16 March 1993) claimed the French and Germans only get on in border firms in places like Strasbourg. Elsewhere it is Protestants against Rationalists throughout the working day in the 3000 or so companies with Franco-German management. John Mole (1990) warned of culture clash in *Mind your Manners*: don't take your jacket off in Germany, avoid levity in the office in France, in Holland be blunt and direct, and make it a point of honour in Italy to get round regulations. His principal advice is 'learn the language'.

That is just what everyone is doing all the time in Midshires University's Department of Languages, where a curious cultural contamination rather than cultural clash may be witnessed taking place. The British lecturers appear to take on the cultural characteristics of the people whose language they specialise in. So the staff in the Spanish section do everything *mañana,* while in the French section negotiating in abstractions, like justice and equality, is normal, and the long-suffering students have to acquire a very un-British rational approach to every bit of work they do. The secretary in the Russian section says her lecturers are an Eastern European version of the Spanish, the head of Italian is renowned for working her way around the bureaucracy, and as for punctuality in the German section, well the hapless secretary arrives each morning to be met in the entrance by the otherwise thoroughly English head of section who has been pacing up and down for ten minutes waiting for her.

There is clearly not much hope of the global village occurring in *that* particular organisation.

APPLICATION 6

For this one we're still at Midshires University. Anne (our candidate from Chapter 12) was, as expected, appointed to the post in the Engineering Department and on 1 September that year she duly reported for work. Having gone through the required two days' induction she then set about trying to settle in to the job. Six days later she'd finally got an office (but no computer or telephone as yet) and three weeks later (just as term was about to start) she'd finally been given her teaching schedule, although she hadn't been able to make contact with the relevant course managers because they were still on holiday. It was certainly a far cry from industry and she hadn't found people to be particularly helpful; it wasn't deliberate, she thought, but everyone seemed wrapped up in their own little worlds.

On the first day of term she donned a smart business suit from her industry days and went in to teach her first class. She was surprised to see that her colleagues were dressed in the same way as they had been in the summer except that the shorts had been replaced by a variety of jeans and cord trousers (invariably baggy) and that trainers or loafers had replaced sandals. Here and there a tie was in evidence but it was of the knitted variety last seen outside academia thirty years ago. As the first semester drew on, baggy corduroy jackets appeared against inclement weather. 'This lot are so scruffy,' Anne thought, 'I'm not going to let myself get like them – I think we've got a professional status to uphold and one of the ways to do it is to look smart.' She was determined to retain what she thought of as her image, even though she was aware of the nickname given to her by both students and colleagues – in fact she was quite flattered to be called Mrs Thatcher.

The first semester was drawing to an end and Anne found herself unconsciously replacing her jackets with comfortable sweaters. By the end of the second semester she was to be found in leggings and baggy T-shirts. At a meeting called to discuss a new degree she found herself sitting next to a man in a business suit and tie. 'You can tell he comes from the Business School,' she thought as she drove off in the second-hand Citroën 2CV which had recently replaced her BMW.

The main point to make here is the socialisation of new people into an organisation in order to inculcate them and get them to adopt cultural norms. Here we can see that the process was quite a long one and was accomplished almost unconsciously – quite a different approach from our Army example.

AFTERTHOUGHT

> The difference between involvement and commitment has been described as being similar to a plate of eggs and bacon: the hen is involved but the pig is committed . . . .

23 Management Development and Organisational Effectiveness

CASE STUDY

Employee relations at Midshires College

Midshires College of Technology is a further education college based in the south of England and, in common with other similar academic institutions, is facing a difficult financial future. It deals primarily with full-time undergraduates studying across a range of academic disciplines (see Fig. 23.1). However, approximately 30 per cent of the teaching revenue is derived from part-time vocational courses. Student numbers have been constant over the last five years and there are currently 7000 full-time equivalent students. There are approximately 400 full-time equivalent staff with some 350 managerial and support staff.

Funding for Midshires largely relates to the number of students recruited. Government funding is provided for EU students; however, in real terms this funding has reduced by some 35 per cent per student over the last three years. Buildings are in need of repair and there is a large outstanding overdraft to pay for increased teaching accommodation purchased four years ago. Several strategies have been adopted by the senior academics and managers of Midshires to cope with this shortfall.

Additional students (an increase of 15 per cent) have been found for the academic year 1999/2000 to increase revenue. Most of these have been recruited from countries outside the EU. The fee for each of these students is approximately twice that for the equivalent EU student. This has worked well for cash flow but is causing some difficulties. The balance of students in some programme areas has changed, notably in the subjects of accounting and computing. This has produced a situation where there are more overseas students and EU students studying in some groups. Lecturers are complaining that academic standards are dropping because of this. Overseas students recruited are not always fluent in the English language and entry qualifications are sometimes inferior to home students'. To reduce failure rates, extra tuition and counselling is provided.

A policy of larger lecture group sizes has been introduced to cope with greater numbers and, to offset the problems created, a system of tutorials to provide more targeted tuition has also been introduced. Rooms are often too small for the number of students attending lectures and often students sit on the floor or stand for short lectures. In comparison with last year, staff this year will be expected to provide 10 per cent more tutorials and will be expected to set and mark 20 per cent more work. Staff are also

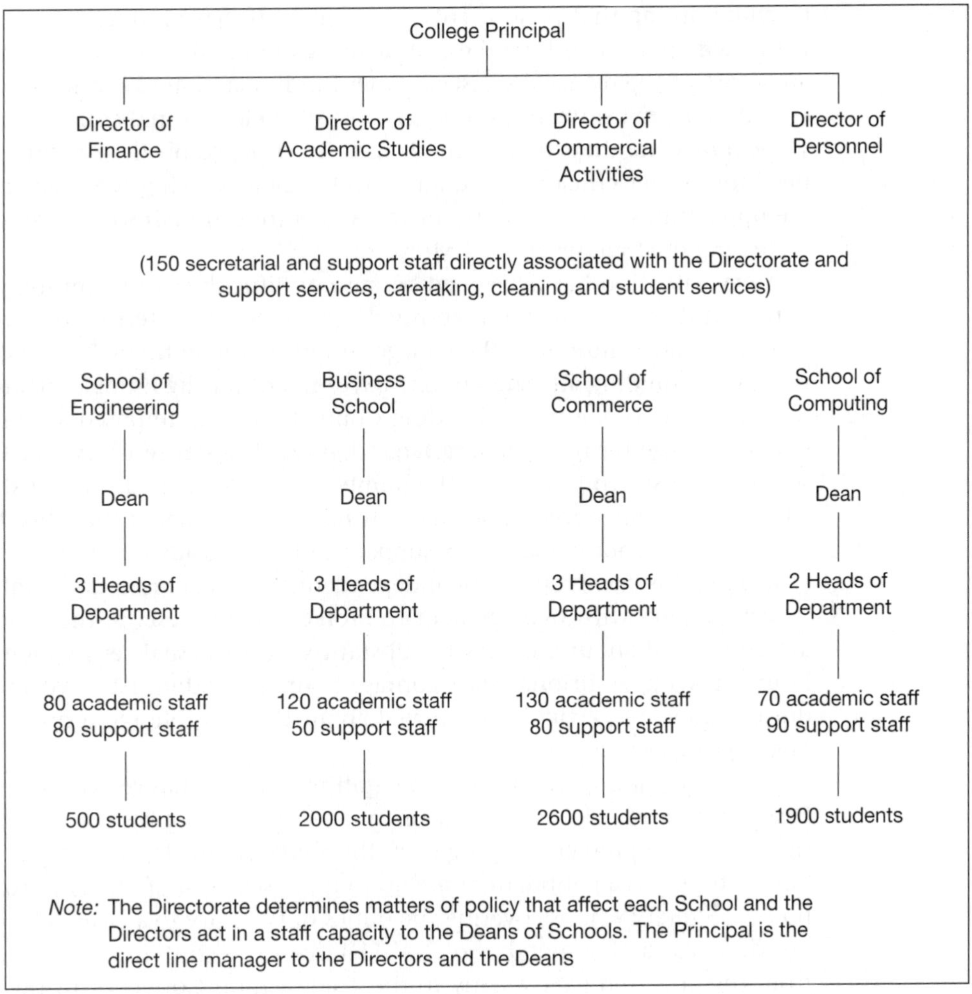

Fig. 23.1

being asked to manage and undertake a range of administrative duties relating to these larger groups that are, again, time-consuming processes.

One suggestion put to staff by senior managers is that it provides an opportunity to consider innovative teaching and learning strategies that could reduce the class contact and assessment burden on staff. No funding is available to support this initiative. However, staff have been encouraged to find ways to reduce contact time '. . . for your own good'. There is great pressure on support facilities provided for staff and students. Car parking is more difficult and it is proposed that next term both staff and students will pay parking charges for using college car parks – currently this facility is provided free of charge. Refectory facilities are no longer adequate with large queues forming at peak times and there are often shortages of seats and table space to eat cooked food.

This term, college opening hours have been extended in an attempt to reduce the pressure on teaching space. However this has meant that some staff are on the college premises from 8.00 a.m. to 10.00 p.m. with perhaps five or six hours of teaching during that period. This, for some staff, has produced domestic problems with their spouses and families. All is not gloom and despondency, however. Staff are aware of the external constraints on funding and are keen to provide a quality educational environment as long as some of their personal concerns are addressed. They appreciate that their own job security depends on their ability to accept the need for greater efficiency and adapt to the new working requirements. They also see opportunities to compete for research funds and short course training, thus increasing the total revenue of Midshires.

A new situation has developed because of difficulties in recruiting sufficient student numbers in the Engineering Department this term. As a result of not recruiting target numbers, the college suffers a double financial penalty. They will not receive funding allocated by the government for the number of students under-recruited. The Government Funding Council had also imposed a financial penalty on the College for not reaching target figures. The net result is that the College is seriously considering reducing the number of academic and support staff employed within the Engineering Department. It has been estimated that this department is overstaffed by approximately six support and eight academic staff.

Against this background, the independent and recognised trade union, NATFHE, is seeking talks with management to protect the interests of their members. They are concerned about changes to substantive contractual terms such as extended hours of work, additional class contact hours and administrative and managerial duties. They are particularly worried about the possible reduction of staff in the Engineering Department.

The Principal is worried about low staff morale and has convened a meeting with Deans of Schools, Heads of Department and members of his Directorate to consider the major staff problems arising from the above issues. The agenda for this meeting has been sent as a confidential memo to these senior staff but unfortunately a temporary secretary who is covering the duties of secretary to a Dean left the agenda on her desk. An active member of NATFHE read the contents, removed the agenda from the desk and gave a copy to the Trade Union Convenor in the College. The covering note to senior staff and the agenda is shown in Figs 23.2 and 23.3.

The Convenor is extremely concerned abut the agenda items and the apparent secrecy surrounding the meeting. The union has a bargaining agreement with the college and expects to be consulted over changes to working conditions. As well as the legal requirements relating to consultation there is also a collective agreement that requires the employer to give one year's notice of any possible redundancy situation.

The Convenor immediately sought a meeting with the Principal and showed him the photocopy of the agenda, asking for an explanation. The Principal defended his position by suggesting that the meeting with senior staff is a preliminary meeting to find out the size of the problem. Normal discussions with the trade union will follow if necessary. He also asked how the union obtained a copy of the agenda, suggesting that he considers the disclosure of confidential information a fundamental breach of contract which he may have to pursue through disciplinary action. After a good deal of heated discussion the Convenor suggests that the motivation and morale of staff are exceptionally low and the Principal would be well advised to consider how best to look after the interests of staff rather than to take disciplinary action over petty issues.

CONFIDENTIAL

To: Members of the Directorate
Deans
Heads of Departments

From: The Principal

A meeting to discuss the financial crisis facing the college will be held in the Board Room on 10 February at 9.00 a.m.

A copy of the agenda is attached.

Fig. 23.2

CONFIDENTIAL

AGENDA

1 Apologies for absence

2 Funding arrangements
- student numbers
- financial position

3 Change in contract terms for staff
- extending the academic year and staff leave arrangements
- staff reductions in the School of Engineering
- further increase in student numbers for the next academic year
- new contracts for existing staff

4 Change to semesterisation

5 Any other business

Fig. 23.3

Activity brief

1 The recognised trade union is concerned about the agenda items and apparent secrecy surrounding the senior management meeting to be held on 10 February. Critically examine the proposition that this concern is entirely predictable and can be explained by reference to the management styles shown throughout the case study.

2 Taking into account the organisational culture and climate described in the case study, describe ways in which senior managers at Midshires College can improve staff morale and commitment to organisational goals.

3 Demonstrate how senior managers at Midshires can use the principles of organisational development to implement the changes suggested in the meeting.

4 Taking the role of either a trade union representative or senior manager:

(a) Prepare to negotiate the changes to terms and conditions set out in item 3 of the agenda. List the strong and weak points of your arguments, the maximum you believe you can achieve and the minimum you will accept.

(b) Use appropriate behavioural skills and a sound structure to negotiate a settlement within the limits described in (a) above that is acceptable to the other side.

Case study provided by Alan Peacock, University of Portsmouth.

ACTIVITY 1

Assume that you or your group are management consultants whose main area of expertise is leadership training.

Design a leadership training programme for middle managers in a work organisation of your choice.

You will need to:

- specify the objectives of the course;
- detail the timing of the course (number of days etc.);
- outline each day's training in detail, including any tutor input, exercises, etc.;
- prepare an evaluation sheet for delegates.

ACTIVITY 2

Management team-building

The management team in a medium-sized manufacturing company was not performing effectively. There was evidence of a lack of trust and confidence in the team and relationships between individuals were poor. The managers were brought together in a series of workshops and asked to examine their managerial role and how it related to other managers and staff. They explored key issues and 'blockages'. After a short time it was realised that there were a number of misperceptions and misunderstandings. The workshops also revealed confusion over roles and responsibilities. An action plan was implemented to tackle these problems.

1 As management development manager, what steps will you take to ensure that the action plan is successfully implemented?

2 How would you measure the effectiveness of the action plan?

Source: Beardwell, I. and Holden, L. (1997), *Human Resource Management: A Contemporary Perspective*, 2nd edition, FT Pitman Publishing.

DEBATE

'Many organisations waste a fortune paying for the development of staff and then preventing them from using their new ideas in practice.'

Starting points

For

- People can be pigeon-holed in an organisation so that only a small part of their talent is ever recognised or used.
- Sometimes people change, but the perception that their peers and bosses have of them changes much more slowly.
- New ideas gained from courses are often treated with open sceptism by experienced managers ('that's OK in theory, but . . .').

Against

- Many organisations use their appraisal and career development systems to tie the development opportunities for staff closely in to the needs of the organisation.
- It is a good idea to let new ideas incubate slowly, rather than expecting radical changes every time someone completes a new management course.
- The purpose of management development is gradual strengthening of the overall capabilities of the organisation.

Further reading

Stewart, J. and McGoldrick, J. (1996), *Human Resource Development*, Pitman.

Senior, B. (1997), *Organisational Change*, FT Pitman Publishing.

ASSIGNMENT 1

1 List the different methods and techniques used to develop managers.

2 How would you judge and evaluate their effectiveness?

3 Choose two particular techniques from your list and explain how they could be used to make improvements in an organisation with which you are familiar.

ASSIGNMENT 2

Organisations are increasingly turning to self-development as a management technique. Imagine you are the manager responsible for a group of young graduates about to embark upon your organisation's graduate development programme. Write a briefing paper of not more than 800 words explaining ways in which you might encourage them to adopt a self-learning culture.

Source: Adapted from Beardwell, I. and Holden, L. (1997), *Human Resource Management: A Contemporary Perspective*, 2nd edition, FT Pitman Publishing.

APPLICATION 1

Problems evaluating management development

You are the personnel director of a medium-sized manufacturing company. You have had a hard task persuading your board colleagues that they should invest a considerable sum of money in a management development programme for middle managers to ensure succession and the continuing success of the business. However, they finally agreed to your request and the funds were made available a year ago.

The programme is now under way and you have just reported progress to your colleagues. The operations manager, who fought against the programme a year ago because he wanted the money to install a new piece of plant, turns to you somewhat aggressively in a board meeting and says: 'This programme of yours has been running for a year now. In that time I could have saved this company considerable sums of money and increased both quality and revenue. What will you produce and when will we see some pay-back on our investment?' The rest of the board look expectantly in your direction.

- How might you respond?

Source: Beardwell, I. and Holden, L. (1997), *Human Resource Management: A Contemporary Perspective*, 2nd edition, FT Pitman Publishing.

APPLICATION 2

Practical answer to the management skills gap

FT

Smaller companies may value staff training but many feel they cannot afford to lose a manager even for a few weeks, particularly if the benefits are intangible.

Recently, 30 managers from small and medium sized enterprises (SMEs) in Bradford started a one-year Business Masters programme devised by Bradford Management Centre. The centre hopes the pilot course will fill the gap between short courses that may offer SMEs too little and a full MBA that requires a long-term commitment.

'We believe SMEs need access to high quality management support at a pace that fits in with their time and particular needs,' says Robert McClements, chairman of executive development at the centre, which is attached to the University of Bradford.

'Often, they're not looking for management theory, but for practical guidance. Our research showed that SMEs were interested in management training and very interested in solutions to their problems, but they were not terribly keen to go on a generalised course.'

The Bradford course is shorter and more focused than an MBA and geared to practical learning and problem-solving, says Mr McClements. It follows research by the centre, the local authority and Bradford's Training and Enterprise Council that identified a need locally for skills development to improve competitiveness, business survival and growth among SMEs.

'There are many able entrepreneurs who start companies and are fine hands on. But they can become lost as the company grows because they haven't developed the skills to sustain and develop a company,' says Mr McClements.

The 30 managers will attend three evenings a month for a year. The course comprises three elements: formal lectures, best practice visits to companies, and team problem-solving. Parts of the course will be customised to address issues facing individual companies.

Bradford Tec is backing the course with a grant of £250 000, allowing three scholarship places and a subsidised rate of £3600 for local companies. Others will pay £10 950.

Mohan de Silva, the Tec's director of business and economic regeneration, says he wants the course to improve the competitiveness of SMEs in the region. 'Companies that form the backbone of the local economy need more encouragement and access to the latest in management thinking. To give them the edge, that training has to be customised. Smaller companies who have had bad experiences in training will be very cautious about committing themselves again. It's not just money, they cannot afford to waste time and they need to see a pay-off.'

Tony Watson, managing director of Millar Dennis, a Bradford valves manufacturer with a staff of 25, encouraged his new sales director, Nick Whitfield, to apply for a place on the Bradford course. 'I want him to learn about general management so that if I'm not here he can take the reins,' says Mr Watson.

'It's important that we develop people but difficult if your sales are relatively small and the training budget dependent on the success of the company.'

Mr Watson says that evening classes allow for training without disrupting the business. 'As a small company, I can't afford to lose a key person for days at a time.'

Source: Sheila Jones, *Financial Times*, 27 April 1998.

APPLICATION 3

Why workers relish hard graft

FT

Strong trade unions can help organisations implement total quality management, one of the most popular management objectives, according to a report published recently by the Department for Trade and Industry.

Such a message, enthusiastically endorsed by ministers, is scarcely surprising, given Labour's commitment to partnership between both sides of industry. Yet this study – by researchers at Warwick University – was commissioned and completed under the previous Conservative administration. The study, which surveyed 280 employees in six public and private sector organisations, came to some unexpected conclusions – not least that most workers enjoy working harder.

The academics said several organisations were willing to discuss the outlines of their quality initiatives, but 'became very coy when we suggested independent analysis of employees' reactions'. The six 'brave enough' to submit to scrutiny were: British Steel (Shotton works), Halifax Building Society, Lewisham Borough Council, Philips Domestic Appliances (Hastings plant), Severn Trent Water and South Warwickshire NHS Trust.

While some critics of TQM suggest it increases pressure on workers and heightens management control, the academics found little support for this and developed instead a 'disciplined worker' thesis: that workers can accept working harder and often welcome the precision and sense of direction involved in TQM.

The report found most workers enjoyed working as hard as they did. The authors classified 57 per cent as 'committed' in that they were working harder and said they liked doing so. Only 19 per cent were pressured: working the same or harder and disliking it.

The organisations where workers were most likely to say that they were working harder and were more subject to managerial monitoring were also those where trust in management and an acceptance of quality programmes were highest.

The survey also identified important conditions promoting successful implementation of TQM. Across all the organisations, workers who felt their job security was highest were most likely to favour quality initiatives. 'High job security at the Halifax was part of a climate of mutual confidence. In other organisations, and at Severn Trent in particular, perceived job security was relatively low.'

The researchers also believe it important that short-term pressures be kept in check. At the Philips plant, acceptance of quality principles was qualified by problems over product design, which stemmed from a short timescale for the development of new products. 'A sense of division between shop floor and staff tended to undercut the atmosphere that TQM aims to promote.'

The Warwick academics challenge the claim, focused on by supporters and critics, that TQM 'empowers' workers, by giving them resources and discretion to make their own decisions.

They found a much more pragmatic view, with most managers denying the term empowerment was used, or that they ever intended to cede discretion to the shop or office floor. 'The structure of authority was not radically changed by TQM initiatives, and managers and supervisors continued to exercise traditional powers,' says the study.

Workers likewise had pragmatic expectations of TQM programmes. They did not necessarily seek 'empowerment' and they retained a sense of distance from management.

'On balance, employees identified with the principles of quality management and involvement in problem-solving, even though this involvement remained limited to immediate work tasks.'

Source: Andrew Bolger, *Financial Times*, 30 June 1998.

Appendix
Guidelines for Chapter 9

GENERAL ASSESSMENT OF YOUR HANDWRITING

Below you will find the general meanings of the movements of handwriting that you looked at in Chapter 4, 'Activity two'. If you feel that any interpretation is totally wrong it is probably because there is a modifying factor in your writing which needs deeper analysis than this brief test allows.

1 Size

(a) Large middle zone

You are aware of your own worth and have good confidence levels. Because you enjoy meeting and being with people you find work with an aspect of social activity particularly rewarding – personnel, conference office, public relations, and so on. Sometimes you find concentrating a bit difficult if there is a lot going on around you.

(b) Small middle zone

You are able to concentrate well no matter what is going on around you. You like to immerse yourself in the work in hand. You are not pushy by nature. You enjoy working in an academic environment and are excellent with fiddly, detailed work such as figure work, data entry and working with your hands on intricate work.

(c) Mixed

You are a highly strung person and as a result can work fast without tiring easily. You get a lot done in a short space of time. Variety is the key to maintaining your interest and keeping you mentally stimulated. You enjoy activity in your work rather than pure administration or deskwork.

2 Letter connections

(a) All joined up

You have a very logical train of thought. You don't like being interrupted from what you are doing and are keen to achieve what you set out to do. You are good at work where you need to use deductive thinking.

(b) All disconnected

You are an intuitive person. You can sense an atmosphere when you walk into a room. You will know instinctively if you like a working environment or not, without knowing why. You are excellent at coming up with ideas and relate well to other people's creative ideas. Although you get along well with others you keep emotional distance. You find you are sometimes distracted from what you set out to do.

(c) A mixture

You have a combination of good ideas and a logical mind enabling you to put those ideas into action. You are able to come up with practical solutions to problems and find alternative ways to reach your goals. You are a good troubleshooter.

3 Loops

(a) Loopy

You have imagination and a visual mind and will get more job satisfaction in a creative or artistic environment – graphic design, art studios, interior design companies, fabric manufacturers, photographic companies, and so on.

(b) Loopless

You are a practical and down-to-earth person with good technical skills. You have a natural aptitude for working with electronic equipment and an innate feel for technical matters.

4 Overall shape

(a) Rounded

Affectionate and warm-hearted, you are a good pacifier and look to others to give you work to do. You relate well to people, especially children, and teaching or administrative posts, amongst others, are well within your scope.

(b) Angular

You are prepared to work extremely hard for your employer and are therefore an asset to any company. You are thorough in whatever you undertake and don't give up easily. You are a natural researcher and are good at finding essential information quickly. You can find a needle in a haystack if required!

(c) Stretched

You are interested in anything new and exciting and variety is the keyword for you. You find it difficult sometimes to make decisions and work more happily in an environment where decisions are made elsewhere. You love challenges and are prepared to have a go at anything.

(d) Mixed

Adaptability is one of your strongest assets. You are able to turn your hand to a variety of jobs and are also able to handle chopping and changing tasks when necessary.

5 M's and N's

(a) Humped

You are a patient person and can deal in a kindly way with others and won't push them to do anything they don't want to. You learn best by hands-on experience.

(b) Angular
Determined and thorough, you complete what you set out to do. You love research work and have an analytical mind that can be put to good use in business. You like to get your teeth into a problem and can be relied upon not to give up until it is sorted out.

(c) Pointed
You are very curious and inquisitive and always want to know a little bit more about things. You pick up new information quickly and are therefore easy to train. You respond well to state-of-the-art environments and innovative atmospheres.

(d) Mixed
Versatile and adaptable, you are able to handle differing situations in differing ways and can find alternative solutions to problems.

6 Margins

(a) About equal
You are a visually minded person with an eye for the aesthetic. You appreciate well-designed and harmonious surroundings and will work best in an environment that pleases the eye.

(b) Wider on the left
You are a person who is a little bit on the shy and formal side. You are happier if you are introduced to a newcomer than having to go up and meet them. You also feel ready to meet change head on.

(c) Wider on the right
You are a little apprehensive of what the future holds for you and will need to feel that a job is absolutely right for you before you will commit yourself.

Note: *Very narrow margins all round* are the sign of a natural communicator who is never at a loss for something to say and therefore is excellent at putting others at their ease.

7 Capital 'I'

(a) As large as the other capitals
You have a good sense of your own self-worth and a realistic level of confidence.

(b) Larger than the other capitals
You have a good level of self-confidence but need to be careful not to take on more than you can really handle as you take disappointments and failures very much to heart.

(c) Smaller than the other capitals
You are modest by nature and prepared to work in an undemanding way. It takes you more effort to blow your own trumpet. Your confidence levels could be improved with an insight into assertiveness training.

8 Signature

(a) Larger than your writing

You are good at putting forward a lively and confident image even when you don't feel brilliant underneath. You have an excellent interview technique and the ability to make others feel at their ease and think well of you.

(b) Smaller than your writing

You like to be private and dislike intrusions into your personal affairs. You need to be recognised for your professional merits more than for your personality.

(c) Same size as your writing

You are a person who can be taken at face value and you expect the same of others. You are natural and spontaneous and neither oversell nor undersell your capabilities.

Note: *Underlined signature.* Underlining is a sign of self-assertion and a desire for recognition. It helps confidence levels and indicates that you are satisfied with your talents and ready to put them to good use.

9 Spaces

(a) Fairly close together

You are an excellent team member and work best as part of a group or team. You need to have others around to maintain a feeling of enthusiasm and spirit.

(b) Fairly wide apart

You are happy working on your own and relish being given responsibility to get things done without interference and supervision.

(c) A mixture

Very flexible in your working methods, you are happy working on your own or with a team or a combination of both. You are adaptable and enjoy variety in the work you do.

10 Slant

(a) Vertical

You are a person who likes to know all the facts before making a decision. You manage to stay cool-headed in stressful situations.

(b) Right slant

You are an emotional person who relates in a friendly way to others. You need to have people around you with whom you can establish a rapport.

(c) Left slant

You tend to be a very cautious person and are wary of new situations and acquaintances. You are excellent at telephone communications. Job satisfaction is a very important priority for you.

(d) Mixed

You are adaptable and impressionable. You prefer to have decisions made for you, and variety and changes in routine in your work are essential for you as you thrive on a varied programme.

11 Legibility

(a) Clear and easy to read

You are a natural communicator. You are good at explaining complicated facts in an easy to understand way. You are thorough and conscientious in what you undertake.

(b) Some letters skimmed over

You get things done quickly and can be considered a fast worker. You don't particularly enjoy fiddly work but always keep sight of the end result in whatever you undertake.

12 Lines

(a) Going up

You are enthusiastic and optimistic and have good energy levels.

(b) Going down

You need to make sure you are getting enough rest and relaxation so that your energy levels are replenished and you can put your best foot forward.

(c) In an arc

If the arc goes *up* in the middle you tend to take on more than you can handle and need to learn to pace yourself better so that you can complete the jobs you undertake. If the arc goes *down* in the middle you are a bit unsure that you can undertake the jobs you are given but you always manage to fulfil your commitments.

(d) Horizontal

If you say you will do something then you stand by your word. You are reliable and prepared to take on responsibility. A steady worker and employee.

Assessment provided by Corinne Bible, Chairman, British Institute of Graphologists Examinations Board.

References

Adam-Smith, D. and Peacock, A. (eds) (1994), *Cases in Organisational Behaviour*, Pitman.

Arnold, J., Cooper, C. L. and Robertson, I. T. (1998), *Work Psychology*, 3rd edn, FT Pitman Publishing.

Beardwell, I. and Holden, L. (1997), *Human Resource Management: A Contemporary Perspective*, 2nd edn, FT Pitman Publishing.

Belbin, R. M. (1993), *Team Roles at Work*, Butterworth-Heinemann.

Bengtsson, A. (1993), 'Stardust, Fantasy and Performance Excellence', *Training and Development*, September.

Berger, P. (1963), *Invitation to Sociology*, Penguin.

Burnes, B. (1996), *Managing Change*, 2nd edn, Pitman.

Canals, J. (1994), *Competitive Strategies in European Banking*, Clarendon Press.

Drucker, P. F. (1961; first pub. 1955), *The Practice of Management*, Heinemann.

Feldman, D. C. (1981), 'The Multiple Socialisation of Organization Members', *Academy of Management Review*, April, 310.

Ferner, A. and Hyman, R. (1994), *Industrial Relations in the New Europe*, Blackwell.

Festinger, L. (1957), *A Theory of Cognitive Dissonance*, Stanford University Press.

Graham, H. T. and Bennett, R. (1998), *Human Resource Management*, FT Pitman Publishing.

Hall, L. and Torrington, D. (1998), *The Human Resource Function*, FT Pitman Publishing.

Handy, C. (1989), *The Age of Unreason*, Business Books.

Handy, C. (1993), *Understanding Organisations*, 4th edn, Penguin.

Hellriegel, D. and Slocum, J. W. Jr (1974), 'Measures, Research, and Contingencies', *Academy of Management Journal*, June, 225–80.

Hoffmann, S. (1967), 'Heroic Leadership', in L. J. Edinger (ed.), *Political Leadership in Industrial Societies*, Wiley.

Kanter, R. (1983), *The Change Masters*, Simon & Schuster.

Keuning, D. (1998), *Management: A Contemporary Approach*, FT Pitman Publishing.

Kimmage, P. (1990), *A Rough Ride*, Stanley Paul.

Lambert, R. (1968–9), 'Processus d'influence et performance de groupe', *Bulletin de Psychologie*, 22, 800–10.

Lawrence, P. R. (1958), 'The Changing Patterns of Organizational Behavior', *Harvard Business Review*.

Lee, R. and Lawrence, P. (1985), *Organizational Behaviour: Politics at Work*, Hutchinson.

Legge, I. (1989), 'Human Resource Management: A Critical Analysis', in J. Storey (ed.), *New Perspectives on Human Resource Management*, Routledge.

Legge, K. (1978), *Power, Innovation and Problem Solving in Personnel Management*, McGraw-Hill.

Lenk, H. (1969), *Sport, Culture and Society*, Macmillan, 393–7.

Lewis, R. (1989), *Stage People*, Weidenfeld & Nicolson.

Lord, R. G., DeVader, C. L. and Alliger, G. M. (1986), 'A Meta-analysis of the Relation between Personality Traits and Leadership Perceptions: An Application of Validity Generalization Procedures', *Journal of Applied Psychology*, August, 402–10.

Maccoby, M. (1988), *Why Work: Motivating and Leading the New Generation*, Simon & Schuster.

Meudell, K. A. and Gadd, K. (1994), 'Culture and Climate in Short Life Organisations', *International Journal of Contemporary Hospitality Management*, 6 (5).

Mole, J. (1990), *Mind Your Manners*, Industrial Society Press.

Morgan, G. (1993), *Imaginization*, Sage Publications.

Mullins, L. J. (1992), *Hospitality Management: A Human Resources Approach*, Pitman.

Mullins, L. J., Meudell, K. A. and Scott, H. (1993), 'Developing Culture in Short-life Organisations', *International Journal of Contemporary Hospitality Management*, 5 (4).

Peters, T. J. and Waterman, R. H. (1982), *In Search of Excellence*, Harper & Row.

Roddick, A. (1991), *Body and Soul*, Ebury Press.

Sashkin, M. (1991), *Pillars of Excellence: Organizational Beliefs Questionnaire*, Organization Design and Development Inc.

Semler, R. (1993), *Maverick!*, Century.

Senior, B. (1997), *Organisational Change*, FT Pitman Publishing.

Sheldon, W. H., Stevens, S. S. and Tucker, W. B. (1940), *The Variety of Human Physique*, Harper.

Shubert, A. (1990), *A Social History of Modern Spain*, Unwin Hyman.

Staw, B. M. and Ross, J. (1980), 'Commitment in an Experimenting Society: A Study of the Attribution of Leadership from Administrative Scenarios', *Journal of Applied Psychology*, June, 249–60.

Stewart, J and McGoldrick, J. (1996), *Human Resource Development*, Pitman.

Taguiri, R. and Litwin, G. H. (eds) (1968), *Organizational Climate*, Graduate School of Business Administration, Harvard University.

Tolman, E. C. and Holzick, C. H. (1930), 'Introduction and Removal of Reward and Maze Performance in Rats', *University of California Publications in Psychology*, 4, 257–75.

Torrington, D. (1994), *International Human Resource Management*, Prentice Hall.

Torrington, D. and Hall, L. (1991), *Personnel Management: A New Approach*, 2nd edn, Prentice Hall.

Townsend, R. (1985), *Further Up the Organisation*, Coronet Books.

Whyte, W. (1956), *The Organization Man*, Doubleday Anchor Books.